WARTIME LETTERS HOME

by

LOIS MACDONALD COOPER
CANADIAN RED CROSS CORPS OVERSEAS

Borealis Press,
Ottwa,Canada
2005

Published by Borealis Press Ltd., 2005

Canada

The Publishers gratefully acknowledge the financial assistance of the Government of Canada through the Book Publishing Industry Development Program (BPIDP) for our publishing activities.

National Library of Canada Cataloguing in Publication Data

Cooper, Lois Jean, 1920-
Wartime letters home / Lois MacDonald Cooper.

ISBN 0-88887-314-X (bound)
ISBN 0-88887-302-6 (pbk.)

1. World War, 1939-1945—Personal narratives, Canadian.
2. Cooper, Lois Jean. 3. Canadian Red Cross Society—Biography.
I. Title.

D811.5.C654.2005 940.54'771'092 C2004-907301-X

Cover design by DRT
Printed and bound in Canada on acid free paper.

th & Wilts Chronicle & Herald. 6/6/1944 Black-out: 11.7 p.m.—5.10 a.m. Lighting-up: 11.22 p.m.—4.55 a.m.

Bath and Wilts Chronicle and H

Est. 1776 The Evening Paper for N. and Mid-Somerset, Wilts and S.

No. 19,367 TUESDAY One Day Nearer Victory UNE 6

WE INVADE T

Air-Sea Descent: "Hopes Of Tactical Surprise"—*Churchill*

Communique Number One" set the world agog to-day. It was issued from Supreme Q. Allied Expeditionary Force—SHAEF for short— at 9.33 a.m. and said:— Under the command of General Eisenhower, Allied naval forces, supported by ong air forces, began landing Allied Armies to-day on the north coast of France."

THE LANDINGS, IT IS UNDERSTOOD IN LONDON, RE MADE IN NORMANDY BETWEEN 6 A.M. AND A.M., MINESWEEPERS CLEARING A WAY. NAVAL MBARDMENTS, IN WHICH U.S. BATTLESHIPS OK PART, WERE CARRIED OUT, AND AIRBORNE NDINGS MADE. FIRST REPORTS ARE DESCRIBED "GOOD."

W. E. West, Press Association correspondent at S.H.A.E.F., says that General Montgomery is in charge of the Army Group carrying out the assault, with British Canadian and U.S. forces under his command.

A confident Mr. Churchill in the House of Commons ay gave the world dramatic news about the cross-nnel invasion.

"There are already hopes that actual tactical surprise has been attained, and we hope to furnish the enemy with a succession of surprises during the course of the fighting," he said.

mong the facts which Mr. rchill gave the House e:

An immense armada of up-rds of 4,000 ships, with eral thousand smaller craft, e crossed the Channel.

Massed airborne landing suc-sfully effected behind the my lines.

Landings on the beaches are ceeding at various points.

Fire of shore batteries "largely lled."

KING TO BROADCAST TO-NIGHT

The King is to broadcast to his people at 9 p.m. to-night.

General de Gaulle, who has arrived in London and has had talks on military matters with General Eisenhower and Mr. Churchill, is also scheduled to

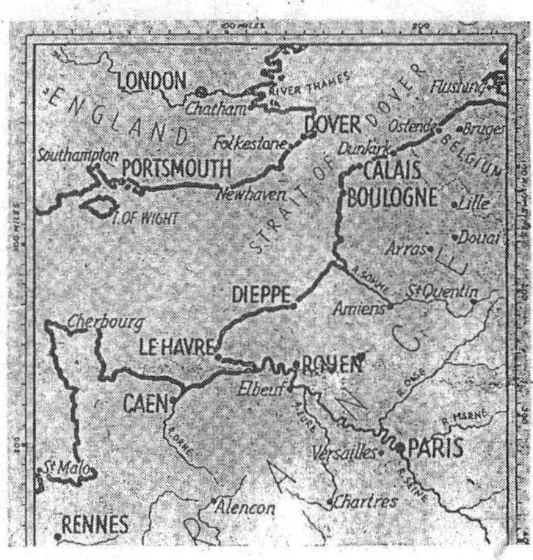

The landings have taken place on the Normandy coast. German reports out the area of operations as including the Cherbourg penin-

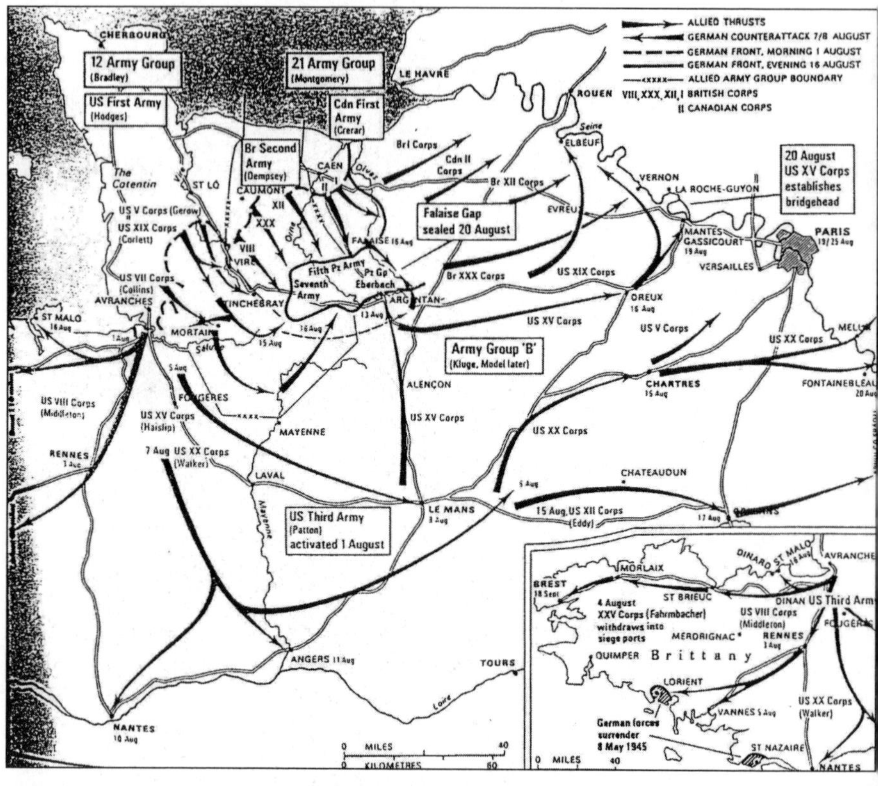

The Battle for Normandy &
advancing south into France

Team of Canadian Red Cross welfare officers with No. 12 Canadian General Hospital in July 1944, in Whitby, Yorkshire, mobilizing to go to the continent. Left to right: Lois MacDonald, Ottawa; Sheila Birks, Montreal; Mary MacDonald, Ottawa; and Laura Sharpe, Montreal.

Red Cross Corps members cycling to Headquarters
Burlington Gardens

WAR ORGANISATION
OF THE
BRITISH RED CROSS SOCIETY
AND
ORDER OF ST. JOHN OF JERUSALEM

Presented to

Lois. J. MacDonald.

Canadian Red Cross Society

in recognition of devoted service to
the cause of humanity
during the second world war
1939–1945

George R.I. — Sovereign Head, Order of St. John of Jerusalem.

Elizabeth R — President, British Red Cross Society.

With heartfelt appreciation
to
Douglas Fisher,
noted Canadian journalist,
who gave me initial encouragement
to compile these letters,
and
his expert guidance along the way.

Sincere thanks
to
Glenn Clever and Frank Tierney,
Borealis Book Publishers,
for their expertise and enthusiasm
in bringing this book to completion.

In loving memory
of my dear parents,
the recipients of these letters.

Dedicated
to
my beloved family:
my late and dearly loved husband,
who was always there for me;
our four very precious daughters;
four wonderful sons-in-law;
a dearest only grandson; and
eight beautiful, thoughtful granddaughters
who have all brought so much joy
and affection into my life.

Special thanks to
daughter Laurie and granddaughter Christy.

Our Partners

The Canadian Red Cross wishes to thank the following companies and organizations for their generous support and assistance for our VE-Day 60th anniversary commemoration project. This project includes the publication Wartime Letters Home by Lois MacDonald Cooper and the commemorative poster series "Women of the Canadian Red Cross."

GENERAL DYNAMICS
Canada

Contents

PICTURES

MAPS

Foreword by the Secretary General of the Canadian Red Cross

The Canadian Red Cross Society has a long and proud history of humanitarian service. An important chapter of that history was written during the Second World War by the Canadian Red Cross Corps Overseas Detachment and the enthusiastic young women who volunteered to serve their country and humanity in a time of dire need. Lois MacDonald Cooper is one of those women. A 23 year old resident of Ottawa when she joined the Red Cross to go overseas in August of 1943, Mrs. Cooper was part of a contingent of over six hundred women who served their country with great pride and patriotism. There is indeed little doubt, as Mrs. Cooper notes in her letters, that they went to England as "girls" and returned to Canada as "women."

Mrs. Cooper's *Wartime Letters Home* provides the unique perspective of a young Canadian woman in the Red Cross who had a front row seat on history. She took advantage of the opportunity presented to record the routine of daily life and impressions of tumultuous events unfolding around her in the letters she wrote to her parents.

On a personal level, her letters capture very concisely the spirit of the day; the many quick friendships that arise as people's lives intersect briefly and the smaller number of more enduring friendships where similar experiences under difficult circumstances forge life-long bonds. They resonate with anticipation as she and her colleagues await the invasion of Europe, and with sorrow as Canadian casualties mount in the battle for North-West Europe.

Within the Canadian Red Cross Society, there is a bridge between those who have gone before and those now serving. That bridge is the humanitarian principle and the desire to help those who are most vulnerable. Mrs. Cooper and the women who served with her epitomize the very best traditions of the Canadian Red Cross and the Red Cross movement. We are indeed proud she is one of us.

Dr. Pierre Duplessis
Secretary General
Canadian Red Cross Society
May, 2005

PREFACE

The Canadian Red Cross Society

It is time to pay a special tribute to the Canadian Red Cross Society, particularly those wonderful people who held office in major cities across the country during those early years of the war. They recognized the need and had the courage and vision to set up the four branches of the Canadian Red Cross Corps.

The Transport Branch was the first one organized, in Montreal, under the name Canadian Women's Transport Service. Then came the VAD, or Volunteer Aid Detachment, who were trained and worked in hospitals. Soon the need for extra help in wartime offices became apparent and hence, the Office Administration Branch was formed, followed by the Food Administration Branch, and later, General Duties.

The first recruits to these branches did not realize that the opportunity to serve overseas might be an option. Later, however, girls did join the various branches specifically to go abroad. There were many, perhaps thousands, of young women across Canada serving long hours on a strictly voluntary basis in their particular branch.

Then the call came to go overseas. Very small groups were chosen from the four branches and sent on their way to set up the nucleus of the Canadian Red Cross Corps overseas detachment. The Red Cross Society had already obtained suitable sites in London to establish the 4 Maple Leaf clubs: one for junior officers, two for other ranks, and one for Nursing Sisters. These clubs provided overnight accommodation and meals for these military personnel, on leave or courses in London.

Suitable housing was quickly acquired in South Kensington, which became "Corps House". All this must have taken considerable effort and funding. It is obvious that a very knowledgeable and able group formed the basis of the Canadian Red Cross Society in Canada, and accomplished these tasks. It was a marvellous opportunity for young women to serve their country and, at the same time, it provided much needed and valuable service for our Armed Forces, in military hospitals in Canada, and in the clubs and hospitals in England and on the continent. Consider the transport drivers who performed so nobly, the welfare officers on the continent and in the Far East, the girls who worked in HQ in London, the escort officers for the War Brides and, eventually, the Civilian Relief Team that served in Normandy in 1946.

There were 641 of us who left Canada for service in the overseas detachment and 640 returned safely to Canada. One girl died with a medical problem.

In the 60 years that have passed since the end of the war, over 300 of our Corps members are gone. Each newsletter that arrives carries a few more names "In Memoriam". Although we did not know all the members, usually I see a couple of familiar names and have a few moments of sadness, remembering those long-ago days and special friendships.

The Red Cross Society, through Corps HQ in Toronto, looked after our welfare extremely well. Our uniforms, travel expenses on duty, and room-and-board on duty were all covered by the Red Cross. We received approximately $35 per month. We did work hard; long hours, often under difficult or stressful circumstances. The girls were a great group, and shared the wish to serve their country and fellow man. They were "doers" and also possessed a spirit of adventure.

I have always felt a deep sense of gratitude to the Canadian Red Cross Society for giving us this very special opportunity. We left Canada as girls. We grew up in those few years and returned as women.

Canada's Armed Services

Canada's military services of the late 1930s must have had a monumental job to do when war was declared in September '39.

It was necessary to immediately mobilize and drastically boost enlistment in the various branches of the services. It must have been a very difficult and daunting task—to increase the manpower of the Army, Navy and Air Force simultaneously. To find, and put in place, capable leaders in the top ranks of each branch of the service—transforming it from a comfortable peacetime group to a well-trained, battle-ready organization.

The time-honoured regiments were already in place all across the country, which must have been a tremendous help. Then recruiting filled out their numbers as well as beefing up the rest of the Army Services and the Navy and Air Force. It was evidently done with efficiency, speed and success. By early 1940, we were shipping troops overseas.

Our interest here is mainly in the Canadian Medical Corps and how it was built up so quickly. There were military hospitals across Canada, dealing principally with veterans of the First World War and permanent staff members needing hospitalization. But suddenly, it was necessary to recruit many top medical specialists in various fields, registered nurses and trained orderlies, as well as all sorts of other personnel. It must have required much careful planning and complicated logistics to put together these new large hospitals. The Canadian Neurological and Plastic Surgery Hospital at Basingstoke, along with No. 1 CGH and No. 14 Canadian General Hospital, were the first to arrive in England

Hospitals with 600 and 1,200 beds were planned, staffed and completely equipped. They could set up their own tent city or move into a vacant building and be admitting patients in a matter of days. Every department in the hospital had all the necessary equipment to do its particular job.

Each hospital had an administrative group headed by a medical doctor with the rank of Colonel. There were also two Lieutenant Colonels, one heading surgery and the other medicine, a Matron carrying the rank of Major, with an Assistant Matron, a Captain.

The usual complement for a 1,200-bed hospital included approximately 50 medical officers comprising many specialists, plus pharmacists, dentists, padres, quartermasters, etc.

As well, there were 100 Nursing Sisters, plus a dietician, 2 physiotherapists, a Home Sister who ran Nurses' Mess, and 4 Red Cross welfare officers.

There were roughly 300 other ranks headed by a Sgt. Major overseeing cooks, drivers, mechanics, clerical personnel, the post office, lab and X-ray technicians, the dispensary, the dental clinic, Q.M. stores, batmen, and others, adding up to a staff of roughly 450.

They had to keep mountains of supplies coming to look after 1,200 patients, and supplies of all kinds, for each different department in the hospital. Plus food to feed 1,650 people three meals a day!

Each hospital had an enormous fleet of trucks and other vehicles, carrying 1,200 beds and mattresses, stoves, refrigeration, tents, and other essential items. It certainly must have seemed an impossible task. Logistics must have been horrendous.

The military planners of that day surely deserve our praise and special tribute. They had a huge job to do and, obviously, it was done expeditiously, with much care and thought to every detail.

INTRODUCTION

Here I am at 85 years, and my one question is, "How did I get here so quickly?"

As I begin to go through the three hundred letters, pictures and memorabilia that I had sent home while overseas during the Second World War, and that my parents had carefully kept for me, those years come back to me quite vividly.

Jack and I married a month after we returned to Canada, and settled in North Bay, where he had accepted a position with the Ontario Northland Railway. We built a life there together, and established a family of four daughters. Had a log cabin built on nearby Trout Lake, then a home on Browning Street. It was a busy and happy family life as our daughters grew up, finished high school, attended university, then married. We travelled frequently, enjoyed summers at the lake, and went skiing in winter. Our girls all developed a great love for the outdoors. North Bay was a fine choice to bring up a family. It was a very social place—in a smaller community, you tend to make your own fun—and friends became very dear.

I never opened the box of letters that my parents had so lovingly saved for me until the 40th anniversary of VE Day celebrations on TV. I was suddenly seized by an urge to recapture some of those days. I found the box, opened it and started to go through the letters. Some were amusing, others sad. I considered trying to condense them into a record for our family, but never did it. By then we had retired and were living in Florida for six months each year. The box was put away once more.

Last winter, when one of my Florida grandchildren was doing a project on the Second World War, and the teacher suggested that they should try to find a veteran to interview, Diana chose her grandmother! Again I opened the box and we talked about some of the experiences. She wrote her essay and presented it with pictures and illustrations. An older granddaughter who was visiting at the time asked if she might see some of the letters. Christy did go through many of them and expressed the hope that I would do something with them.

Then I had the good fortune to meet Douglas Fisher and Jeanie. I discovered that Douglas had served in the Manitoba Dragoons Regiment. His regiment had become very special to some of us at No. 12 CGH in Belgium. When he heard that I had these letters and records, he encouraged me to try to put a book together, even if only for my own family. So after many months, here it is!

In 1941, while in the employ of the Metropolitan Life Insurance Company at the Canadian head office in Ottawa, I joined the Canadian Red Cross Corps Office Administration Branch. We were volunteers and were assigned to wartime offices several evenings a week, doing office work to help with wartime overload. We also drilled weekly in the local armoury. I had somehow reached the exalted position of Sergeant Major, barking orders and hoping not to make a mistake that would send the whole parade headlong into a wall!

Women were beginning to think of wartime service, so it was very exciting when the Red Cross announced that they would be forming an overseas detachment made up of members of their four branches, Office Administration, Food Administration, VADs, and Transport. The minimum age was 23. I applied and my application was accepted soon after my 23rd birthday in mid-March.

I should add that as I was an only child, my parents were not thrilled with my decision, whereas I felt that as I did not have brothers, I had an obligation to take part. In those years between the wars, we were brought up with a strong sense of patriotism. If there was a war to be won, we needed to be there!

The long tedious wait began. I had completed courses in first aid and home nursing and had sufficient hours accumulated. We went through physical exams and shots for various diseases. Uniforms were ordered (we were switching from our Office Admin. grey to khaki), photos taken, and necessary documents completed. Excitement heightened as family and friends gave parties and gifts. I left my job at the Met Life at the end of June. Finally on August 12th, 1943, the following message was received:

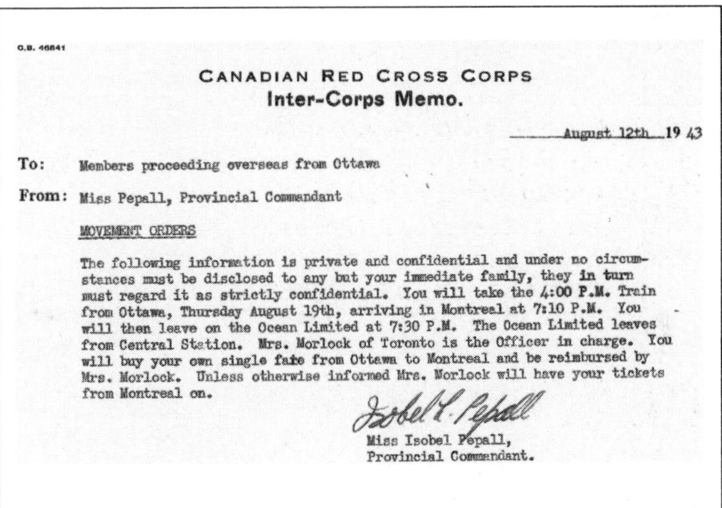

C.B. 46841

CANADIAN RED CROSS CORPS
Inter-Corps Memo.

August 12th 1943

To: Members proceeding overseas from Ottawa

From: Miss Pepall, Provincial Commandant

MOVEMENT ORDERS

The following information is private and confidential and under no circumstances must be disclosed to any but your immediate family, they in turn must regard it as strictly confidential. You will take the 4:00 P.M. Train from Ottawa, Thursday August 19th, arriving in Montreal at 7:10 P.M. You will then leave on the Ocean Limited at 7:30 P.M. The Ocean Limited leaves from Central Station. Mrs. Morlock of Toronto is the Officer in charge. You will buy your own single fare from Ottawa to Montreal and be reimbursed by Mrs. Morlock. Unless otherwise informed Mrs. Morlock will have your tickets from Montreal on.

Isobel L. Pepall
Miss Isobel Pepall,
Provincial Commandant.

After tearful farewells in the old Union Station, four of us boarded the train for Montreal on August 19th, 1943. That evening, we met the Toronto and Montreal contingents, which also included girls from across Canada. We were a group of forty.

After two nights in the Nova Scotian Hotel, during which we had a day to explore Halifax, we were transported to the harbour. Rumour had it that we would be sailing on the *Queen Mary*, as it was in port, so it was quite a shock when the tiny *SS*

Cavina swung into sight, docked, and we marched aboard.

This little ship of the Elders and Fyfe Line had plied the Caribbean for many years, carrying bananas, then was pressed into service and had made numerous Atlantic crossings carrying troops. We were fortunate to cross in August, as we heard many tales of their trials during winter trips, with gale force winds and the ship encrusted in ice.

OUR VOYAGE

Place: Unknown
Time: Unknown
Destination: Unknown

Dearest Mother and Dad:

I shall begin this with my first day on board. My only regret is the many things I cannot say. It does seem a shame not to be able to write everything down because I do want you to know all about it. Our ship is an extremely trim craft and very comfortable. We are four to a cabin, rather crowded, with two sets of bunks. Probably in peacetime, it accommodated two persons. May and I are sharing with two Montreal girls, Mary and Laura. We are all about the same age and we are having a great time together.

Another day dawns—perhaps we shall sail today. We have had boat drill and various instructions. We are to sleep in slacks and sweaters and carry our life jackets at all times, keeping them in our bunks beside us at night. We will wear civvies during the day and our uniforms for dinner at night. Our food is wonderful.

Breakfast consists of fruit, cereal, liver and bacon, or eggs or fish, rolls and coffee.

Luncheon is soup (very good), salad (tossed), cold meat or roast, hot vegetables, dessert and coffee in the lounge. We have tea, cake and cookies at 4.00 pm.

Dinner is soup, a fish course, meat and vegetables, pie or pudding, plenty of rolls and butter, and again, coffee in the lounge. Also, coffee and sandwiches before bedtime. We are all worried that we may burst out of our uniforms before we ever reach England.

WE DID SAIL TODAY! It was absolutely thrilling. Everything seemed so quiet and orderly as the tugs moved us out into the harbour. No peacetime shouting or fanfare. I think everyone had mixed feelings, rather sad leaving Canada, and we all turned and took one long, last look as we headed into the open sea. So very excited about what lay ahead and also wondering when and if we would ever return!

While in Halifax, some of us had climbed Citadel Hill and watched a huge convoy of ships assembling. We joined this formidable group, 80 ships in all, escorted by destroyers, corvettes and minesweepers of the Canadian Navy, the little corvettes shouting their distinctive "Whoop, whoop!" as they scooted along. We are lined up beside an enormous flat-top or aircraft carrier. We have to be completely blacked out at night, so first thing each morning, we raise the porthole shades to see if our sister ships are still with us and breathe a collective sigh of relief that we are still all bobbing along together. We are all fully aware that there are packs of German submarines lurking beneath the shipping lanes, searching for convoys like ours.

Today we saw porpoises rolling and leaping, also a whale spouting! How I wish that you could both be here to enjoy it with me! We were lying on the deck in the sun when another boat signalled and the brother of one of the girls shouted to her through a megaphone. She had not seen him for months and was so thrilled. That was our excitement for the afternoon! Wish I could go into detail about everything but am trying to keep the censors happy, so must be careful. It is the most beautiful and inspiring sight I have ever seen—something like that scene from Mrs. Miniver. The gently rolling sea with its glorious colour, the bright sunshine and our marvellous collection of ships, moving along so majestically.

Life on board is fun indeed. We play deck tennis and quoits, walk the measured mile around the deck several times a day, play bridge and cribbage, relax in the sun and get to know the rest of our group. They are a delightful mix. Our leader is a charming girl from Toronto and all seem lively, good-natured and fun. We have had many laughs together. Drawn from many backgrounds but with the common goal of going overseas to try to contribute to the war effort. Some of the girls are married and looking forward to joining their husbands, many of whom have been in England for several years.

By the way, did I tell you that five of us are sitting with the First Officer at meals? He is 2nd in command on the ship, and is extremely interesting. A rugged sort of man, thoroughly British, as are all the crew. He looks quite stern but has a twinkle in his eye and a keen sense of humour. One of the girls darns his socks, so he thinks we are all right!

There are many RAF officers and men on board. The other ranks sing their hearts out. All the old wartime tunes and a few we had not heard. "Roll Me Over in the Clover" seems a top favourite and we think it is pretty funny. One of their senior officers, W/C "Merry" Oakes, flew with Billy Bishop. He has been extremely kind to us. Saw me struggling up the gangplank, laden down, so he came to my rescue and carried some of my gear to our cabin. I had bought grapefruit and lemons in Halifax, thinking they would be a treat for folks in England. Had tied the cuffs of my trench coat and great coat, then filled the sleeves with citrus, forgetting just how heavy it would be. It was like dragging an anchor!

Other passengers are civilians returning to their homeland from various places. Some are from the Far East. There are approximately twenty young children on board. Angelic-looking little blond twin boys and their younger sister. We call them the "Holy Terrors". Their mother was laid low for a few days, so some of us endeavoured to look after them. I drew the Terrors for dinner one evening and it was an absolute nightmare! Almost decided never to have a family! One young mother survived the Fall of Singapore and had managed to escape with her small daughter, after her husband had been taken prisoner. She has been months trying to get home. Our mascot is a huge grey-and-black striped cat. His name is Barnacle and he has made countless crossings.

Our weather has turned foul, with rain, wind and rough seas. The waves seem to be rising by the minute. We struggled out on deck briefly and it really is an awesome and magnificent sight. The towering waves; one minute we are away down in a trough and then climbing a huge hill of water. It amazes me that with all these ships travelling so closely together, there have been no collisions. It is surprising, the feeling of safety and security that pervades our ship. Guess we have complete confidence in our crew and our escort. The RCN was with us the first half of the journey, then the British Navy took over escort duties and will carry on, while the Canadian ships headed home.

Last evening, in the bar, glasses flew off the tables and chairs slid across the room. Suddenly, we lurched in a strange fashion and our leader, who was sitting with a glass in her hand, flew off her chair, did a complete back flip, sailing through the air in a slow-motion somersault and rolled across the floor. When we realized that she was not hurt, we all hooted with laughter. In the past few days, people have disappeared from the dining salon. They struggle down below, weave to their place, take a look at the food, turn a pasty white and bolt for the door. Fortunately, our cabin is well amidship so it is a bit smoother than the lounge and other cabins. Laura and I must be fairly good sailors as we are still making it to meals.

Today we were told that the fastest ships would leave the convoy and go on ahead. Surprisingly, our little Cavina is one of them, so we broke free of the group, speeded up and away we went in a smaller fleet. After zigzagging our way across the Atlantic at the speed of the slowest ships, it is exhilarating to feel the wind rush by and see the wake churning behind us.

WE HAVE SIGHTED LAND! It's perfectly beautiful and looks like Canada. Don't know what I expected, but thought everything should look completely different.

As last evening was our final night on board, we had a dance. Someone had scads of records so they played them on the public address system and we danced in the lounge. It was a great party—complete with cabaret. Some of our members participated and it was a very good show. Our Margo was hilarious—dressed as the "Gay Nineties" in a motley collection of wearing apparel scrounged from the other cabins. The party lasted on into the morning and then we all adjourned to the galley for sandwiches and tea. I thought we ate a great deal in good old Canada, but these people never seem to stop.

We have not been sure where we will land, but finally word got around that we were entering the Mersey Estuary and would go into Liverpool! I guess this is the end of our cruise as we are sailing into our berth. It has been a marvellous experience and I have loved it all. Wish you could have both been with me! We have been treated so very well and everything has been taken care of for us. It has been wonderful so far and it is a thrill to reach England on the 4th anniversary of her entrance into the war.

I do want you both to know just how much I appreciate everything you did to help make this trip possible for me. You understood that I really wanted to do it and sent me on my way!

Heaps of love,
Your loving daughter, Lois

September 4th, 1943
Dearest Ones:

We disembarked with great joy. After thirteen days at sea, we were finally in England! We were met by a local Red Cross official with a single station wagon. He was expecting a party of FOUR instead of forty! Poor man had to rush away and make other arrangements. A large red double-decker bus rolled in, followed by a truck for our luggage, and we were soon on our way to the railway station. Devastation in Liverpool was shocking as we viewed bombed-out buildings and some whole blocks, completely gone. Our first look at the bomb damage.

Trip to London was fascinating, as we rolled past towns and villages and saw endless rows of houses, each with its share of chimney pots! Landscape seemed to be in miniature with narrow winding roads, small fields separated by stone fences. Each little house had its tiny garden plot. But all was very green and lush. Beautiful flowers everywhere and vines and flowering shrubs massed together. There were small hamlets and large cities. We stopped at one station, all got off, wearing our hats and gloves, and filed past a table where the local ladies' group had sandwiches and tea in paper cups ready for us. As the sun disappeared and the daylight dimmed—we suddenly realized how dark and utterly black the world had become. Quite eerie, to roll towards London, with not a light showing anywhere.

Arriving, we were greeted by our Corps House leaders with a fleet of vehicles, and on to Maple Leaf II, one of our Red Cross clubs in London. Corps House was filled at the moment, so this would be our temporary home. We received a very warm welcome and a hot supper. There were familiar faces from our own units back home. It was a marvellous feeling to finally be in London. Such a wonderful trip and now we are all anxious to see what lies ahead. Will keep you posted.

Love you both dearly, Lois

ARRIVAL IN LONDON

September 5th, 1943
Dearest Family:

We are settled in at Maple Leaf Club II on Cromwell Road, London, SW1, until we are posted to our hospital. Have our ration cards and registration cards. Our luggage all arrived safely. One gal lost her dunnage bag. When the stevedores were tossing the gear ashore, one bag went over the side and that was the last we saw of it. Of course, as they were all identical, no one knew who had lost it. They are huge bags, as you know, and we were all trying to remember just what we had packed in our bag, in case the lost one was ours!

Today we went downtown. The traffic is horrendous, flying in all directions and you surely have to watch your step. The streets are filled with Americans—it looks more like New York. I am dying to see someone from home who even looks familiar. We have seen many well-known places. Pall Mall, Piccadilly Circus, Trafalgar Square, Buckingham Palace and so many other spots. We went to Canada House and British Columbia House, then thought we should see the famed Beaver Club. We had no idea that it was strictly a men's club. We sailed gaily in the door and the doorman rushed after us. When we explained that we had just come to town and were very anxious to see the club, he took us to Miss Crow, the manager, who kindly took us on a tour of inspection. It's really a marvellous place—a small village in itself. We were delighted to see it.

Laura and I had to attend to our banking. We first went away down into the "City", which is the financial section. We wandered around in circles for ages and saw the most amazing sights. All sorts of old-fashioned markets, places and things I have read about and always hoped to see. We did find her bank, then back to Trafalgar Square. My bank was right there, so easy to locate. We went to a very attractive restaurant, which may possibly become a favourite. L'Ecu de France, on Germyn Street. It was more like a spot in New York and we had an excellent meal.

We have been granted a week's leave, and those without family or friends in England are encouraged to request hospitality. Laura and I saw Lady Donegal at HQ this morning and she will make arrangements for us. We asked for a place in the country, preferably in the South, so it will be interesting to see what she comes up with.

Life at Maple Leaf II is fun. A great crowd of girls there and they run the place as a hostel for other ranks on leave in London. We have helped them with some of their chores. Making those dozens of beds every day, with the heavy army blankets, is surely hard on the arms and fingernails! They need all the help they can get!

We are to leave tomorrow morning for Brenchley, Kent. Have not heard much about it, as we seem to be the first Red Cross girls going there and are to report back to Lady Donegal when we return.

Will write again from Kent.
Much love, Lois

September 10th, 1943
Dearest Family:

Here we are in Brenchley, Kent. We travelled to Tunbridge Wells by train, through glorious countryside. Everything so green and lovely. Mrs. Langer, our hostess, met the train and we drove to her home. She is a former Canadian, from Northern

Ontario, who married an Englishman and has lived here since. She is most charming and gracious. We learned that she lost her husband to cancer earlier in the war. Has one son, Charles, recently graduated from Cambridge and presently at home. Before the war, her life centred around bridge, shopping in London, cocktail parties, entertaining and travelling. Her husband was a successful businessman, commuting to London during the week. There were servants galore and everything was looked after, but then came the Blitz, and at this point, in 1943, the servants have all been drafted for war work. She is left with one Land Army girl and one very old gardener.

The drawing room and dining room are closed and we eat in the kitchen, which is very nice. The library is beautiful with a huge fireplace and lovely casement windows opening into the garden. It is like a small farm and Mrs. Langer, with the help of Charles, does much of the work, but still finds the time and motivation to entertain an endless parade of young Canadian service people. She is surely a tower of strength and does so much to make our visit pleasant.

The house, "The Warren", is absolutely perfect. Large, rambling, beautifully furnished and centrally heated! That is a real luxury in England. It is set back in the trees, at the end of a lovely winding lane. Landscaping is marvellous—a sunken pool with a variety of goldfish and water lilies. Exquisite rose arbour, and a running stream through the other colourful gardens. You would love it, Dad! There are greenhouses with tomatoes and melons, a kitchen garden with every kind of vegetable. There are chickens, geese and jersey cows. Gladys had to learn to cook, run the house and even milk the cows! They seem to be managing very well, although it is pretty difficult to keep the landscaping looking as neat and trim as when they had a larger staff. There are five cars in the garage but four of them are put up for the duration and they use bikes for most short trips.

We shopped with them in town, taking a fishing creel in to the fishmonger, who was called "Fishy". He dumped the little fish into the creel. Then on to the bakery, where cakes and buns were placed in Gladys' fancy basket, wrapped in the clean towel she had brought along. Then we joined their friends, at a nice little restaurant, for coffee and cake—a weekly ritual. We sat there until it was time for lunch—then started over again! By this time there were eight or nine in the crowd, so all went to a show. After the show, back to the restaurant for a substantial tea. Then we said goodbye to the others and drove home in time for dinner! They do eat well, these British!

It is hop-picking season, and Kent is well known for its hops. There are many migrant workers in the fields and the crop is being picked and hauled to the oasthouses to be stored and dried. An important ingredient in beer, it is a good cash crop in the area. Charles took us to one of the hop farms and into the oasthouse so we could see the process. Very interesting.

We walk wherever we wish on their large property. There are three beautiful dogs and we take them along. Picked blackberries with Charles and rode the countryside on bikes, after we had taught Laura to ride! While she was practising, I rode around to the front of the house, where there was a huge parking area, surrounded by a 5-foot cedar hedge. Forgot that the bike had brakes on the handles, and as I approached the hedge, reversed with my feet, to slow. My feet simply spun around backwards, and I seemed to go faster than ever, flew over the handlebars, headfirst into the cedar hedge. Laura and Charles came around the corner just as I was picking myself up, covered in mud, with sprigs of cedar in my hair! We help bring in the cows, walking a mile and a half with Charles to get them. We must be a funny sight in our shorts, each armed with a large stick, herding the cows along. The ancient gardener collapsed in a fit of giggles when we came in sight.

Delightful holiday. This serene, lovely part of England, and the Langers, with their sincere kindness and hospitality. I guess it was not always so quiet and serene. They tell us that during the Battle of Britain, the planes were roaring overhead and some of the dogfights were close enough for them to watch, in fascination and horror. We left The Warren with a warm invitation to return.

Now back in London, our group of forty are destined for hospitals or transport duty. The girls already here are all working in London, in Red Cross HQ or Corps House or the four clubs. There are to be two girls assigned to each hospital. The married girls were given first chance so they could choose a spot near their husbands. Laura and I had hoped to go together; however, as there were no places left for two, Aileen Corkett suggested I go with her, to No. 1 Canadian Neurological and Plastic Surgery Hospital in Basingstoke, Hampshire. Her husband, George, is a patient there.

Heaps of love,

Lois

Coombehurst, Basingstoke, Hants, England

Meren Gemmell, Canadian Nursing Sister with Mrs. Simon and Bengy

Coombehurst

LIFE IN BASINGSTOKE

September 20th, 1943
Dearest Family:

Now we have moved into a lovely spacious old home, another country estate. Mrs. Simon, a delightful Scottish lady, is in charge here, keeping it going for the owner, Colonel Blythe, who is away serving with his regiment. His wife and young child have moved to smaller quarters.

Our new home, Coombehurst, is on the outskirts of Basingstoke, a couple of miles from the hospital. Situated on a hill, with a gatehouse down at the road and a winding drive leading up to it, lined with huge dark green holly bushes. Plenty of land around it—a lovely walled garden with fruit trees—pears, peaches, apples, etc. growing flat against the walls. Flower gardens and the ever-present kitchen garden. There is a conservatory or greenhouse at the back of the front hall or foyer, with lovely green and blooming plants. The house has central heating, but fuel is in short supply, so we will only enjoy the luxury of heat for the week between Christmas and New Year's. Apart from that, must depend on the fireplaces for heat. Our room is pretty crowded with the twin beds and my bed is right against the hearth, so we cannot have a fire, but will live in a pretty chilly room as winter advances. Mrs. Simon has a huge coal-fired range in the kitchen, so that helps to heat the ground floor. It is a stately old home, vine-covered and with gorgeous wisteria in all its purple glory. We have a cow, old Bessie, who provides our milk, and Neddy, a dear little old donkey, who seems to be a pet. There are chickens, geese, Moscovy ducks, also pheasants strutting the lawns and a covey of partridges that appears from time to time. We are indeed fortunate. It seems to be a delightful place to live.

Later—a word about the other boarders at Coombehurst. Mrs. Hubbard and her daughter Shirley, age 11. "Mother Hubbard" is very prim and proper. Poor child is fussed at from dawn till dark. Mother H. has not much of a sense of humour and takes life very seriously. Her husband is in London but insisted on evacuating them to the country for safety. Shirley is a pretty child with a sweet face, lovely eyes, rosy cheeks and two long braids. She wears a school uniform and takes all sorts of lessons, music, dancing, singing, riding, etc., and is constantly being stuffed with vitamins and tonic.

Then there is Captain Hedges. "Oscar", a British Army Officer, is the original Mr. Five by Five! He has a round merry face, a great booming laugh and thinks everything is terribly amusing. He teases poor Mother Hubbard unmercifully.

Next is Dr. Weston, a civilian doctor, youngish, dark and rather sloppy-looking. He seems to have a perpetual cold, always carrying a huge white handkerchief. He has a girlfriend in a neighbouring town, who calls him punctually at 9.00 every evening. He almost breaks a leg leaping to the phone.

The staff consists of Elsie and Mary, two old family retainers, both a little slow, otherwise they would have been drafted for war work. They try Mrs. Simon's patience severely. Mrs. S. runs the house, does all the cooking, with Mary helping in the kitchen.

Dewes and Mrs. Dewes live in a small house on the estate and he does much of the outside work. He also looks after Colonel Blythe's greyhounds and takes them to race at White City during the season.

Mrs. Simon is a very motherly soul, jolly, and loves people. She often entertains medical staff from the hospital, and it was the padre from the hospital who was able to arrange for us to live here. We are encouraged to invite our friends and it is truly a home away from home for us.

We all gather for breakfast and dinner at night. If we are in for the evening, we assemble in Mrs. Simon's sitting room, which is cosier than the large drawing room. Tea and cookies are served at 9.00 pm while we listen to the BBC news.

Our jobs at the hospital are very busy and interesting. We do mostly handicrafts. The Up patients come each day to our workroom, and we go to the wards in the afternoons, with our crafts, for the bed patients who, if able, are eager to start a project. A large part of our job is to talk with the patients, look at their pictures, hear about their families or girlfriend back home, write letters for them if they are unable to do so, to be there for them in place of their families, so far away.

The handicrafts are very popular. They make string or leather belts, sew leather gloves and slippers, make felt stuffed animals, do needlework, other leather work, wallets and handbags, do hooked rugs, and anything else that we or they can think of.

It is very rewarding, seeing the interest they take in a project once they start. Competition spurs them on, too, finding who can do the best job in the shortest time. It is very good therapy for them, helping to fill the days while their bodies heal. Also boosting their morale and self-esteem.

We work with two English women who were employed by the Canadian Red Cross before we arrived. They seem to feel threatened that we, as Corps members, will take over their jobs and authority, so working with them is not completely congenial. However, everyone else in the hospital is marvellous to us—from the Matron and the Colonel in charge, to all the Nursing Sisters and medical officers—so we keep smiling and put up with the two of them. The English pair prefer to sit in our nice comfortable Red Cross Room, close to their teapot, so Aileen and I do the wards, which we really enjoy.

It is tiring work, pushing our laden carts along the long, damp, freezing corridors with their cold concrete floors, to the endless rows of Nissen huts. However, it is all very worthwhile and rewarding as we do seem to bring a little diversion and joy to the patients. It is fun being amongst them, sharing their stories and jokes, hearing where they are from and we may discover a mutual friend, or be familiar with their hometown. It is a thrill to see a lonely lad's face light up at the mention of something dear to him.

The hospital is located on Lord Camrose's estate, a large acreage called Hackwood Park. An imposing structure of creamy stone, several stories high, with great wings curving out to each side. This is used for the medical staff residence and administration—with dozens of Nissen huts erected at the rear, in two long rows, connected by long corridors. These house the wards and all the other necessary departments of a hospital. The Red Cross Room is in the ballroom. A beautiful spacious room with high ceilings and many tall windows looking out on the gardens and swimming pool (which is covered over and out-of-use for the duration). It is a magnificent and impressive establishment, with lush green lawns rolling down to the gatehouse. There are tennis courts, stables with horses as well as a huge flock of prize black sheep, with darling fluffy little lambs that wander and graze on the beautiful lawns. There are fascinating walks through the woods, with one wonderful area, surrounded by tall leafy trees meeting overhead, called the Cathedral. We walk there often on our noon break, or ride our bikes around the grounds.

(I returned to Basingstoke in February 2000 with daughter Diane and granddaughter Christy. Was surprised and pleased when they were so eager to see the places that had meant so much to me. Basingstoke had grown from a sleepy, old-fashioned town to a busy city with tall buildings and paved pedestrian malls. Many new roads made it difficult to find some of the old haunts. Coombehurst had been levelled and the property divided with many small homes. Only thing recognizable was the gatehouse and drive, called Coombehurst. Sad, but then that is progress!

But Hackwood Park, being such a large property and mansion, had been declared a Heritage Estate and protected from the developers. Could only be sold as a single acreage, and the house could be restored but not changed in any way.

We drove up the winding drive to the house. The beautiful black sheep were gone, replaced by a herd of lovely deer! The house looked neglected and in need of repair. As there was a car parked and the large front doors appeared to be ajar, my family insisted that we knock and I could enquire about my long-ago friend, Diana, one of the Camrose daughters who had lived there. A gentleman appeared, said he was the estate agent. He knew nothing of the Camrose family. The property had been purchased two years earlier by a family from the Middle East. They were now ready to start the restoration and prepared to spend untold funds to do so. We were indeed fortunate to have happened along that day when a meeting was planned for an hour later; otherwise the place would have been locked and deserted. The estate agent was very kind, ushered us through the ground floor and into the ballroom, which had been our Red Cross workroom. It was empty, except for the elegant but dusty drapes and the massive chandeliers. The other gentlemen, young men from London, architects, contractors, interior decorators, began to arrive to plan the coming project. When introduced to us, they were obviously very surprised to learn that Hackwood had served as a Canadian hospital. I surely must have seemed like a relic from the past!

We left happy, delighted to know that Hackwood will regain its stately beauty and elegance.)

Many old friends show up in England. They come to Basingstoke or I meet them in London. There is so much to do and so many marvellous places to visit. One long-time friend was in our area, and he surprised me by wanting to see so many sights in London. We went to St. Paul's Cathedral, saw the Marble Arch and Hyde Park, where we watched the orators on their soapboxes. Saw Petticoat Lane, with all its merchants. Really a giant flea market. Also Madame Tussaud's Wax Museum, a fascinating place. Everyone looked so natural and lifelike. I was trying to decide who one figure was, when suddenly, he walked away.

We ride the subways and double-decker buses—wonderful way to see London. A favourite place is the London Zoo. Saw lions, tigers, zebras, leopards, parrots, reptiles, bears, camels, monkeys and a huge giraffe. A tall bald-headed man was standing in front of his cage, and suddenly, the giraffe lowered his giant head on his great long neck and licked the bald head!

We went to Reading, walked along the Thames and saw enormous white swans sailing along so effortlessly, while fancy rowboats moved between them.

Did I tell you that we went to Royal Albert Hall last weekend? It was a real treat. Such a tremendous building with so many tiers and balconies. Really breathtaking, all in scarlet and gold. There is no stage, as the building is circular, but entertainment is staged on the lower floor in the centre. The whole setting is magnificent. We heard the London Philharmonic Orchestra play Balshazzar's Feast, with Dr. Malcolm Sargent directing. It was truly wonderful.

This letter has gone on for ages, so must finish and get it in the mail.

So much love to you and all the family, Lois

October 4th, 1943
Dearest Mother and Dad:

Time rolls on and another week has passed. We did our stocktaking in the Red Cross Room and it has been busy, indeed. Days have been glorious. Football weather at home!

Sunday morning I dug out my jodhpurs and went riding—with Shirley, the little girl at the house. We cycled three miles to get the horses and rode for an hour. It was absolutely beautiful—through country lanes, past quaint villages, thatched cottages, ancient stone churches, very old cemeteries, over delightful little bridges, the horses clopping along over the cobblestones. I loved every minute of it. We cycled back in time for dinner, which is served at noon on Sunday.

Your old friend, Captain Cahill, now a padre, had been in to our hospital during the week and arranged to come for me Sunday afternoon. We went to Salisbury and Winchester in his Jeep. To the cathedral in Salisbury first. It is over 500 years old and quite beautiful. Hard to imagine how they were able to build these very tall magnificent buildings so long ago, without the aid of modern building equipment. In Winchester, we saw the cathedral there. So much history and sheer beauty in these places. The buildings are huge and rambling, with their marvellous old stonework, wood carvings and cloistered gardens. We went to Wyckham College—a very famous old boys' school. The students all wear the funniest straw hats with coloured hatbands. It is amusing to see the young boys all dashing about in their peculiar headgear.

Last evening Mrs. Simon took me to church in the neighbouring village. It was the Harvest Festival and also a special service commemorating "the Battle of Britain". The church was quite small, stone, very narrow with a high-beamed ceiling. The interior was completely decorated with the most luscious fruit, vegetables and flowers. I was greatly impressed. It was all so colourful and I do wish you could have seen it.

Here I am again! I do love to get your weekly letters, Mother. They come in about five weeks. I was all set to write a note yesterday on the joys of the English climate. It was teeming rain—just coming down in buckets in the morning and I had to cycle to the hospital. Aileen had a cold and was staying in bed. I put on my high rubber boots, trench coat and pulled my hat down over my hair and ears, and looked like a member of some lost legion. We have to go over a mile on country roads and the final part through Hackwood Park, uphill all the way. The water dripped off the peak of my cap and splashed all over me, running down into my boots. I thought a hundred nasty thoughts about the English climate—all that nonsense about the rain in England never wetting you! It's an absolute fable! I was soaked to the skin. However, I got to the hospital, put on dry stockings and clothes and had a cup of tea. Then in about five minutes, the downpour stopped, and the sun blazed forth and I completely forgot about the rain.

Another weekend, and another old family friend entertained me. Colonel Underwood was in London and contacted me during the week. He had come to England on a short trip to check on the Canadian Postal Corps, his responsibility. I met him after lunch on Saturday, in London. As he had grown up in London, he was a marvellous guide. We did a walking tour, through St. James's Park, Birdcage Walk, saw many waterfowl, including giant white pelicans. Tremendous wingspread.

Walked past Westminster Abbey, along past the Houses of Parliament into Whitehall, past so many famous old buildings, saw No. 10 Downing Street, then to the Royal Automobile Club for tea. That was a welcome respite after our hike. Next we went to a musical comedy, The Magic Carpet. It was the first big stage show I had seen, and it was fabulous. Beautiful costumes, great music, wonderful dancing and very fast moving. I was absolutely fascinated. Because of the Blackout, the shows start very early in the evening, then you go to dinner later. We proceeded to the Kingston Close Club to enjoy a delicious dinner. It was a lovely day. I really did appreciate him taking me to all those great places. I will write to him but perhaps you will tell him, too, how much it meant to me. He should be home again soon.

The following day, Sunday, we had a church parade. Seventy of us lined up in front of Corps House in Queensgate Terrace. It is a very wide street, with little traffic, so a good place to assemble. We marched to St. Paul's Church in Onslow Square, where General Price of the Canadian Red Cross and the Honourable R.B. Bennett took the salute.

Perhaps I should tell you about Corps House. It started as one house in row housing. No. 20 Queensgate Terrace. As the Corps in England grew, the houses beside it, No. 18 and then No. 16, were both obtained and doors opened in the walls on the ground floor, so we could all move back and forth. These houses are very solid with large white pillars at the front entrances. They line the whole block! They are five stories high. If you are on the fifth floor in one unit and wish to visit a friend on the fifth floor in one of the other houses, it is necessary to go down five flights, into the other house and up the stairs there. The kitchens are in the basement. Rather dark and gloomy. I have great admiration for the Food Administration girls who labour there and manage to turn out such appetizing meals. A variety of food is difficult to obtain and ration rules are strictly enforced.

Before we left Canada, word was that Mrs. Lee, our Corps Commandant in London, was very strict and difficult. I have no idea who spread that nasty rumour but it could not be more wrong. She is warm and charming and we soon found out that she really does have our welfare at heart. We who are stationed out of London are told that we are always very welcome to stay at Corps House. There will always be a bed for us, as the girls living there often leave for weekends. It is wonderful to have a spot in London and I do spend many weekends there.

Corps House is in South Kensington and not too far from the Underground Station. In the Blackout, it is difficult to find your way. We have learned to count the blocks, then the houses, and hope we are going in the correct door. With possibly 40 houses side by side, all identical, it is very easy to make a mistake.

In London, there are air raids most nights and they are pretty scary, as the sirens sound, then we hear the planes and the "ack ack" guns, and wait for the explosions as the bombs hit. Hoping all the time that they will miss us! But wondering, too, how many poor souls did get it. When the sirens sound, we are required to leave our warm beds and go down to the basement, a cold and dreary place, where we all stand, leaning against the cold stone walls, waiting impatiently for the "All Clear". It is a great temptation to simply pull the blankets over your head and stay put! Must admit I have done this on a few occasions.

The ordinary Londoners are a brave and stoic lot. They have been enduring these night raids for over three years. Many of them trudge down into the bowels of the earth, the Tube or Underground Stations, night after night, carrying babes and young children. They bed down on some of the bunk beds placed there, or on the cold concrete, with a few blankets and pillows, with heads against the wall and their legs and feet extending out towards where the boarding passengers walk. Little tousled heads and the odd teddy bear peek out from blankets. How they can possibly sleep, with the roar of the rushing trains a few feet from them, and hundreds of people literally stepping over their feet! People in the streets look genuinely weary, tired and shabby. London looks dusty, damaged and sad.

The devastation in London is dreadful, and shocking to behold. Bombed-out buildings, cordoned off, work crews are there, round the clock, trying to clean up the rubble as soon as possible. What can be repaired quickly is done to get business back to work. People from demolished homes move to family or friends'. Some poor souls have lost their homes and possessions several times. But life goes on in beleaguered London. The theatres and cinemas, nightclubs and restaurants are crowded. The famous hotels of London keep going, despite shortages of fuel, food and beverages. Completely black and dark on the outside—but ablaze with lights and gaiety inside.

This has been a long one. Please keep the letters coming.

Much love, dears,
Lois

Canadian Neurological and Plastic Surgery Hospital
No. 1
Basingstoke, England

Hackwood Park, location of the hospital in the background

November 11th, 1943
Dearest Mother and Dad:

I was utterly shocked to hear of Grand-daddy MacDonald passing away. Had no idea he was so ill. Do wish I could be with you now. We will surely miss him. He was a special person.

Your cable was at the hospital when we got there this morning. I did not send a reply from there, as they seem to go more quickly from town so waited until 6.00 pm and pedalled to the post office before coming home. It was just getting dusk when I got there, so stood my bicycle against the building while I went inside. When I came out, my bike had disappeared—my heart sank into my boots, as Aileen and I had bought the last two bikes in town. Suddenly, I saw my friend, the "Bobbie", strolling down the other side of the street. I flew across to tell him my bike had been stolen. He appeared concerned and then, after a few minutes, led me around to the back of the post office where he had hidden it. He was trying to teach me a lesson—not to leave my bicycle unlocked—because there have been numerous thefts lately. He saw me leave it there, so hid it and then waited for me to emerge!

Fun to be so busy and we do love the work. We cut the felt toys, also pairs of gloves, for the bed patients. The others come on foot or in wheelchairs to get what they want. I had so many gloves, Scottie dogs, rabbits and ducks to cut today—but it is worth it when we go into the wards and the men are all working away. I really think it does help them. They think they can't do anything, having been injured, but then they start on a simple little toy or belt and are so pleased when it turns out well, then are anxious to try something more complicated.

It's surely an experience to work in the hospital. Often wish I had gone in training—when I see how capable and efficient the Nursing Sisters are. It must be gratifying to see a man who has been badly wounded making a good recovery in a short time.

I am so sad about Grand-daddy and know you both must feel the same way.

It never occurred to me when I said goodbye to him that I would never see him again. Expect the Montreal family are with you now.

Thinking of you.
Much love to all, Lois

November 15th, 1943
Dear Family:

Parcels have been arriving very well. The whole household thanks you both for all the goodies you have sent. Aileen and I share many of our things with the others here. We give Mrs. Simon whatever will help her with cooking. She does like to get pudding powders, cake mixes, Tea Bisk, etc. She makes fine meals for us and is so happy to be able to offer a variety. So many of the family have sent wonderful boxes, too. I surely do appreciate it. The church and the Met Life have sent candy and cigarettes, which we give to the patients on special occasions. I realize, too, that many of the things you send, nylons, candy bars, so many things, are very difficult to obtain, and know you are doing without yourselves, in order to send them to me.

Mrs. Hoyle, one of our co-workers who boards at the estate beside Coombehurst, invited us over one evening. We had never been there and as both houses were up long driveways, paralleling each other, it seemed to make sense to try to go across at the top. We fought through bushes and hedges, climbed a fence in a miserable drizzle and finally arrived at a forbidding-looking mansion. We had glimpsed it through the trees but on this moonless night it looked almost forsaken. A housemaid of the old school admitted us to the Victorian reception hall, asked our names and announced us very formally. And we had just come to sit by the fire with our knitting!

More about the front hall—walls were covered with cloth in a dazzling pattern. On this were hung rows of pictures of Empire soldiers in period uniforms. Above these was a series of antlers—no deer heads, just dusty antlers, horn to horn! We were ushered to the drawing room, looked in and more or less charted a course, through masses of furniture, to the fireplace. Mrs. Hoyle and the lady of the house were sitting there, and beckoned us forward. The room was jammed with antiques and the walls completely covered with tapestries and dozens of pictures. The mantel was laden with Dresden figurines crammed together. There were some lovely things but so crowded you could not appreciate any of it. We wondered how Mrs. Hoyle could bear to live in that dusty museum and quite relieved that she had not checked us in there, too!

The Blackouts have become a way of life for all of us. Every home and other building is completely equipped with heavy blackout curtains over windows and on the inside of exterior doors, so not a ray of light can shine anywhere, even when a door is opened. It's the queerest feeling, to stumble along a blacked-out street, with every building in complete darkness, not a sign of life or light anywhere. It's as if you had entered a ghost city or recently deserted town. I have to keep telling myself that the houses we pass are brightly lit inside and filled with laughing people.

Every vehicle is blacked out as well. Only tiny slits of light are permitted from headlights. I surely respect our transport drivers, who weave through the London traffic, day or night, finding their way, when it is impossible to read the signs, circling the roundabouts, manoeuvring in masses of traffic, and doing it all on the wrong side of the road!

Love and hugs, Lois

November 18th, 1943
Dearest Ones:

Aileen and George went away last weekend to celebrate their fourth Anniversary. The very first one they have ever spent together! He had gone overseas soon after they were married. Mrs. Simon suggested I might like to ask a friend as Aileen's bed was available. Mary MacDonald had arrived recently from Ottawa and was happy to come to the country.

Saturday morning, we biked to the riding stable and the groom got us organized on the horses. Mary looked quite confident and it never occurred to me that she had not ridden before. My horse moved off and Mary's lurched ahead. She flew forward, threw both arms around his neck, slid sideways and hung, momentarily, under the horse's chin! Then slid to the ground. Fortunately, she was not hurt. The groom rushed up, pulled her to her feet and said, "Have you ever been on a horse before, Miss?" Mary said rather indignantly, "No, but I do ride a bicycle!" Mary, good sport that she is, did mount again and we had a rather sedate but pleasant ride.

Aileen and I, being classed as civilians, were required to do a firefighting course. We had to go to the local ARP place. It was bitterly cold as we cycled along, looking for the address. Finally found it, a hut in a field! We had worn our warmest clothes, and were given overalls, huge navy blue ones. The floor of the hut was covered with wood shavings and had charred old furniture standing around, for atmosphere. There was another girl there, so we had a team of three. They set fire to the shavings, and we took turns manning the stirrup pump, keeping the pails full of water and crawling around in the fire with the nozzle, putting out the flames. It was a new experience. So now we are prepared to take our turn on Firewatch duty, which means we are scheduled to report for duty for four hours, one night a month.

Keep well, Much love, Lois

Corps House
20, 18, and 16 Queensgate Terrace
London, England

November 23, 1943
Dearest Mother and Dad:

Our work at the hospital goes on each day. There are many moments of sadness as we realize that some of these young lads will never walk again, be permanently disabled or disfigured. The patients become our friends, we look forward to seeing them every day, try to remember their names and something about their families, hometown or regiment, so we can chat with them.

The Burn Ward is a special place—where the badly burned patients are treated with the newest methods. Some completely swathed in bandages. The Nursing Sisters are very compassionate and certainly give these lads tender loving care.

The medical officers are a fine group as well. Many are highly trained specialists in their fields. Dr. Wilder Penfield of Montreal, a noted neurosurgeon, is here, along with a very competent staff. The plastic surgery team is very skilled—with Dr. Gordon and Dr. Hoyle Campbell. Dr. Campbell lets us watch some of the surgery and it is most fascinating. They work on many of the burn cases and have distinguished themselves with their fine and dedicated efforts. The Neurological Ward is also staffed with highly trained professionals who treat the mentally troubled. It is a top-flight hospital and it's a privilege to be part of it.

Basingstoke is a 600-bed hospital and runs to capacity most of the time. These patients are casualties from the North African and Italian campaigns. A few Naval personnel, wounded in action at sea. Also, some from training accidents or traffic accidents, especially the DR's (Despatch Riders) who, sadly, pile their motorcycles into the road roundabouts in the Blackout and sustain some severe head injuries.

December 2nd, 1943
Dearest Folks:

We are suddenly into December and had our first snowfall—huge white flakes, and it did make us a bit lonesome for home. It is very cold with a penetrating dampness. We went to a movie in town, biking a couple of miles. We were in heavy wool sweaters and our great coats, buttoned up to the neck, heavy wool socks, hats and ski mitts! And this was inside! The lack of heating facilities is really appalling; of course, there is a real shortage of fuel, and I guess a movie house is away down on the priority list!

You should see us in bed, in our heatless room. I wear my yellow flannel pyjamas with the hood, often a sweater over it and heavy housecoat on top and snuggle up to a hot water bottle! Never thought I would use one! The only heat in our bathroom comes from the heated towel rack, which is chrome with hot water running through it. At least you can count on a nice warm towel to wrap up in!

Had a note from Captain Cahill, written on the boat, heading for foreign shores.

Heaps of love. Think of you both so often, Lois

December 19th, 1943
Dearest Family:

I returned to The Warren in Kent to pay a pre-Christmas visit to Mrs. Langer and Charles. She had invited me for the holidays, but Mrs. Simon was going to much trouble to make it festive, so planned to stay at Coombehurst. It was the weekend before Christmas, and the weather was cold, dreary and wet. Missed my connection in London so it was late Friday evening when I arrived. Mrs. Langer and Charles and two of the dogs, Sam and Alfie, met me. Their home was as lovely as ever, and all decorated for Christmas. I was in the same beautiful guestroom. Such a joy to be in a warm bedroom! To be able to sit up in bed without wearing three sweaters, a parka and mitts!

Saturday the rain continued, so Charles showed movies of The Warren about six years earlier in 1937, with his father still alive. Also pictures of their place in Switzerland—a marvellous spot in a lovely valley, on a beautiful little lake. They spent summer holidays there and ski vacations as well. Country life in the pre-war days in England must have been idyllic but by 1943, it was a struggle to keep going. However, they were doing their best to hold it all together. Probably hoping for the good life again, if and when hostilities cease.

It was a very pleasant weekend. Friends and neighbours were invited for Saturday evening. They had stacks of records, so we danced by the lights of the Christmas tree. I had to leave Sunday on the afternoon train. The gentleman who lived across the road, a fruit farmer, appeared with a very large basket of marvellous-looking apples for me. He was very nice, English, and greatly impressed with Canada's effort in the present struggle. He said how much we were doing and how very much they appreciated it—I think the basket of apples, to me, a Canadian, was part of his spirit of gratitude, so I could do nothing but accept them graciously.

There I was, rushing across Waterloo Station, in muddy rubber boots and greatcoat, carrying my fur coat, suitcase and the huge basket of apples, topped by a bunch of holly and a big red bow. Of course, just then, the handle pulled off the basket and the precious apples flew in all directions. A very nice young American came to my assistance and got me on the train, with all my gear, complete with apples. He was the nicest lad and was going beyond Basingstoke so we each munched an apple and talked of his hometown, Chicago, and dreamed of hamburgs and milkshakes.

Life has become most complicated. I find that the weekends are far too short and too few to see all the places I want to see. There are seven very nice invitations for Christmas dinner. Everyone has been so kind and thoughtful, knowing it is my first Christmas away from home. However, we are putting up a tree, and Mrs. Simon got out the decorations, lights, etc., that have not been used for several years. She has ordered a turkey and is planning plum pudding and all the trimmings. We are even going to each have a boiled egg for breakfast! A very special treat!

Have a lovely Christmas.

I will miss you all so very much.
Love and kisses, Lois

December 21st, 1943
Dearest Ones:

One evening a week we have a Ping-Pong and Dart Tournament for the patients. It seems very successful and last evening there were about 60 taking part. It runs from 6.30 to 9.00 pm and the Knights of Columbus supply coffee and biscuits. Darts is almost a national sport over here. Everyone plays it and it is quite complicated.

We have just heard that some of our Red Cross girls, en route to Italy, with their hospital, were torpedoed and had to take to the lifeboats. Evidently all were safe but it must have been pretty frightening when it happened.

Have seen quite a few old Ottawa friends in the past few weeks. Always so exciting when someone from home shows up. There have been quite a few dates for lunch or dinner, sometimes with new friends here. Have been to a couple of dances.

We went to the Police Ball recently. Big event on the social calendar here. Dress was optional, although there were many tails and tuxes and long dresses. Some very pretty ones. I wore my short black dress and it was fine. We are permitted to wear civvies when off duty, although we usually travel in uniform. Am so glad I brought my fur coat as it seems to be the only thing that keeps out the dampness.

It was a very good party—a super floor—fairly good music—fine floor show and delicious food. The English go all out for their dances. Forget the war and get all dressed up and everyone has a wonderful time. I guess that is what has helped keep them going through these rough years.

Sunday, I went to Farnborough with Miss Sturges, the Matron of the civilian hospital here. She is from Wales, is a dear, and we have become good friends. Her brother and six other chaps live together in an old rambling house. They have a housekeeper to look after them, they are engineers and work in an aircraft plant there. It's the most amazing household—they have all been there for three years and everything runs so smoothly. One is in charge of the gardens, another the groceries, another the fires, etc. When we arrived we had a small tea. Then about 5.00 pm they said we would have tea, so we all went in and sat around the dining table. Everything was in huge dishes, bread, butter, tinned fish, large bowl of tomatoes from the garden, jam, cake and the inevitable pot of tea! I thought it was the evening meal and was hungry as we had an early dinner. Then we all retired back to the living room to listen to the wireless, as they call the radio. About 9.00 pm they said we must have supper. I thought we had already had it, but followed back into the dining room, and had the same menu all over again! It is odd, that so many of us in Canada are descended from the British Isles but our customs are so very different.

Miss you,
Much love, Lois

CHRISTMAS 1943

December 23rd, 1943
Dearest Family:

It's December 23rd, and everything is so Christmassy. The hospital is a mass of decorations. Each ward has tried to outdo the next one and they are all very clever and most original. We have given them whatever we can and helped with some of the decorating and the Sisters on each ward have helped, too. We have our Red Cross Room looking quite pretty with a small tree. Some of the Sisters and doctors dropped in this afternoon and we had a little party. My Christmas parcels all seem to have arrived. All the aunts have checked in and the parcels all look so pretty. Can hardly wait to open them. Do tell them all that I have received their gifts, surely do appreciate it and will write after Christmas.

Aileen caught the bus to Borden at noon, to spend the weekend with George. They were given the use of a house for over Christmas. Needless to say, they are thrilled. I went to the bus with her as she was laden with luggage. She is a fine person and a wonderful friend. I did some shopping for Mrs. Simon, then dropped in at the local hospital to see Miss Sturges, and she took me around to see the colourful decorations in the wards. The Children's Ward was really a picture.

Then back to Hackwood. Our English women had left, but Mrs. Reford, our lovely transplanted Canadian friend, had asked me to come back and help her distribute the Red Cross Christmas stockings. Her daughter, Marian, a WREN, home for the holidays, was helping, too. Marian had spent a couple of years at McGill, as her parents are from Montreal, but had returned home to join up. The

Refords have been very kind to Aileen and me and we always enjoy going to their home. The three of us went around to all the wards and wished all the patients a Merry Christmas. I was so glad to have the opportunity to do that, as I had felt badly, closing shop at noon and just disappearing, as Mrs. Hoyle had decreed we would do.

When I got home for tea we decorated the Coombehurst tree. It looks beautiful, with lights, tinsel, etc. Captain Hedges is away but Dr. Weston is here and has a friend, Reggie, with him for the weekend. Also, Father Hubbard has arrived. Then carol singers appeared at the front door and sang several numbers for us. I loved hearing them. Without snow—it's hard to believe it is Christmas.

Love and hugs, Lois

December 24th, 1943
My Dears:

Here it is, the eve of my first Christmas in England. It's after midnight and I just opened my presents—couldn't stand the suspense any longer. Love everything you sent. The pretty housecoat and the beautiful blouse, the pyjamas and the lovely scarf. Of course, the stockings are absolutely precious here. All the other good things that you thought of will surely come in handy, too. Thank you both so very much. Will hope to be home with you next Christmas. Suppose you will have the usual family dinner, at the grandparents. Can visualize the whole scene, with most of the family there.

Tonight I went to the Christmas Eve Party at the hospital, the medical officers' Mess. They are a great group and we do appreciate being included in their festivities. It was surely a fun evening. Then it was time to head home. We donned our fur coats, boarded our bicycles and off we went, in the pitch black. Imagine coming home from a dance on Christmas Eve—on a bicycle!

Happy Happy Christmas!
Your loving daughter, Lois

December 28th, 1943
Dearest Mother and Dad:

Our Christmas dinner was excellent. Mrs. Simon outdid herself! The turkey was delicious. Dressing had chestnuts in it, and the gravy plenty of mushrooms. Only thing I missed was cranberry sauce, which does not seem to be part of their tradition here. We all enjoyed the plum pudding and the sauce was different and very good. Mary had come for Christmas and we went to the hospital for a buffet supper. It was a lovely party. We were with such a friendly group and it was great fun.

Today was rather exciting. We were in the movies! Aileen and I and some of the patients. An army picture—do hope you will have a chance to see it sometime. They will shoot a few more scenes tomorrow—in our workshop. Today was done in the wards.

Must get to bed and get our beauty sleep for tomorrow's shoot!

Let's hope our New Year will bring peace.
Much love to you both, Lois

January 1st, 1944!

First of all, a very Happy New Year to you both. Here it is my first New Year's in England and it has been so very gay! This would be the day for the family party at our place, when everyone wears a paper hat and plays all those silly games.

To get back to last evening, there was a dance at Hackwood, and a very good one, too. The nurses and doctors are such a carefree, friendly crowd—and all have such a good time together. Some of them had asked guests but the majority were on the staff of the hospital. Meren, the Nursing Sister from Winnipeg, had asked me to stay the night with her and that was fun. There were 12 young Yankee officers—lined up like a bunch of wolves—they had been invited from a nearby unit that had just set up in the area—so you can imagine what a fun time we had.

One of the Americans is coming over tonight. They are all such nice lads and Mrs. Simon wants to meet him, so he is coming for dinner. Mrs. Hubbard and Shirley are away for 10 days. The Captain is on two weeks' leave and Dr. Weston is gone for the weekend; we are having the house to ourselves. It's really a treat to be without them for a while—especially the Hubbards.

It was rather a cosmopolitan group last evening. I had supper with an RAF officer, two Canadian officers and three of the visiting Yankees. Safety in numbers!

Oceans of love, Your loving daughter, Lois

January 4th, 1944
Dear Folks:

Gerry did come for dinner. He is a lanky Yankee with red hair and a Jeep. A decent sort and much fun. Mrs. Simon thought he was very nice. You can rest easy—she checks out all my new friends! Gerry, his name is Phillips, came again the next evening. We went out with a fellow officer and his girlfriend, an Army nurse from Brooklyn.

We have been very busy at the hospital, with so much handicraft going on in all the wards. Aunty Marjorie sent me some new patterns for felt. We are thrilled with them. Great to have something new to offer. The weekly Ping-Pong and dart tournaments are very popular and the Up patients bring as many pals as they can, in wheelchairs. The patients come and go, convoys move out and others move in. It's surprising how many we can make some connection with—know something of their town or regiment, or have a mutual friend or acquaintance. Happily, we can usually find something or some interest to chat about. They don't care as long as we talk!

Have received some lovely boxes. All the ones you sent, and others from friends and relatives. Met Life has been very generous. A lovely box of canned goods and then today, a beautiful large box of Laura Secord's. Must write to thank them.

Friday, I'm going to a formal dance with Gerry at Park Prewett Hospital. Quite a large affair, so am trying to decide what to wear. It's such a problem! I did go shopping in London, but could not see a thing. Everything was either very expensive or downright shoddy. Even the high-priced things were not very nice. Did not see anything that I liked as well as the clothes I have.

Enough for now.
Much love and God Bless! Lois

January 12, 1944
Dear Family:

Here I am again after a rather long silence. We went to the formal dance. It was a marvellous party and everyone was dressed to kill. I wore my long black skirt and white frilly blouse and Aileen's pretty coloured belt and had a beautiful red corsage. There was a cocktail party first, then we all went to the dance.

Saturday, I went to Corps House and Harvey Fenton called for me. He had come to Basingstoke unexpectedly one day and we planned a weekend in London. Always special to see an old friend from home! We went to a super place for dinner and dancing. Everywhere in London is absolutely crowded—especially on weekends. We had a lovely time. Great to see him.

I went back to Basingstoke Sunday. There was a very nice RCAF officer there, Alan MacDonald from Winnipeg. Aileen and George had returned, so the four of us went to Brigadier and Mrs. Reford's for dinner. They are wonderful people and so good to us.

Tonight was our Ping-Pong and darts evening. There must have been about 80 patients there. They really do enjoy a little diversion. It is tedious for them, being confined to the hospital. One lad is a whiz on the piano and he soon had a group around him, singing many of the old favourites. Great fun for all of us. We are making plans for another evening each week, perhaps bingo or some card games. Just something they can look forward to and enjoy.

Gerry picked me up at 9.00 pm and put my bike in the Jeep. We dropped into one of the local pubs where we played "Shove Ha'Penny", a very simple game but quite amusing. Everything closes at 10.00 pm so we came home and had tea and cookies. The whole family was assembled, even Mrs. Blythe, who is staying here for a few days. She is charming and I am happy to meet her. Have not seen the baby, Penelope Jane yet. Perhaps tomorrow, if I am home when she is awake.

(Colonel and Mrs. Blythe owned Coombehurst. He was serving with his regiment and she lived in a nearby town, but came periodically, to spend a few days. As a wartime measure, the large homes had to be filled with boarders. She preferred to live elsewhere for the duration.)

January 16th, 1944
Dearest Mother and Dad:

Another Sunday and time for another note. Aileen and George are having a weekend in London. I worked yesterday morning, and it was very busy at the hospital. With only two of us instead of four, it does make a difference. Hospital still runs to capacity and guess it will continue.

Last evening was the Yankee Dance—I went with Gerry—we went to a buffet supper first at their Mess—a very good meal and such a nice party. Then on to the dance. They had their own band, so the music was really super. We had a wonderful time and they are such fun.

You asked about my finances, Dad. The situation seems very well in hand. I have very little to spend money on. Only railway fares, and we do get a service rate when we travel in uniform. In London we stay at Corps House, free of charge for food and bed, and here in Basingstoke there is literally nothing to buy—because our board is paid and we eat at the hospital free. When I do go to London, it's usually Saturday afternoon and all the shops are closed. All the candy we can buy is one shilling and 6 pence—about 35 cents worth a month! So you can see, I don't have many expenses. When in London and here too, we are usually taken out, so I don't even get a chance to spend my one pound, eight shillings that we get every week.

Wish I could get home for just one short visit!

Much love, Lois

WEEKENDS IN LONDON

January 17th, 1944
Dearest Mother and Dad:

We have been so busy at the hospital lately. The wards are all full and it keeps Aileen and me busy trying to see every patient every day. It's quite rewarding when they seem to be waiting for us when we appear in the entrance of the ward. They vie with each other for our attention and look for things that they need help with. Some of the wards have the badly injured and the post-operative cases. They cannot do much handicraft, but we do go from bed to bed and have a short visit, after checking with the Sister in charge to see which patients we should see. It is usually 6.00 pm when we leave, so a dark trip home at this time of year.

I caught the 9.00 pm train to London Friday night. There was a raid on and of course everything was late. It was 11.40 pm when I finally got to London. I knew the Tube would stop running soon, so rushed out to look for a taxi. I'm now safely tucked in the guest room in Corps House. A tiny room, but it has central heating and a lovely soft bed! Here it is Sat. morning—a real doozie of a raid last night—I woke up to the tune of guns blazing and planes roaring overhead—took a peek out the window and saw flares dropping like fireworks, decided that bed was the place for me, so dove back under the covers, head and all. Have just had breakfast and am going to do the shops again.

Had two letters from you today, Mother. I love to hear all the news. Enjoyed London but it is complete bedlam on weekends. The shopping was an absolute fizzle. Didn't even see a thing! Dreadful-looking clothes and so expensive. Certainly makes my own things look pretty good after all. You asked about a cotton or silk print dress. Either would be marvellous. We do wear civvies usually going out in the evening.

I came back yesterday, Sunday, after lunch. Met a lovely girl on the train. A British WREN. She was coming to Basingstoke, too. She is Diana Berry—youngest daughter of Lord Camrose, who owns Hackwood. She has eight older brothers and sisters. She was only home overnight, but will be back on leave shortly so will call and we will get together for some riding.

Love to all the family.

Lois

January 29th, 1944
Dearest Family:

Last night was the Pub Keepers' Ball. Gerry had acquired a beautiful case of pink eye and had one eye firmly closed. It looked like a permanent wink. It was pouring rain, and we trailed from one pub to another in the Blackout and downpour! Such a stupid custom. Then we all went to the dance. As usual, there was all sorts of evening wear. We left when they started the auction.

Mrs. Simon had left milk for me and cider for Gerry, and cookies. Put drops in his eye and he was on his way. I locked up very carefully—because Mrs. Simon had given me her key and that is quite a privilege! To get to the point, I thought the doctor had the key for the conservatory door, so locked and bolted the front door. The doctor arrived, very late, had a key for the front door, but could not get in. He slept in his car for the remainder of the night. If you only knew him, you could appreciate it. I did feel dreadful this morning when we opened the front door and he wandered in looking so bedraggled.

We are very busy at the hospital, patients coming in a steady stream. Our handicraft supplies have improved and we have a greater variety. The men are doing so many interesting projects. Quite a bit of needlepoint, and they do a great job. There are two patients, sitting up, side by side, working away with their needles and wool, one doing a huge sailboat and the other, a scene with horses. It will be quite a surprise for their families when they arrive home with these tapestries rolled up in their packsacks! Many of the Up patients are doing leather work, tooling some attractive designs, making handbags and wallets. Some are quite meticulous and do a professional-looking job.

We seem to be forever bidding them goodbye, hoping we may see them again, perhaps years from now, when this war is long over. Am sure we will see a familiar face and connect it with the young lad who struggled with a twine belt.

Much love, Lois

February 1st, 1944
Hello Folks:

Gerry drove Sally, the Jeep, up to the front door, misjudged the distance, and we ran over the concrete step and broke off the corner. I was really upset about it. However, we did get a man to come the following day and he made an excellent job of repairing it, so all was forgiven. Mrs. Simon was very nice about it and said she had no idea that "Perambulator" could do so much damage!

Aileen and I finally caught the mouse. It has been eating our candy for weeks and we haven't been able to catch it. Last night, after we had turned out the lights and opened the Blackout curtains, we heard it rustling around and we were both too scared to move. Then there was a bang and that was the end of Mr. Mouse. He was in the trap this morning and Mother Hubbard came and removed him.

I hope I am not picking up an English accent. The doctor and the Captain tell Aileen and me that we are losing that "dreadful Canadian twang" and our English is really improving! Somehow, they feel free to make personal remarks—something we would just not do. The English people insist that they have no accent, but speak English as it should be spoken and that we "colonials" (I hate that reference) have the accents. However, Aileen and I don't think we speak differently, at all. We are with Canadians all day, so perhaps they are just teasing us. I hope so.

Love to you both, Lois

February 3rd, 1944
Dearest Ones:

Must tell you about going to lunch on Sunday with the Camrose family. Their family name is Berry, but they are Lord and Lady Camrose. He is a newspaper baron on Fleet Street. Hackwood is their family home, but it was needed for war purposes, so they moved to a "small house" nearby. Diana had given me instructions to find it, so I biked over, a mile or two from here. It was a colossal house on top of a hill. An old family retainer bowed me into the drawing room, a gorgeous room with lovely antiques, soft elegant colours in the upholstery and drapes, huge fireplace with marble mantel and wonderful paintings. One by one, the family made their appearance. The mother and granny came first—very nice, beautifully dressed and quite human. Then Diana and one of her married sisters, Countess so-and-so, sailed in, wearing dirty old slacks and sweaters. Her father came in—a very stately and charming man. A couple of other guests and a young grandson rounded out the group. Sherry was served and after a short period, we all went into the dining room.

What a charming room! Beautifully decorated, huge table and matching chairs, all in gleaming dark wood, the chairs upholstered in burgundy velvet. Table was set with much silver, gorgeous crystal and lovely flowers. There were two uniformed footmen, wearing white gloves, who served us. A very nice dinner—delicious soup, then roast lamb and vegetables, and finally, a rather exotic dessert. When we had finished and the young grandson had left the table, our hostess informed us that we had just eaten a portion of Lucy—erstwhile family pet (lamb). There was great consternation and everyone felt like a cannibal!

Then we walked over to the stables to see the horses, returning to Diana's for tea, and we hope to ride next weekend. England in peacetime really must be something special. I mean, living in the country the way they do, yet with a flat in London. It is very obvious what a class difference there is. The majority, the ordinary people, live very simply. Lucky if they have the bare necessities. Have only had indoor plumbing for a few years! The lower classes don't expect very much and don't seem to strive to rise above what they have been born to. The wealthy, and they are very wealthy and titled, live like royalty. The wealth is handed down to their children along with the titles, and they continue to live in the same manner. Lovely country to visit but I would never choose to live here.

Much love, dears, Lois

February 7th, 1944
Dear Ones:

Have just returned from London. It has been hectic, but fun. Friday, Aileen and I went up to London after work to attend the Corps House Anniversary. A number of the girls were there and it was a thrill to see them again. Many we had not seen since we came over on the boat. Corps House was jammed, food was delicious and we did a great deal of chatting and laughing. We had to leave at

9.45 pm to catch our train back to Basingstoke. There was not a seat left and we were in the corridor where two RAF lads let us sit on their packs! It was rather a dreary journey and we kept saying to each other, "Is your journey really necessary?" This slogan is plastered on signs all over London.

Gerry and I caught the train to London after lunch. Went to the K. of C. (Knights of Columbus) Hut to pick up the theatre tickets. We went to his club, then on to Corps House, then back to the West End to the Park Lane Hotel for tea. After a short walk, on to the Piccadilly for cocktails and then to the theatre. We saw a very good play, Pink String and Sealing Wax. *It has been running for a long time. A mystery and very cleverly done. Then we went to Scott's for dinner as the show was over at 9 pm. Then on to the Trocadero for a while. A busy evening!*

Gerry returned at ten in the morning and we went to Westminster Abbey. The service was nothing special but the building is magnificent. The stained glass windows are wonderful. We walked all around after the service and looked at everything. Then along Whitehall to Trafalgar Square—up the Haymarket and along to Piccadilly Circus. Went to the Regent Palace for lunch. Then I called Colonel Underwood as he had said he would like to see me again before leaving for Canada. He and Colonel Lawrence came to meet us and we walked through Hyde Park. They showed us many points of interest, then they had another engagement at 4.00 pm, so parted company and we headed back to Corps House.

General Price, head of the Red Cross Overseas, was there with Mrs. Tudball of Toronto Red Cross, who had come with the new group. They were all having tea with Mrs. Lee in the drawing room. It was quite amusing. I had left Gerry sitting in the hall while I went upstairs to collect my things. He was sitting right outside the room where they were all having tea. There was a young Canadian Lieutenant with them and he told a joke about two American soldiers in London. The story ran that they were fresh to a couple of ATS girls and an ATS police came up and ordered them away. They replied that they would not take orders from the ATS and that they had come over here to win the war. Whereupon the ATS is supposed to have replied, "'Oh, I thought you were a couple of fugitives from Pearl Harbour!'"

Of course, the facetious young Canadian who told the joke had not seen Gerry sitting in the hall. Gerry practically choked when he heard it—or sputtered with rage. Anyway, the General looked out and saw him and they immediately asked him in for tea. He had met Mrs. Lee before. Guess they all felt a little sheepish when they saw the American uniform and realized that he had heard. Anyway, someone asked him where he was from and he promptly said, "'I'm just a fugitive from Pearl Harbour!'" When I returned, they were all laughing and thought it quite amusing. Good thing he was a good sport about it.

I was pleased to have an opportunity to meet General Price. He is such a nice man. His daughter Helen came over in our group.

We went to see James Cagney in Johnny Vagabond. Then dashed to Waterloo and caught the train home. A fun weekend.

Heaps of love to you both.

Take care, Lois.

February 10th, 1944
Hello again!

Another week well under way. Looks as if I will have to hold the fort all by myself; today Mrs. Hoyle, Mrs. Perry and Aileen are all sick with colds. That is what I get for being so tough! Some of the Up patients will help me.

The early flowers are all in bloom—snowdrops, crocus, etc. It is really lovely here now. Will soon be spring and the place will be a mass of daffodils. They don't just grow in gardens, but spring up through the grass in great profusion. Dad, you would love the flowers.

Gerry is going away for two weeks, leaving tomorrow, and cannot say where he is going. We are having a Valentine Dance at Hackwood, so have asked Harvey to come out for the weekend. Mrs. Simon can always find room for a visiting Canadian!

Thank you so much for the cigarettes. Gave some to Mrs. Simon and will save the rest for the patients who don't receive any from home. I love it here at the hospital. It's terribly interesting and there is always something new. The patients don't tell us much about the action they have been in. Think they just don't want to dwell on the horror, but the odd time something slips out and we realize just what these very young men have been through. Some are maimed or crippled for life, but they don't whine or become bitter. They are surely a fine lot, our Canadian soldiers, and we can certainly learn a lot from them and be very proud. It's really a privilege to be able to be with them and try to help in some small way.

The movie film I mentioned, taken here at the hospital, should be shown in Canada during March. I believe there is a Red Cross Drive on then, so do try to see it

Last night was really a fizzle. After the Ping-Pong tournament, I came home from the hospital about 9.00 pm. It was to be Gerry's last evening before going away, so he was coming over after I got home. He and his pals had been celebrating their departure, and by the time he finally arrived, he was really slap-happy—not objectionable, but terribly funny. I didn't know what to do with him, as the whole family was in the drawing room and they would all tease me so. Hoyle can be quite a tease, too, says he never had a sister, and as I am the only single girl living here, he and the doctor and Capt. Hedges take great delight in kidding me about the young gentlemen who come calling.

Thought a bit of fresh air might smarten Gerry up, so I went upstairs to get my coat. First of all, I had to put him in the drawing room and hoped that no one would look at him very closely. Told him not to say a word and not to giggle! Mrs. Simon realized what had happened and poured some strong tea into him. The rest of the lodgers must not have noticed, because they did not say anything, and they never miss an opportunity. We got as far as the front door and I realized it was hopeless, so packed him off home. Fortunately, he had a driver for the evening.

Their departure was delayed a day, so he appeared tonight, all apologies and bearing a beautiful box of chocolates—Lofts of New York. Remember, we used to go to Lofts whenever we were in the U.S. He will be gone for several weeks on a course.

Heaps of love to you both, Lois

February 13th, 1944
Dearest Folks:

When my three co-workers were all sick on Friday, Mrs. Hoyle said we must close at noon, so I went home to Coombehurst, put on old clothes and helped Mrs. Simon in the garden. We tied up the rose bushes and straightened up that part of the garden. Then Dr. Weston came in and said he had a couple of calls to make in the country and would I go along for the ride? It was a lovely day and this is the prettiest county. Hampshire is a beautiful spot, with all its tiny narrow lanes and quaint old houses. Not the lakes and rivers that we take for granted in Canada, but wonderful pastoral scenes—in miniature. Got home for tea and the house was overrun with Canadians.

Aileen had come home from her stint as a patient. John Gemmell, the young Air Force officer who is Meren's brother, had arrived on leave. Meren and Vic, Ruth and I, then after tea, Hoyle arrived home with the news that he had just become a Major. Ruth was terribly thrilled—of course we all were, so all trooped down to the Golden Lion to celebrate his promotion.

As mentioned, I opened the shop and carried on alone Sat. morning, in spite of Mrs. Hoyle. She feels she is indispensable. It was not difficult and the patients pitched in and enjoyed doing it.

George and Harvey arrived in the afternoon. After dinner we all got ready for the dance. Had helped the Sisters decorate one evening and it looked so attractive. The dance was simply terrific. All the parties at Hackwood are. We finally boarded our bikes for the ride home. Fortunately, it is downhill for the first mile or so, but quite a climb the last part in to Coombehurst.

There are so many Canadians staying here this weekend, it is like a house party. Sunday, we all slept late, then have had a very pleasant day walking around the grounds, playing games and just chatting over our meals and tea. Mrs. Simon is a marvel. Always so cheerful and makes all our friends so welcome. She never knows just how many she will have to feed, but always rises to the occasion. Aileen and I went to the station with George and Harvey tonight and then bicycled back.

There is a new American Red Cross club opening in Basingstoke, and they have asked us to help, so Aileen, Ruth and I will possibly go one evening a week.

We still have our large Canadian household. Last night, Monday, there was another party at Hackwood—rather an impromptu one—but great fun. John and Alan and I went. As usual, we biked. Don't think I will ever get used to getting ready for a dance, then tying a scarf firmly over my head and climbing on my bike—then riding home again at 1.00 or 2.00 am.

Harvey is being presented with his DFC at the next Investiture at Buckingham Palace—to be at the end of the month. I am going in for it. Should be quite a thrilling affair. Am looking forward to it.

Do take good care of yourselves.

Very much love,
Lois

February 19th, 1944
Dearest Family:

Am so thrilled to hear about cousin Bill and Billie, and shall write to them both immediately. Bill is fortunate. She is a lovely girl. Happy that you will be meeting her soon. So glad I had the good sense to introduce them! Have they set a date for the wedding yet?

Yesterday afternoon we went to the cocktail party at the Refords. We went in a large truck from the hospital—Ruth and Hoyle and Aileen and I from Coombehurst, so they came and picked us up. There must have been twenty of us in the back of the truck, sitting on benches—every time we went around a corner, the benches collapsed and we all landed in a heap. We were a dishevelled-looking crew when we emerged from the rear of the truck. They have a beautiful home and we all enjoyed it. We got home about 8.30 pm and Mrs. Simon had a lovely supper for us.

It is now Wednesday and I am still in the middle of this note. Just returned from the evening at the hospital—Ping-Pong and darts. We play too, and the patients seem to get a kick out of it.

Saturday I am going to London with Alan MacDonald. He is the young RCAF officer who has been spending his leave here. Then Tuesday is the day we go to Buckingham Palace.

Have not stayed at Corps House for a couple of weeks. Bombs came very close there the other night and shattered some of their windows.

Gerry is back from his course. They are stationed about twenty miles away now and B-Stoke is out-of-bounds, which makes it awkward.

We saw The Battle of Britain *at the Hospital today. A very good film—living here, one is apt to forget how marvellous the English people have been through it all. They take everything so matter-of-factly and go on living, very seldom even mentioning the horrors of war or the tragedies they have gone through. We get the alerts for the raids, but we are pretty well out in the country and can only hear the guns rumbling in the distance. If you read of the raids in the paper—please don't worry about me because the Canadian papers always exaggerate the situation.*

Do remember to watch for that army film shot at Hackwood.

Love and Hugs to you both and all the family,
Lois

February 25th, 1944
Dearest Mother and Dad:

In London again—in bed at Corps House after quite a day. I worked this morning then caught the noon train to London. Alan met me at Waterloo Station. We went to Corps House and I changed, then back to the Savoy Hotel where he was staying with a fellow officer, a very nice lad from Port Hope. We had a super tea. Oceans of sandwiches—on a huge platter, covered with tiny nasturtium leaves. Also, Alan produced a bottle of huge olives and Howard had a box of Laura Secord's, so we had a feast.

Then we went to see an extremely good show. It was a Terence Rattigan play, While the Sun Shines, a comedy and very amusing. It was about an Englishman, an American officer and a Free French officer—very topical of present-day London, when one sees uniforms of all the Allied nations. The American was exceptionally good. Just typical of Gerry and his friends. He was terribly funny because he was so true to life and behaved exactly as the Americans do in England but in an exaggerated manner. I was glad I didn't see that show with Gerry because I appreciated the antics of the Yankee—and I couldn't have laughed quite so hard if Gerry had been there.

Then back to the Savoy—to the dinner dance. Very good music and a lovely meal. Such nice lads to be with. Now I am back at Corps House, hoping it will be a quiet night!

Here it is Sunday night—I shall finish this note. It has been a busy day—I called Coombehurst this morning to see if there had been any messages for me—Mrs. Simon had everything under control, but she had been busy. Gerry had got leave unexpectedly and had arrived in Basingstoke Saturday afternoon. Of course, I had left right from the hospital—so missed him. Mrs. Simon took the situation in hand and asked him for dinner and the night. Then another American Lieut. I had met arrived at the door. Mrs. Simon got rid of him before Gerry arrived, and told him I would not be back until Monday. Then Harvey called—to let me know about details for the Investiture on Tuesday, so Mrs. Simon talked to him and made all the arrangements for me. Then the third Yankee Lieut. arrived and she sent him on his way. They all seemed to show up at once! Mrs. S. was just about tearing her hair out at this point; however, she managed it all beautifully. When I heard that Gerry was there at Coombehurst, thought I should get back. Spent a lazy afternoon. Aileen and George were here too. After an early tea, we went to a movie, then dropped in to a pub on the way home—being careful because this town was now supposed to be "off-limits" to Gerry's outfit. In the pub were most of his fellow officers and we even bumped into his Colonel!

We came home in time for tea and cookies, then Gerry had to leave to catch his train. Mrs. S. was afraid he would be hungry when he got back to camp, so sent him off with a package of sandwiches. Gerry is an awfully nice person and we do have a marvellous time together—but that is as far as it goes. Not the time to make any kind of a commitment in the middle of a war!

Am glad that Colonel Underwood approved of him.

The Investiture is Tuesday morning, so I shall go into London again tomorrow night, to be there in plenty of time. I seem to do such a lot of gallivanting—you will wonder when we do any work—we really have been working pretty hard—we work from 9.00 am till 6.00 pm—but love it and the time just flies.

Had a letter from Jack Cooper yesterday. Remember him? The Naval officer who was hurt skiing at Camp Fortune last winter. He is stationed not far from here and we are going to meet in London sometime soon.

There is to be a dance Saturday at George's Station. He and Aileen are going and they have asked me to join them, so am thrilled about that. Will know more about it later. Also, will write and tell you in detail about the Investiture.

Much love, Lois

BUCKINGHAM PALACE

March 1st, 1944
Dearest Family:

Well, we have been to Buckingham Palace!

I went into London Monday after work and Harvey met me and we went dinner- dancing at the Mirabel—a very nice spot. Had a delicious dinner and enjoyed it, but made it an early night as we wanted to be on hand in good time in the morning. We knew it would be best to be there early in order to get decent seats. We arrived at 9.30 am, just as people were beginning to queue up.

Bill Woods, a longtime friend of Harvey's, was there, too, so we were able to sit together. Harvey went in with the rest of his crew. All five of them were being decorated—two DFCs and three DFMs. We went through the gates of the palace—under an arch—into the courtyard. It was a glorious morning. Clear blue sky and bright sunshine.

Then a bus drove up and out stepped the court attendants. At first I thought it was a group on their way to a Fancy Dress ball! They were elderly men, about twenty of them, all dressed in short brocaded scarlet tunics and short skirts, long red stockings, black shoes with huge shiny buckles—great white ruffs around their necks and tremendous big black hats, with rosettes of red, white and black all around the band. Each one held a gigantic staff. Their chests were covered with Boer War and First World War medals. They formed a guard of honour as we all walked between them, into the palace.

We entered a lobby, then up a few steps and into an oblong room, with a raised platform or stage along the wide side in front of us. There were probably ten rows of chairs facing the stage. We had wonderful seats—second row, right in the centre. Here we were, sitting in a great hall in Buckingham Palace! It was most impressive. A lovely room, beautifully decorated in gold leaf and indirect lighting. The walls were lined with paintings of royalty—Queen Victoria and Prince Albert graced either side of the door, with many modern royalty represented. Officials were buzzing about and one pompous-looking gentleman was wearing a monocle. There was a band in attendance and they played softly in the background.

It was all very colourful—the lovely old room, the courtiers in their picturesque costumes and the regal-looking portraits. Suddenly the music rolled to a stop and at the far end of the room, a door opened and the procession appeared—in single file, all those to be decorated. There must have been close to 250, and lo and behold, there was Harvey, leading the procession! Bill and I were amazed and practically speechless. They moved slowly up to the front of the platform, Harvey looking very handsome and most impressive with his decorations. He has his Observer's Wing, under that his DFC, the 39-43 Campaign ribbon, then "Mackenzie King's Own", complete with Maple Leaf. Under that is the Pathfinder Brevy, it's a lovely gold albatross about two inches across and under that are his Gold Wings, with one gold bar attached, indicating two tours of "OPS".

Mac, his pilot, was right behind him and then there was a miscellaneous assortment of Navy, Army, Air Force and civilians. They stood there—waiting. Harvey did not look at all nervous. I think Bill and I were much more excited than he was.

Finally, the door on the platform opened and out stepped the King, flanked by two high-ranking officials. He was the picture of dignity—in his uniform of Admiral of the Fleet—with rows of gold braid almost to his elbows and masses of ribbons. They played "God Save the King", and of course, every-

one arose. Then the King said, "Ladies and gentlemen, please be seated".

Harvey stepped up on to the platform. The man on the King's right read out his name. He advanced to where the King was—made a left turn—bowed and stepped forward. Each man to receive an award was wearing a hook attached to his lapel. The King placed the DFC on the hook—spoke a few words, shook hands with Harvey and then it was Mac's turn. We were only about six feet from where the King was standing—so were able to see and hear everything perfectly. It went on from there, without a hitch, until everyone had been decorated.

Then it was all over and we all moved out into the courtyard. The RCAF photographers were there and took pictures of Harvey and the rest of the crew. They even took one of Harvey and Bill and me, all looking at his medal. It was a moving experience and a tremendous thrill to be there and witness such a traditional ceremony. It was a very special occasion.

We all went out to dinner—to the Café Royal—a charming place. There were Harvey, Bill, Mac, Holtby, the rear gunner, his two brothers and his cousin. After a delightful meal, the three of us went to a movie, then had tea before Bill and I caught the train. He was going to Bournemouth, on the same line as Basingstoke. It was surely a day to remember!

If Mr. and Mrs. Fenton could have been there, they would have been so very proud of Harvey. Do tell Mrs. Fenton all about it, will you, Mother? I forgot to ask for her address, so will you please send it to me and I will write them a note.

Heaps of Love, Lois

The Warren
Brenchley, Kent

OTTAWA FRIENDS AT INVESTITURE OF FLYER. After Flying Officer Harvey W. Fenton, son of Mr. and Mrs. George Fenton, 278 Second Avenue, Ottawa, received his D.F.C. from the King at a recent investiture at Buckingham Palace, he and two friends, Miss Lois J. MacDonald, daughter of Mr. and Mrs. W. Elwood MacDonald, 330 Driveway, of the Canadian Red Cross Services in London, and Lieut. S.W. Wood, son of Mr. and Mrs. S.J. Wood, 333 Second Avenue, left, posed for a picture in the palace courtyard. (RCAF photo)

March 3rd, 1944
My Dears:

It was just six months ago today that we arrived in England. The time simply flies although we have done so much and seen so many fascinating places. I have loved every minute of it.

Wednesday we had a visit from Mrs. Lee and Mrs. Tudball. They came in the morning and had lunch with Matron Charlton, saw the hospital and thanked the Matron and Col. Harvey, the C.O., for being so nice to us. They were very impressed and said how very lucky we are to be stationed here. Aileen and I were so glad they had come. They are both charming and we were pleased that they should see our hospital. Being at Corps House for the reception and having a chance to speak with some of the girls we had come over with and hear about their places, both their work and living quarters, we do realize that we are indeed fortunate. The hospital is great and the Canadian staff so very pleasant. And how we ever found Mrs. Simon, I'll never know. She is just marvellous. So thoughtful and caring and does so many little things for us. Has really created a lovely homey atmosphere for all of us living there. Mrs. Tudball took your names and address and said she would write to you on her return to Canada.

Tonight Cliff is coming over. Another U.S. Lieut. Gerry's company is having a party tonight, too, but I already had the date with Cliff when he got around to mentioning it. Three invitations for tomorrow night—but am taking the one with George's fellow officer, at their dance. Always nice to be with George and Aileen. Three offers for Sunday, too, but Gerry is coming over for the day.

I seem to keep our household amused with my social life. With so many young men around and so few single girls, it is not surprising to be busy, but rather fun! Hoyle has turned into quite a tease, too.

He and Ruth are a great couple and so nice to have them living here. He is a plastic surgeon from Toronto and does some very fine work.

Later Friday evening—here I am in bed. It was quite an evening. The most amusing I've experienced for a long time. Cliff arrived, with driver and Jeep. It was a very cold evening, so he sent the driver off to a movie and we stayed in. All the family were home, and he certainly got the once-over. Ruth and Hoyle, Mrs. Simon. Dr.Weston, who waltzed in with some new underwear he had purchased to have Mrs. Simon sew on some name tapes. He waved great white shorts and shirts in front of us—so we could see what a bargain he had found. Captain Hedges was the next arrival, with a huge smelly cigar and horn-rimmed glasses, with his great booming laugh and somewhat vulgar jokes. Then Mrs. Hubbard crept into the room, as prim and proper as ever, with her hair drawn back in a neat bun and her skirts almost to her ankles. It is a pretty diverse group and I'm sure Cliff was fascinated by them all.

Now that our numbers have increased, we have been using the drawing room instead of Mrs. Simon's small den. There was a bang on the front window—the doorbell was out of commission—there was Barfield, Cliff's driver. He had found the nearest pub and never got to the movie. In he came, well-oiled from the pub, the sloppiest creature in the world with cross eyes and a great wad of chewing gum. He sailed into the room and slapped Cliff on the back as if they were buddies—you should have seen the eyebrows raised all around the room. Barfield chatted away, taking over the conversation, until he was quite warm. Then Cliff decided it was time for them to leave. Barfield struggled to his feet, tossed his coat to the Lieutenant to hold for him. By this time, we were all chuckling. The Brits are all so class conscious that this was all foreign to them. They finally got organized and left. I expect

Cliff took the wheel on the way home, as Barfield was in no condition to drive.

Love and kisses, Lois

March 6th, 1944
Hello again!

Whatever you choose in a suit would be lovely, Mother. Another suit would be wonderful, as it is all we wear over here. It's too cold to wear just a dress or skirt and sweater without a jacket.

Will start off where I left off in the last letter. George and Aileen were staying in the loveliest place. A very old quaint inn. It used to be a mill and was built in 1760. Wish you could see it. The mill wheel still runs—to produce electricity for the place. I was quite intrigued and want to go back there in the summer. We had tea in the town, then back to the mill for dinner and got dressed for the dance. I went with one of George's fellow officers, Bill James, a very nice lad from Hamilton. They are the Princess Patricia's and a great group. They brought me home after the dance.

Gerry arrived at noon and we went to the Red Lion in town, then walked up to Hackwood and picked up our bikes. Aileen and I had left them there on Saturday. It was a lovely day, cold but very bright, so we rode around Hackwood Park. It's a beautiful place—so many pretty paths and drives. You should have seen Gerry on my bike—all folded up like an accordion.

Jack Cooper called tonight—before I was home from the hospital as it was Ping-Pong night. Here it is Tues. night and I will finish this. Aileen and I and Ruth and Hoyle had dinner at the Venture Restaurant, not far away, as Mrs. S. had a cold and we didn't want her to have to worry about cooking for us. Then Aileen and I came home, as Jack was calling me at 7.30 pm. He called and we are going to meet in London on Saturday. We shall see a show and dinner.

It is now Friday, and I will continue. Cliff came over Wed. night. His last name is Kendall, is from Missouri and a very nice lad. Has quite a drawl. Gerry had called while I was out and Mrs. Simon had asked him for dinner the next night. I think she is trying to protect his interests! Anyway, he arrived, a little late, sailed up to the door, or rather, his Colonel brought him in a jeep—such service! His own uniform was at the cleaners and not back in time, so he was all dolled up in his Captain's outfit, complete with his battle ribbons—the Captain's, I mean. The Yanks amaze us—but they are a lively lot and fun to be with.

You would think Cliff and Barfield quite a panic. The whole family gets quite excited when they are coming. The other night, when Cliff was here, Barfield came back for him—it was quite cold, so we brought him in for tea. The reception hall is dark because of the Blackout. Aileen was at the phone—she had been trying to get George. Just as Barfield sailed into the hall, Aileen said, "Oh hello, darling!" Barfield stopped dead, his eyes crossed and uncrossed—he shifted his great wad of gum and said, "Gosh, does she mean me?" We all had a good laugh.

I love to get cigarettes. No, I still don't smoke but do love to have them, as there are so many boys in the hospital who don't get many. The Red Cross gives each patient one pack a week, but that doesn't go very far. I keep the ones I get at the hospital and give them to the lads who are short. I love the work at the hospital and get so much pleasure talking to the men. The majority of them are very cheerful and going into the wards every day—we get to know many of them individually. Besides helping them and getting them interested in handicrafts—our job is just to talk with them—ask them about their homes and families—look at their snapshots and souvenirs and admire their efforts at handicrafts. Our hospital is truly a wonderful place and it is surely an honour to be here.

Heaps of love to you both and Timmie, Lois

Red Cross Corps members cycling to Headquarters Burlington Gardens

JACK ENTERS MY LIFE

March 13th, 1944
Dearest Ones:

Ruth and I got up early and caught the train to London and I went to Harrods. It is the most wonderful store. Was meeting Jack Cooper for lunch. We went to the Royal Automobile Club.

Then we did a bit of sightseeing—went to the Tower of London—I was really thrilled. We walked over the Tower Bridge and through a bit of old London. Back to the Strand Palace Hotel for tea. Then to the theatre to see Strike a New Note, a musical comedy, a George Black production. On to the Haymarket Club for dinner. It is a nice place—small and intimate, frequented mostly by Canadians. Many Navy as it is close to their HQ in the Haymarket. We joined a group of his fellow officers and their ladies and had a very pleasant evening. It was great to see Jack again.

I came back to Basingstoke after lunch on Sunday. It was lovely when I got home, really spring-like. Some mornings, during the winter when we were bicycling to the hospital, through cold, wet fog, I wondered why anyone would choose to live on this miserable little island! However, when the sun shines, you realize what a truly lovely place England is. Am so glad you received the snaps of the house and grounds. It is surely beautiful here now and wish you could both be here to enjoy it. I always loved the country and it is surely a thrill to live out here and just go into London the odd weekend.

Well, we are finally wearing our "Pips". After all these months. It seems that they didn't have any in stock, but now we have them up. They are metal, gold with tiny Red Crosses on the top. Really quite pretty. We took down the Canada badges and put up new flashes on our epaulets. They are very small gold letters, saying "Red Cross—Canada". They really do look smart although we feel a little conspicuous, suddenly blossoming forth under such shoulderfuls of gold.

The parcel for Mrs. Simon arrived today. She is so pleased and will write to you. Thank you for my birthday cable. It was phoned in this morning and Mrs. Simon took the message. She thought today must be my birthday and she called the hospital as Aileen and I were not coming home for supper as it was Ping-Pong night. I assured her that it was not until Wednesday, so all was serene.

The household are insistent that we "Wet our Pips" in the time-honoured manner and take them out to the corner pub. Being my birthday, we will all go to the Golden Lion before dinner.

Mary and I are applying for leave April 16-23 and planning a trip to Scotland. We will ask for hospitality in Edinburgh—being in a private home, it is easier to meet people and see the points of interest. We will have a long weekend over Easter, and I will go to Kent to see the Langers. Do hope the weather will be good and not too much rain. Am certainly looking forward to it all.

Here it is March 16th, and I have had another birthday. The parcels have not arrived yet, so I still have them to look forward to. Have been very fortunate with all the things you have mailed coming through safely. Will enjoy them when they get here. Mrs. Simon had a beautiful birthday dinner for us last evening: lovely soup, roast chicken, then ice cream with chocolate sauce.

There was a bouquet of flowers at my place in a vase, with tissue paper around it. There were lovely yellow daffodils and I thought just the flowers were for me. Then Ruth said, "Aren't you going to open your gift?" Mrs. Simon was up at the buffet, serving dinner. I tore off the tissue and there was a beautiful antique sterling silver bud vase and I could not believe it was for me. But Ruth assured me that it was, and Hoyle muttered that it was the first time he had ever seen a landlady give a present like that!

I was very pleased with it and it was certainly sweet of Mrs. Simon to go to so much trouble and to give me such a lovely gift. I am very fond of her and she has been especially kind to me. I wonder, perhaps, if in some small way, I have managed to fill in for the daughter she never had?

It has been a quiet week but a very busy one. Aileen and I still feel quite gorgeous in our "Pips". The only drawback is that everyone salutes us! Even great black U.S. soldiers who do so with a broad grin. It is a little disconcerting when someone jumps in front of our bicycles with a salute! We have got to the point where we cross the road to avoid these encounters.

The doctor came home tonight with a new uniform. He has not been officially in uniform, and now he will wear the outfit of the Civilian Defence. He modelled it for us at dinner—navy blue with a fancy beret. He certainly looked swish and we all had a good laugh. It is the craziest household. Every time poor Mother Hubbard opens her mouth, she promptly puts her foot in it. Then Captain Hedges and Dr. Weston jump on it and make something out of it and the poor woman blushes furiously and titters helplessly. I am sure she likes the attention.

Much love to you both, and to Grandmother and Grand-daddy Kelly.

Lois

March 23rd, 1944
Dearest Family:

The birthday boxes arrived today and I love everything. The red and white print dress is perfect! Fits just right and can hardly wait until weather is warm enough to wear it. It was just like Christmas when I opened them all. So many wonderful things. The candy and things for Mrs. Simon to use cooking. Everything will be enjoyed so much.

Thank you, thank you! The skirt is fabulous. English-looking and such a good fit. I don't know how you do it, Mother. I am well fixed for clothes now. After being in khaki so much, it is a treat to wear pretty bright colours. The two cotton dresses are so pretty and fresh looking.

Sunday was a beautiful morning and everything is blossoming. Glorious time of year. Gerry and Mac came over after lunch. It was rather a lazy day. Gerry was exhausted after so many route marches, so he slept and Mac and I listened to the Canadian-U.S. football game on the radio. Such a flop. 18-0 for the Yanks. Of course, Mac was elated! Guess they had been practising ever since we trimmed them last time.

John Matheson, a nephew of our McCuaig relatives in Edmonton, is a patient here. I had no idea who he was. He did mention having attended Queen's, and we spoke of friends who had been there. Then his name struck a familiar chord and I asked if he was Eric's cousin. He was quite amazed and said he was. He is a Capt. and was injured out East several months ago. Such a nice chap. He did know that cousin Eric had stayed with us in Ottawa while there in the Navy.

(John Matheson had been severely wounded and returned to Canada aboard a hospital ship, then spent many weeks in a veterans' hospital, where he met his future wife. He completed a law degree and for many years had a very successful law practice in Brockville, Ontario. He was elected as a Member of the federal Legislature, serving for several terms, and has been the recipient of many honours.)

Saturday morning, Syd Frost came over. He is an Up patient in the Officers' Ward. A Princess Patricia, he was seriously injured in Italy but has made a great recovery. He was getting a little bored with hospital life, so I asked him to come for coffee. We walked around the grounds, saw the greyhounds, and gardens, then met the rest of the family. We went to the Venture for a very nice lunch.

(Sydney Frost graduated in law after the war, then had a fine career in Toronto. He always remembered the promise he had made to himself to return to Sicily, Italy, Holland and Cyprus where his beloved regiment, the Princess Patricia's Canadian Light Infantry, had fought so valiantly and many had paid the supreme sacrifice. He has made ten pilgrimages back to these places to follow the route the regiment took and to visit the cemeteries to honour his fallen comrades. All recorded in his two excellent books, *Once a Patricia*, published in 1988 and the recent book, *Always a Patricia*. In the past two years, Aileen and I have had two delightful visits with Syd. Great fun to recall Basingstoke and fine friends there more than 60 years ago!)

Jack came for the weekend. It was the kind of weather that must have inspired that poem, "Oh to be in England now that April is there". We went biking—stopped at noon for lunch. It was just like June weather at home. Then on to Winchester. We were surely bears for punishment, being that far from home, on bikes. We still had to get back to Coombehurst. Winchester is such a lovely old town and Jack was anxious to see it. We went to the cathedral and a few famous places, home by a different route. Quite hilly, walked some of the steeper ones. We biked about forty miles. The last few seemed the longest! Great way to truly see the countryside.

Much love to you both and my dear doggie. Lois.

March 27th, 1944
Dearest Folks:

The mail situation is improving—I had two letters from you, Dad, and one from you, Mother.

Aileen and I have been very busy stock-taking. We did finish today so all is well. Many of the men are doing handicrafts. They pick it up very quickly and it is interesting to see them all working away. There are two lads side by side, both doing needlework; they started together so it has become a marathon and they are both working like crazy. Ted broke his needle today and was delayed until we got the message and rushed another one to him. There was great consternation in the camp as his bedmate surged ahead. Then Ted said Eric worked until lights out last evening and was hard at it again at seven this morning.

We do get a kick out of seeing such enthusiasm. They really do seem interested and do things beautifully. We get to know them—where they are from—all about their girlfriends, wives and children. When some lad who had been with us for weeks leaves, we really miss him. They are such a great group and very easy to get along with. Our workshop is a bright, lively place. Such a lovely large room, with huge tall windows. The sun streams in and we keep the radio playing most of the time. There is a Ping-Pong table and several dart boards. Also long tables and benches where they do their leather work.

Mrs. Perry has been away for six weeks and Mrs. Hoyle has been ill, so Aileen and I have been on our own. Very pleasant! We have been extremely busy, but the patients are eager to help and that is a blessing.

Here it is April 1st. April Fool at home! When I got here at noon, Bill James called to say that he had been away on a manoeuvre and just arrived back to discover that there was to be a dance at their Mess tonight. He is George's friend in Borden.

He picked me up after dinner and we went and had a super time. The Princess Patricia's do have great parties. I'm a little late now but will write a few lines.

Am reading an exceptionally good book, So Little Time, *by John Marquand. Read it if you have a chance. I haven't done much reading since I have been here. We never have a spare moment—so perhaps that is why I am enjoying this book so much. Jack sent it. He had just read it before he was here last weekend and was quite enthusiastic about it.*

Monday we had a hectic day and the Ping-Pong tournament was in the evening. Aileen and I had to arrange it and everything seemed to go wrong. However, it all turned out very well and everyone seemed to enjoy it. They all play, officers and other ranks and we enter, too. Some of them are extremely good and we never get past the first few rounds. They all appear—with cups clutched in hand—because we serve coffee and biscuits to everyone possessing a cup.

Gerry called in the middle of it. He had just arrived in town after being away for two weeks. He was "Jeepless" so said he would go to Coombehurst and meet me there. We were late getting home and when we finally arrived, he was having tea with Mrs. Simon. The whole family was in and Hoyle had slides of his work, plastic surgery, so he showed them. All very interesting.

All the regiments and other units are so busy. We all know what they are preparing for and it scares me, just thinking about what lies ahead for all these brave and fine young fellows. Gerry may be over tomorrow night as I am going Friday for the weekend and expect to stay until Monday. Aileen and George were to go on leave, beginning at Easter and for the following week. It has been cancelled and she is so disappointed. I am sorry because she was surely looking forward to it.

Ruth and Hoyle left for Glasgow this morning and Mrs. Simon went with them to London for the day, where they would do a show.

Heaps of love and I do love to get your letters. Lois

Easter Sunday, April 10th, 1944
Dearest Mother and Dad:

Guess you are in Montreal right now—while I am at The Warren with the Langers. Arrived Friday about 8 pm. Caught the 4.09 from Basingstoke. It was late and each time I changed trains I was late and missed the connection. It's an experience, travelling in England—not an enviable one—because crowds are terrific, trains late and very little food to be had in transit. Of course, being a holiday weekend, it is more crowded than usual. Most interesting, as the train dashes through the crowded suburbs with their narrow streets and much evidence of bomb damage, through the quiet countryside with very green fields and masses of spring flowers, and through sleepy villages with tiny thatched cottages. It really is a cross-section of England.

I always wonder about the people who live in the various places. In the smoky suburbs with their unending rows of little houses, all joined together and each one exactly like its neighbour—with tiny windows, short front walks, trim box hedges and numerous chimney pots. They all present a neat appearance from the front—but the backyards as viewed from the train window leave much to be desired. Small, untidy plots of ground, with perhaps a tiny Victory garden, an air raid shelter, outside plumbing, all buried under inches of soot and grime.

As the train gets out in the country—it's Kent, and much more pleasant—everything is very green, rolling hills, quaint old stone churches, pretty little cottages and flowers abound. Daffodils and prim-

roses grow wild and come up everywhere. I always pictured England entirely built-up, with scarcely a field or bit of uncultivated land, but not so. The crops are beginning to come up in long even rows, and the flowers, fruit blossoms and flowering shrubs make it a virtual garden.

Places like The Warren, Coombehurst, Bylands (Refords) are all country houses and more or less farms with a few animals and a few acres around them. There are other similar homes nearby and the various families socialize. Children attend boarding school, and are only home for the holidays.

This place, The Warren, is certainly the most complete home I have ever been in. There are not too many rooms, but they are large and spacious, very comfortably furnished and have an air of being lived in, used and loved.

We must come back here, when the war is over. I'm hoping by the time I return to England, there will be speedy air service and we will all be able to fly over for a few weeks.

There are the places like Hackwood Park—estates or more correctly called Country Seats—I think they must be something like hotels. Colossal places—run by an agent or manager, with a whole retinue of servants. Various members of the family have their own suites and go their own way. These places are steeped in tradition, some of them belonging to the same family for generations. Most have flats in London and spend weekends and summer months in the country.

It would seem much more pleasant to live in country homes like this one and Coombehurst—where you could enjoy the garden and everything else about it, without having a great staff running everything and always underfoot.

Their home, The Warren, is still as lovely as ever, even nicer, with the spring flowers. We went to help decorate the town hall for the dance in the evening. Friend's son had just returned from duty in the East, and it was a party for him. Then off to a cocktail party, dinner and the dance.

Sunday we went to the village church—a lovely day and such an enjoyable service. Gladys Langer works so hard, but makes it all look so easy. It was warm, with flowers everywhere, and so many birds, all singing. We biked in the afternoon, then neighbours came in for the evening.

Monday morning Charles and I went fishing bright and early. The stream was recently stocked with trout. It was great fun. You know how much I like to fish. We got half a dozen beauties and took them home for breakfast.

Now I am getting ready to go off to Scotland. We are leaving Friday night.

Much love, Lois

SCOTLAND

April 16th, 1944
Dearest Mother and Dad:

Here I am in Scotland! Mary and I are in Melrose, a lovely little town in the hills.

To get back to the beginning of our trip—I caught the train after work on Friday and met Mary at St. Pancras Station. Oh yes, I was in the same railway compartment as George Formby! They are evidently shooting some scenes in B-stoke. At first I wondered who the celebrity could be on the station platform—in the beige Jaegar coat and peak cap—but when he turned around there was no mistaking that face. He sat in one corner across from me, and hummed to himself.

Mary was waiting for me and we got some little boys to help with our luggage. The urchins in London have a little chant that goes like this: "Say Chum, have you any gum?" If they see a Canadian or Yankee uniform, they immediately expect you to have a great pocketful of gum. The Yanks usually have, and consequently the children in London, in fact all over the country, are fast becoming enthusiastic gum-chewers. I am sure most of them had not even seen it a few years ago. I very seldom have gum for them—but usually keep Canadian candy in my pocket—they love that.

We could not get berths, but managed to get good seats. We had sandwiches, cookies and coffee, so about 11.00 pm we shared it with the other passengers in our carriage. They all had something, too, so we had a little party. We arrived in Melrose at 9.00 am on Saturday morning. It was lovely, travelling along on the train—up through the hills. Do tell Mr. and Mrs. Clark that I am much impressed with their native Scotland. The rugged beauty is entirely different from the south of England—although I still think southern England is a pretty nice place.

We are staying in Melrose over the weekend with Miss Low. She is in charge of the local Women's Voluntary Service here and she is such a kind person. Met us at the station, rushed us home to breakfast, then we went to bed and slept until noon. She took us to Melrose Abbey—quite a picturesque and historic spot. Saw the ruins of the museum there. A lovely old place—full of tradition and old tales. This is such a pretty town, right on the Tweed and is an ancient place. Buildings are of stone—grey, in contrast to the familiar red brick of England. The hills are spectacular and must be a picture when the heather is in bloom.

There are three hills that form the background of Melrose—Tri Montiem, as the Romans called them—and they can be seen for miles. We saw Darnick Tower—the oldest inhabited house in the British Isles. Has been in the same family for over 800 years. We walked along the Tweed which, with all due respect to Scotland, is just an overgrown brook, Stag Creek in early spring! People were wading across it, fly-fishing. It is very pretty and I was most intrigued with the fishing. There are Polish troops in the vicinity and somehow, it seems odd to see them here, wielding a fly rod.

This morning we went to church, a Presbyterian service much like ours at home. The church, the minister, the hymns, and even the accents were more like ours than anything I've seen in England, where the churches are stone and terribly cold.

Sunday afternoon we went to Lowood, to Lady Middleton's home. She is the daughter of Earl Grey—former Governor General of Canada. Lady Grey was there, also. Quite a stately old lady. Rather exciting to meet her. It's a beautiful location—right on the bank of the Tweed overlooking the water—and the flowers, especially the daffodils, were lovely. Our hostesses were most gracious and we enjoyed tea with them. As Mary and I had both grown up in Ottawa, we found much to chat about with Lady Grey and her daughter.

Monday morning we went on a salvage campaign with Miss Low. She was in charge for Melrose and vicinity. It was a wonderful opportunity for us to see the countryside, as we drove along—through outlying and rural districts—to all the hidden villages, nestling in the border hills. We had a loudspeaker attachment on the car—also a gramophone and records—so we entered the villages, in a burst of music, then Mary and I took turns making little speeches about the importance of salvage and the need for books for the Forces. It was really pretty funny. However, the people came out of their homes in droves, with books and all sorts of other things. We drove miles, all through Sir Walter Scott's famous Border country. We heard the ancient tales and quaint superstitions and saw the "Meeting of the Waters"—where the Ettrick flows into the Tweed. It's the loveliest country—mountains, streams, forests, and fields, divided with old-fashioned stone fences and filled with shaggy sheep and many baby lambs, gamboling in the spring sunshine.

In the evening, we went to a Whist Drive. Quite an experience, like something you might witness in Sandy Creek. Mary and I got a big kick out of it. We were not very good at Whist and always were several jumps behind the locals who really seemed to be sharks.

Tuesday morning we went to Abbotsford—Sir Walter Scott's home and one of the most attractive places I have seen. A lovely setting and beautiful architecture. Sir Walter Maxwell Scott, a descendant of the famous one, lives there now. He was charming and insisted that we should see all through the place. It was most impressive—the library, the stud-

ies, the armoury room and the Chinese drawing room—all just as they had been long ago.

We had a taxi—he waited for us and then took us to Galashiels, then back to Miss Low's. It was a colossal high old vehicle and I felt just like one of those tourists we used to see in the movies—sitting, peering out the window, with a guide book clutched in one hand and making inane remarks.

We went to Darnick for lunch—to Mrs. Andrews'. She was young, pretty and very pleasant, with three darling little girls. Such nice children. Miss Low did so much to make our time there enjoyable. It was quite special to spend time in that part of the country and be entertained by some of the local people. We caught the 6.00 pm train to Edinburgh. The sun was shining and it was really beautiful. I got quite a thrill as the train rolled into the station—to actually be in Edinburgh!

We went directly to the King George and Queen Elizabeth Officers' Club—had dinner and found out where we were to stay. Walked around—through the park in front of the castle, and up to the parade ground. Then we went to the Botts', our hosts.

They are super people and made us feel so much at home, right away. We can come and go as we please. Dorothy is out most of the time, as she works at the American Red Cross. Cyril is such a nice man and Randall, their son, is fifteen and a darling boy. The children here seem to have so much poise—without being bold.

Wednesday morning, we were up bright and early and off to Princes Street. We went through some of the shops, Jenners, Binns and several others. Then met Mrs. Andrews, her husband and children at the Caledonian for coffee at 11.00 am. Such an attractive family. I was disappointed in the merchandise in the stores. Thought I would be able to find something nice to send you both from Scotland, but there was nothing to buy. Even worse than London.

We returned to the Officers' Club for lunch. There were two New Zealand officers there. They were extremely nice and it was their last day of leave. They asked us to have dinner and go to a show that evening. In the afternoon, Mary and I went to the Astley-Ainsley Institute—a hospital—because I was most interested in their handicraft dept. There was a Canadian girl running it—from Toronto—she showed us all over their department, then invited us to have tea with them. That was a very worthwhile visit.

We returned to the club and met Frank and Ted, the New Zealand lads—had dinner and went to see The Gypsy Princess *at the King's Theatre. It was very new—in its first week—was a bit slow in the first scene—but was exceedingly good. We went back to the club where a dance was in full swing. Frank is a pilot, had been a prisoner and had just escaped a short time ago. What extraordinary lives these young men have had. Very reticent to talk about it—but the bits we did hear were pretty exciting.*

Thursday morning, Mary and I were up and off to the Overseas Club, where we were meeting a Mr. Stewart, who was taking us on a tour of Edinburgh. He is a Scottish philanthropist who has made a hobby of entertaining Canadians and showing them the city. He has tour-guided over 5,000 Canadian troops and is always pleased to see new ones. He had two Canadian pilot officers in tow, as well. We went first to the castle—went through it, and saw all the famous old spots, and the war memorial. Then down the Royal Mile—to Holyrood Palace. He explained everything and told us the quaint old tales. We went in a very old church, through John Knox's house and various other ancient places. Then into Holyrood itself—through the cloistered gardens, heard about the rivalry between the various clans, etc., up to the banquet hall, a gorgeous room—must have been marvellous when they held banquets there.

Through Mary Queen of Scots' apartment—heard the story of her life—of her husband, Lord Darnley and the subsequent murder of her secretary, Rizzio. I was most intrigued and hated to leave. Then he took us to Lord Darnley's Pub. A real old-fashioned one that certainly has held its place in history. Andy and Eddie, the two Canadian lads, were thrilled with it. We left Mr. Stewart and the four of us went to Binns for lunch.

We decided we had done enough historical sightseeing for one day. Mary and Eddie climbed partway up "Arthur's Seat" while Andy, Eric Andrews from Sidney, N.S., and I went to Portobello, a nearby seaside resort, because I was dying to see the sea—not having had a glimpse of it since we came over on the boat. We walked the boardwalk and some of the beach. It was fun, then back to town and found a lovely tea dance. We were just in time for tea and several dances.

I had been in touch with Mrs. McAlister, Cally's mother, and she had invited us out there for supper. You remember Cally, one of the Scottish schoolgirls who came to our school when they evacuated the youngsters from Britain. She came to our place on different occasions. Have not seen her since coming over here, but have been in touch with her and she was anxious that we should contact her parents when in Scotland. She is working in southern England and we hope to get together soon.

They live about 15 miles out of Edinburgh, in the most beautiful spot. Cally's dad is Medical Supt. of a large hospital and they live on the grounds, on top of a hill, a magnificent location. Everything so green and windswept. Dr. McAlister met us at the bus and drove us up to the house. Really a lovely place. They were extremely kind and quite disappointed because we could not stay overnight. We saw around the grounds, then had a delectable dinner. They had the occupational therapist (who is also Canadian) for dinner, too. I was delighted to meet her and to hear about their department. We did not have an opportunity to see it—but I hope to go back sometime and will do so then. We caught the 10.00 pm bus back to Edinburgh and a taxi to the Botts'. Dorothy and Cyril were home and had tea and a snack for us.

Mary and I had planned to go to Glasgow and Loch Lomond on Friday, but it is quite a long trip just for one day and also it was a little early in the season—as the steamers don't run until May. It was another glorious day, so we borrowed bikes from the American Red Cross, then biked to Crammond about 5 or 6 miles out of Edinburgh, on the Firth of Forth. The Almond River joins the Forth there and it's a lovely old village. Do ask Mrs. Clark. I seem to remember her telling me that she grew up in that area.

The inn was on a narrow winding street, leading down to the beach. We stayed there for the day—had an excellent dinner at the inn, then walked up the river in the afternoon. It was fascinating. In places there were rapids and little waterfalls, all so pretty, with a shaded walk along the riverbank. We returned the bikes and went to the tea dance because it had been a great success the day before. Met Andy and Eddie again and had such fun. Then we had supper together in a quaint little restaurant. A Mrs. Alexander had asked Mary and me out to her place in the evening, so we caught a bus there, and the lads went off to Lord Darnley's Pub. They had been fascinated and said they must go back and count the flowers embroidered on said Lord's waistcoat that is displayed at the pub.

They called for us about ten o'clock. Mrs. Alexander had baked all sorts of cookies and cakes for us and it was a most enjoyable evening. Then we returned to Dorothy and Cyril's and they invited the lads in and we had a little farewell party as we were leaving in the morning. Randall escorted us to the station, where we joined a queue and stood there for a good fifteen minutes before we realized that we were in the Glasgow queue and we were going to York! We finally found the right one, and Andy and Eddie, who thought we had slept in or were at the wrong station.

We were in a very comfortable air-conditioned club car. I hate the miserable stuffy compartments that make up most English trains. Dorothy had packed us a lunch and we had a thermos of tea and some chocolates. There was another lad with Eddie and Andy and we shared our lunch, then played cards most of the way.

The Scottish people we encountered were all extremely kind to us and made sure that we had a very pleasant time. We will remember them and their gracious hospitality for years to come.

The train rolled into York and we bade farewell to Andy and Eddie. Such nice lads.

The Jobson family were there to meet us. Arthur, Mr. Jobson, Nora and Stanley were all at the station. It had been over two years since Arthur had been in Canada with the RAF in the Commonwealth Air Training Plan. Was delighted to see him again. He had spent quite a bit of time at our place and I remember we took him up to the Gatineau for the weekend. His family were eager to reciprocate and could not do enough for us.

The parents are lovely and made us feel so welcome. Margaret and Nora are both pretty and very nice teens. Stanley is 17, a good-looking lad, with dark eyes and curly hair. Did I tell you that Arthur had married in the last year? A darling girl, Wyn, tiny and dark. She is most attractive and I liked her so much. They gave me a picture taken at their wedding and will send it. She arrived on a later train. She is living at home in Sheffield, and working there, and Arthur is stationed nearby. Great that he is closer to home, as he had that time in Canada, then out East for many months.

We toured York and they showed us all the interesting places. It is an old walled city and really lovely, except for the bomb damage. The wall still stands and there are masses of daffodils on the banks up to the wall. We checked out their local pub, then home for a delicious dinner and very pleasant evening. Sunday morning, we were up early and off to York Minster, the very famous old cathedral. After the service, we had a special tour of the belfry. Mr. Jobson had arranged to take us up there and it was fascinating. We were right up in the top, where the bells are. We saw Big Peter and the smaller ones. Then we went into the room where they ring the bells. I was amazed. Always thought just one man did it all, but there was a team of 12 men, and they stood in a circle. Each one pulled on a rope that came down through the ceiling. They pulled them in different waves and frequencies and this changed the tune of the bells. Most interesting to see it.

We went to see their old home, or rather, where it had stood. Now it is just a vacant lot. Was completely demolished and the only house on the street that got hit. It was amazing that they all got out unscathed. They were crouching under the dining room table. After lunch we all went to the station together. Arthur and Wyn caught the train to Sheffield and we got the one to London. It was an extremely pleasant visit and I was especially happy to meet them all.

Much love, Dears, Lois

(Arthur Jobson, who had grown up in York, Yorkshire, a young RAF officer, had come to Canada in 1941 for flying training in the Commonwealth Training Program. He was stationed in Ottawa after months in Western Canada. I had met him during his weeks there and he visited our home often, before returning to England with his group.)

HACKWOOD

April 26th, 1944
Dearest Family:

Trip back to London was uneventful. We slept most of the way as we were both so tired. I had intended to stay at Corps House overnight and go out on an early train in the morning; however, there was a train just ready to leave, so hopped on and it was much nicer to get right home. There was a Nursing Sister on the train, and we got a taxi together. Of course everyone was in bed, but threw a few pebbles at our window and Aileen came down and let me in.

Our leave in Scotland and York was everything we had hoped and much more. People were extremely kind and the weather, marvellous. We seemed to pack so much in, saw so many interesting and truly beautiful places. Will surely hope to return some day.

Had dinner with Ted Lloyd Monday night as he was leaving Tuesday for the Convalescent Centre. He is fine again but still a bit shaky.

Heard from Joan Bolus yesterday. I did go to their place several times when I first arrived, and they were very hospitable. We reminisced about our days at the Badminton Club when her family spent those years in Ottawa. Her husband Alec is a fine fellow and their little son, Julian, adorable. Alec is away with his regiment and Joan has just had a second son, Peter. I had tried repeatedly to get her on the phone when in London the past few months, without success. They were bombed out and are now in Lancashire. No wonder I could not get an answer, I don't think there was much left of the house. Fortunately, they all got out safely. She is trying to find a place in Tunbridge Wells. That is near Mrs. Langer, so I will be able to see Joan when I go to The Warren.

We have a new occupational therapist—a Canadian Nursing Sister. Aileen and I are delighted because she is really one of us and we will be working partly with her instead of just the English pair.

Have spent the last couple of evenings catching up on correspondence. Believe it or not, I had nine thank-you notes to write for my leave. People were so very good to us, felt I should write to them quickly.

Had a very nice letter from Mr. Norman Holland, in Montreal, saying that he had received my note and that I had been placed on their overseas list, and would receive 300 cigarettes one month and an assorted box the alternate month. Very kind of him and I surely do appreciate getting the cigs and candy as there are always patients who never get boxes and it is nice to be able to have some for them. Last week, I had just received a box of chocolates and opened it at the hospital when a request came in from one of the Nursing Sisters that a dying sailor on her ward was asking for chocolate. That box could not have arrived at a better time. So little to be able to do for the poor lad.

Saturday night was Gerry's Mess dance. We went to the Wheat Sheaf for dinner with a group, then on to the party. I wore my new red and white print dress. That was the first time it has been warm enough to put it on. It was really an elegant party, held in the 300-room mansion his unit has. A colossal old estate. Ten or twelve years ago it must have been one of the stateliest and loveliest old Seats in Hampshire. It was six or seven miles away and we went in the Jeep. When we arrived, the drive and front park were simply jammed with vehicles of all sorts and descriptions—really incongruous in the Old World setting. We had a driver for the occasion and he was obviously bored with the whole thing and really a deadpan, with a great wad of gum. We bounced up to the entrance and climbed ungracefully from our iron chariot. Wended our way through many corridors to the magnificent ballroom—a marvellous room with mirrored walls and huge, glistening chandeliers. French doors opening onto terraces and sunken gardens—with wide steps and tall pillars, overlooking an ornamental pond. The music was great and so was the food—especially the canned pineapple. I ate mine and Gerry's, too, as he was not impressed with it. Said they have it often while, for me, it was a real treat.

Gerry came back at noon today, Sunday. It is really like July weather at home. We had dinner, then went to play golf. There is a lovely little course about 5 miles from here. Hoyle lent Gerry his bike and golf clubs and I had some golf balls, thanks to you, Dad. It was funny, we both drove off from the first tee, mine wasn't bad, not good either, but straight down the fairway. Then, the second shot—I took a mighty swing, the ball sailed through the air, landed on the green—rolled and rolled and finally dropped into the cup! Gerry nearly had a fit and was ready to give up then and there. However, I was pretty awful the rest of the way around—so wiped out after the flying start. We could not have had a better day for it. Just glorious! We biked home for dinner at seven, then all just sat around and listened to the radio.

My beautiful violet suit arrived and I am so pleased with it. Once again you have sent me such a lovely outfit and a perfect fit! Thank you both so very much. I love it.

It is now May 1st, weather glorious. A shame to be inside. Many of the patients are out in the sun, so our work takes us outdoors, too. Hackwood and Coombehurst are both beautiful, with shrubs and fruit trees in blossom. Coombehurst is a picture. I wish you could see the walled garden. It's so pretty. The apple trees, instead of just growing in all directions, as in Canada, are trained to be low and are planted in a row, so that they are flat like a hedge, with the branches of the different trees intertwining. It is indescribably lovely now, when the blossoms are at their best. We have been eating vegetables from the garden for a month now. It is surprising how early they are ready.

Jack Cooper called tonight. He has been away for ten days—he travels quite a bit and will come here again soon if he can get away.

Tuesday evening there was a minstrel show in town to start the local "Salute the Soldier" Campaign. It was staged by the American Black troops at the town hall and was exceptionally good. Ruth and Hoyle and Mrs. Simon and I went. They had their own M.C. I'm sure he must have been on the stage back home—because he had plenty of self-assurance. As a matter of fact, they all had and it was very professional. They sang both popular and classical pieces, tap danced, gave comedy skits, had a boogie-woogie band, also a couple of Negro spirituals. The local audience seemed quite amazed by it—interesting to watch the expressions on their faces. They didn't know just when to laugh or when to look serious.

It was a huge success, and should go a long way towards cementing Anglo-American relations. Wish you could have heard those Blacks singing "God Save the King". They seemed to know all the words and really put so much into it.

Today Mrs. Hoyle, Trudy, the new occupational therapist, and I went to a local British hospital to see their O.T. dept. It was very interesting and we exchanged quite a few ideas with the staff there. Then Trudy and I met Ruth at the Venture, the pub closest to the hospital, for supper. The Canadian Army Show was on at Hackwood, so we went to that. It was great—something we can be justly proud of. The costumes were so colourful and pretty—and one certainly appreciates bright and pretty these days!

Tomorrow night, Mrs. S., Ruth and Hoyle and I are going to the movies to see Jane Eyre.

Saturday, Jack is coming for the weekend. I do hope we have good weather, as we are hoping to get some tennis and a bit of biking. Aileen was in London for a week on a handicraft course, and I am going on the 16th, for a week. Will be living at Maple Leaf Club III, the Nursing Sisters' club. Not far from Corps House. It should be interesting and I am looking forward to a week in London.

Very thoughtful of John Matheson to write to you. He said he would—but I really didn't think any more about it. John was so right—these boys are making tremendous sacrifices every day.

Thank you so much for my beautiful suit.
Much love, Lois

May 8th, 1944
Dearest family:

Here I am again to continue this never-ending saga! We went to see Jane Eyre. *It was quite good but rather depressing.*

Jack came Saturday at noon. I worked in the morning, then went to meet him and we had lunch at the Red Lion. It gives Mrs. Simon a break if we eat lunch out on Saturday. We spent the afternoon over at Hackwood on the tennis courts. Played with some of the medical staff. It was a lovely afternoon—warm enough for shorts. Then we went home for supper and on to a movie. There are three in Basingstoke and I saw them all this week.

Sunday we bicycled miles. Took a picnic lunch and found a very inviting shady place in a field. Climbed the fence and just got settled to open our goodies when we realized that there was a huge bull across the field and he was beginning to approach. You can imagine how quickly we tossed everything back in the bag and made it to the fence in record time, just as he was getting closer. England is glorious now. If I had not seen Canada first, I would think the south of England the loveliest place in the world.

Got home in time for supper and were content to stay in with the rest of the family who were all home. They are surely an interesting group; we have quite a few laughs together. Aileen was off with George for the weekend. She has just told me that they are expecting a baby—not till late fall, so she is not saying much about it yet. Her plans are indefinite, but she will leave here before too long. I will surely miss her.

It is now Tuesday. Jack left early Monday morning. He was going to London for a few days. We did have a fun weekend and it has been great, playing golf and tennis and biking. We do keep busy and I never seem to have a spare moment for all the little things I should do. Am away behind with letter-writing and have trouble keeping my clothes pressed and repaired.

Am getting ready to go to London. Aileen loved the course and seemed to get quite a bit out of it. I am looking forward to it, too. Have not worn my new suit yet, but will probably wear it in London. Mrs. Simon just had word that Colonel Blythe, who owns Coombehurst, is missing in action. She is very worried about him. William, to her. His parents both died when he was quite young and she really brought him up, so he is like a son to her.

It is now Thursday—just before dinner. We have just come home from the hospital and will write a few lines before dinner. Wednesday was Gerry's birthday, so we decided to go to London. I met him at the Venture at noon. We had lunch, then on to the station and caught the train. I wore my new suit and felt quite dressy in it. Gerry got me some yellow flowers from the flower lady in Piccadilly Circus to wear with it. We went to the K. of C. Hut first, lined up reservations for the evening, then went window-shopping. Then to the tea dance at the

Piccadilly. On to the American bar at the Park Lane and then to the theatre. We saw Lisbon Story *and it was marvellous. I have been anxious to see it, but it has been booked for weeks in advance. We were lucky to get seats on such short notice. We went to the Lansdowne, a popular supper club. Had an excellent meal and the music was fairly good but the dance floor was like a postage stamp. However, all those places are alike and it is fun, even if you haven't much room to dance.*

It was a lovely trip to London. I did enjoy it so—rather a weekend in the middle of the week—the best time to go as you avoid the crowds. We met several of Gerry's friends so had a fun birthday for him. He is a long way from Oregon, and has been away from home for months, as his outfit was in action in North Africa with General Patton, and that surely must have been a tough campaign.

The Knights of Columbus does a worthwhile job over here. They always arrange things for you and seem to be able to produce anything at all, for all creeds. Am sure they offer other services as well, but the Reservations Dept. is very well run.

More later. Love you both so much. Lois

ON COURSE IN LONDON

Sunday, May 21st, 1944
Dearest Mother and Dad:

Have thought of you all day, as this is your 25th Anniversary, and have been imagining you all together—with the rest of the family. How I hated to miss it and would have loved a quick visit home. Although I don't want to come home for good yet, not until everything is settled.

A long time between letters as I have been in London all week. Went in on Sunday evening, got to the Sisters' club, which is Maple Leaf No. 3, where I was to stay during the course. Unpacked and then went to Corps House where there was a party in full swing. Many of the girls were there and I met a very nice RCN officer.

Barbara Emmans from Montreal had arrived and was installed in the room, too. She is a great person. We had come over on the ship together and have not seen each other since, as she is also out in the country. Helen, from Hamilton, was sharing the room, too, but did not arrive until Monday. We lived quite luxuriously—had a lovely room, plus sitting room and bathroom. Had breakfast in bed every morning and snacks at night. The food was superb and we had such a good time together. Both Barb and Helen are great fun and it was so nice to have a chance to see them again, hear what they have been doing in their hospitals and exchange bits of news and gossip.

Monday evening we went to see Arc de Triomphe*—it was an Ivor Novello production and really magnificent. I was thrilled with it and liked it even better than the* Lisbon Story *that Gerry and I had seen the week before. The music in the* Lisbon Story *was much prettier and were songs you would remember, but this one was beautifully done and* *had a stronger story. Days were spent at HQ doing handicraft and learning new things. They have an excellent canteen so we had lunch and tea there each day.*

Tuesday night, I went with Bill, the Navy lad, to see The Love Racket*—a musical comedy. It was quite funny. Wednesday night we went to an Allied party at the new American club. It was loads of fun. There were some very nice lads there and I met an American pilot from Kansas City. Thursday night we went to see* For Whom the Bell Tolls. *It was a wonderful picture. I suppose you saw it long ago. It has been running in London all winter.*

The week simply flew. At noon we went window-shopping—one day we went to Liberty's and it is a most amazing place. Not like an ordinary store at all, but full of all sorts of antiques and curios, beautifully displayed, and of course, the famous Liberty prints. Barbara left on Saturday morning and Helen and I went back to Headquarters again. After lunch we saw the new film, Fanny by Gaslight. *I enjoyed it immensely. It was at the Gaumont Theatre—where the premiere was a couple of weeks ago. Then it was time to head back to Basingstoke. It was certainly fun being in London for a while and interesting at Headquarters, seeing how it all works.*

Barb and I were walking home one day, strolling through Hyde Park, along the Serpentine and past Rotten Row, when suddenly it started to pour rain. We were without our trench coats and looked frantically for a taxi, but they all seemed to be filled. Then a massive black sedan came along, with a huge sign on the front—"Priority". We stretched our necks to see who it might be, and there, in one corner, all by himself, was Mackenzie King! They swished by, splashing us well. He never was a favourite. We had a good laugh and then got a taxi.

London is fun—we poked around in all sorts of old places. There are so many antique shops, filled with all sorts of quaint things. Of course, the prices are exorbitant—especially for us Canucks and Yankees, because they always see us coming. You could spend weeks there and still never see it all. We usually have such rushed trips so it was fun to have time to explore. The stores are lovely. Liberty's, Harrods, Fortnum & Mason, filled with so much merchandise, all on coupons and very expensive. We didn't buy anything as there was nothing we needed.

The shows and restaurants are gay and noisy. The theatres have bars, where everyone adjourns between acts. Also, they serve coffee and sandwiches right in the seats, although it is difficult to recognize the coffee. It might be anything! The restaurants and supper clubs on Piccadilly and Curzon streets are similar to those in New York. Bright, almost gaudy places—with chrome and mirrors, thick carpet and fancy stools in the bar. The dining areas are jammed with tiny tables—so you bump elbows with the occupants of the next one. The dance floor is usually very good but small and crowded. The band, noisy, banging out the popular tunes—new over here, but months old at home. There is always a blues singer and sometimes a Black band, playing Harlem music. It's hard to believe that you are really in England!

However, it is all part of life over here in wartime. Old Londoners always hasten to assure you that London is definitely a different place in peacetime. The streets are crowded with uniforms of many nations—Americans predominating. Here and there, one sees the Yankee M.P.s—conspicuous with their snow-white spats and helmets, and the Piccadilly Commandos. I am so glad we are stationed in the country; although I love to go to London for these quick jaunts, I should hate to live there. Basingstoke is such a quiet, peaceful spot and I am always glad to return.

Gerry has left for parts unknown. We had such fun all winter and I shall miss him and hope for his safety. With everything in such turmoil now, you cannot be sure of anything. I don't know where he has gone or if he will return. It is difficult saying goodbye to dear friends when you have an idea what they have ahead. His unit is Infantry, usually in tough spots, facing enemy fire.

Wednesday, Ted Lloyd returned after a month at a convalescent home, so we went out to supper. He looks so much better and really seems to be fine again. He came back here later to see the rest of the family. Thursday I played tennis with him before dinner, then went to supper in the Mess with Trudy Spencer, our occupational therapist. She was doing some dressmaking, so I helped her with the fitting. She is from Vancouver and we have become good friends.

We had something to celebrate at dinner because Mrs. S. had just heard that William (Captain Blythe) is a POW. Remember, I mentioned a month ago that he was missing and she has been so worried ever since. At least she now knows that he is alive. We are all so thankful about Capt. Blythe—for Mrs. Simon's sake. It's strange, through the fortunes of war, we are all living here, in his home, and he is in a POW camp.

Went to the special Whit Sunday Service this morning with Mrs. Simon, then am going to play golf this afternoon. Have been playing tennis quite frequently, with some of the medical staff.

Heaps of love to you both. Lois.

May 29th, 1944
Dearest Family:

We are in the middle of a heat wave! It is really summer at last and we are all wearing summer clothes. This was a long weekend and we all stayed home and enjoyed Coombehurst. Usually we all dash off, and spend hours in the heat or cold, waiting for trains! It has been glorious—part of yesterday and most of today, Ruth, Aileen and I in bathing suits. We all got quite tanned—enough to go without stockings. Coombehurst is really at its best now. The trees in the drive are all beautifully green and the flowers all in bloom. We took some coloured pictures recently and they turned out exceedingly well. Perhaps some day you will be able to see this place and some of southern England.

Here I am again. It is now May 30th, and your letters came today, telling all about your Anniversary celebration. It all sounded perfect and I really missed being there. Will be so anxious to see the pictures. The flowers must have been beautiful, and all the presents. Am so glad you like the silver dish. After I got it, I wondered about it. Found it in Tessier's, a lovely shop in Old Bond Street.

Mrs. Simon was in London today—getting information about sending things to Capt. Blythe. She is so happy, knowing where he is. Aileen and I went to the Venture for dinner tonight, as Mrs. S. was still in London. We had filet mignon! I had not had a decent steak since Larry and I were in London in the fall, and a lad in the Ferry Command had brought steaks from Canada and had the restaurant cook them. We looked so envious when they were taken to his table, beside us, that he said they had more than they needed, and kindly gave us each one.

It is now June 5th, and I shall continue. My McCall's *are arriving very well. I've had three issues and everyone enjoys them. We really have quite a selection. Ruth gets* Good Housekeeping *and* Ladies'

Home Journal, *and with the odd* Cosmo, Red Book *and* Liberty *that you put in my parcels, we do very well. We all see them here, then take them to the hospital and the patients fight over them. All my parcels are arriving very well. Am thrilled with the stockings and all the other good things you think of.*

Aileen is leaving for good on Saturday. It certainly will not be the same without her. She is going to join George. Of course, she has no idea how long he will be there, but she might as well be with him. At present, they are not going to replace her. Moira asked for the job, and that would have been great; however, she was refused, as they did not want to train someone into her particular position in Headquarters, right now.

Friday night Trudy came here for dinner, then about 10.00 pm a call came from the hospital, saying her sister had come from London, unexpectedly. She rushed home and her sister, who is a Canadian WREN, was waiting, with the sad news that Trudy's fiancé had been killed in Italy. What a dreadful jolt for her, poor dear. She had shown me his picture, so proudly.

We are all delighted about the progress in Italy, although am afraid it is at great cost to our troops. A card from Captain Blythe in the POW camp sounded hopeful and he felt that hostilities should be over in six months. Ruth is counting on it and we are all wondering and hoping.

Much love to you and all the family.
Lois.

ath & Wilts Chronicle & Herald. 6/6/1944

Black-out: 11.7 p.m.—5.10 a.m. Lighting-up: 11.22 p.m.—4.55 a.m.

LATE EXTRA

Bath and Wilts Chronicle and He[rald]

Est. 1776 The Evening Paper for N. and Mid-Somerset, Wilts and S. Glos.

No. 19,367 TUESDAY One Day Nearer Victory [J]UNE 6, 1944

WE INVADE T

Air-Sea Descent: "Hopes Of Tactical Surprise"—Churchill

Communique Number One" set the world agog to-day. It was issued from Supreme H.Q. Allied Expeditionary Force—SHAEF for short— at 9.33 a.m. and said:— Under the command of General Eisenhower, Allied naval forces, supported by strong air forces, began landing Allied Armies to-day on the north coast of France."

THE LANDINGS, IT IS UNDERSTOOD IN LONDON, [W]ERE MADE IN NORMANDY BETWEEN 6 A.M. AND [?]15 A.M., MINESWEEPERS CLEARING A WAY. NAVAL [B]OMBARDMENTS, IN WHICH U.S. BATTLESHIPS [T]OOK PART, WERE CARRIED OUT, AND AIRBORNE [L]ANDINGS MADE. FIRST REPORTS ARE DESCRIBED [A]S "GOOD."

W. E. West, Press Association correspondent at S.H.A.E.F., says that General Montgomery is in charge of the Army Group carrying out the assault, with British Canadian and U.S. forces under his command.

A confident Mr. Churchill in the House of Commons [to]-day gave the world dramatic news about the cross-[c]hannel invasion.

"There are already hopes that actual tactical surprise has been attained, and we hope to furnish the enemy with a succession of surprises during the course of the fighting," he said.

Among the facts which Mr. [C]hurchill gave the House [h]ere:

An immense armada of up-[w]ards of 4,000 ships, with [s]everal thousand smaller craft, [h]ave crossed the Channel.

Massed airborne landing suc-[ce]ssfully effected behind the [e]nemy lines.

Landings on the beaches are [p]roceeding at various points.

Fire of shore batteries "largely [q]uelled."

KING TO BROADCAST TO-NIGHT

The King is to broadcast to his people at 9 p.m. to-night.

General de Gaulle, who has arrived in London and has had talks on military matters with General Eisenhower and Mr. Churchill, is also scheduled to give a radio talk ...

The landings have taken place on the Normandy coast. German reports put the area of operations as including the Cherbourg penin-

N[...]

A[...]

THE [...] st[...]
This [...] from [...] miles [...] the sta[...]
Durin[...] man a[...] move.
The [...] said, e[...] seemec[...]
Anoth[...] since t[...] fighter-[...] bombin[...] fences a[...]
They [...] of guns [...] spans w[...]
Allied [...] ing and [...] an abs[...] since da[...]

H[...]
Ni[...]

Last [...] made it [...] on the [...] French [...] tacks, e[...] heavy b[...]
In a[...] patched [...] attacks [...] last nig[...]
The ta[...] naval gu[...] shell. D[...] and how[...] beaches

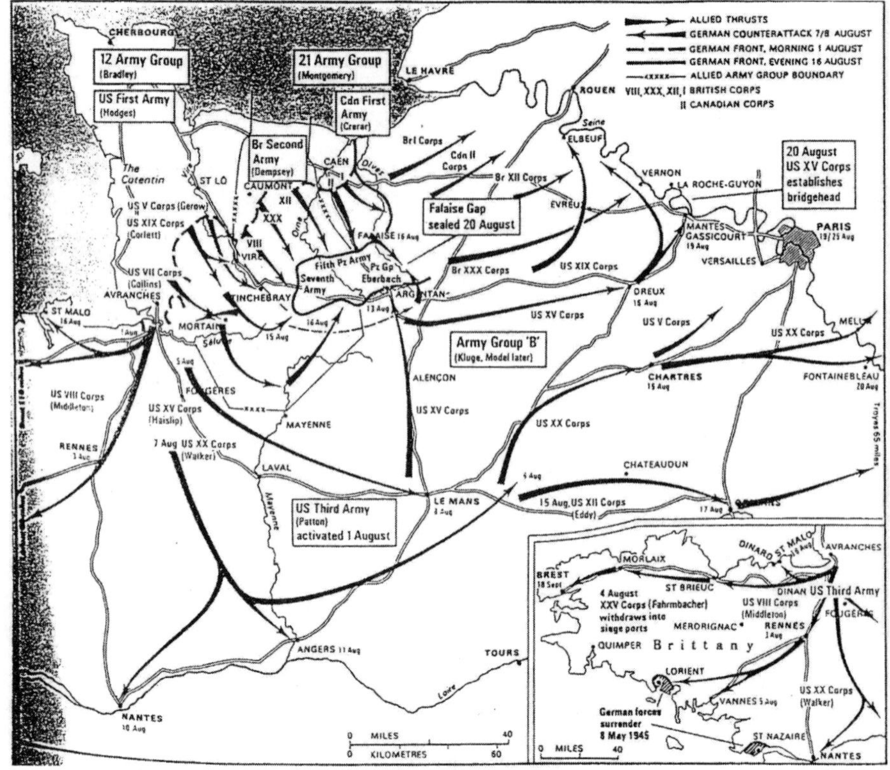

The Battle for Normandy & advancing south into France

D-DAY, JUNE 6, 1944
THE BATTLE FOR NORMANDY

Called Operation OVERLORD, it was the greatest amphibious invasion in military history. Five thousand, three hundred and thirty-nine vessels took part. They crossed the Channel from England to Normandy in twelve narrow lanes with minesweepers leading.

The U.S. were assigned beaches code-named Utah and Omaha to the west, the British and other Allied Forces were east at Gold, Juno, and Sword beaches. The Canadian 7th, 8th, and 9th Brigades landed on Juno Beach.

The entire operation was under the direct command of U.S. General Dwight D. Eisenhower as Supreme Allied Commander, with British General Montgomery as Land Force Commander. The Canadians were led by General Crerar. General Eisenhower was backed up by generals Patton, Bradley, Collins and other very able men. It was vitally important that the location, date and time of the invasion, especially the location, be completely and totally secret. It seems incredible, 61 years later, in this age of worldwide involvement in communication, that it was possible to keep this knowledge from the German intelligence, but this was done.

It took great planning over several years. Even the tide had to be carefully considered as it was important to go in on a rising tide to avoid underwater defences. Dieppe taught many lessons, mainly that it would be easier to go in over beaches than to try to take a well-defended port.

The date was originally set for May 1st, but postponed until June 5th to make more landing craft available. Weather on the 5th was forecast as very stormy; however, prospects seemed more favourable for the following day. The decision to go forward rested entirely with General Eisenhower who, with great moral courage, gave the order to delay a day, and kept his troops confined to the ships, giving the all-important order to proceed in the early hours of June 6th. Evidently Eisenhower said to colleagues, "I'm quite positive we must give the order—I don't like it—but there it is—I don't see how we can possibly do anything else!"

Before the assaulting troops embarked, each man was handed a stirring Order of the Day from the Supreme Commander, saying, "Your task will not be an easy one. Your enemy is well trained, well equipped and battle-hardened. He will fight savagely. The tide has turned. The free men of the world are marching together to victory. I have full confidence in your courage and devotion to duty and skill in battle. We will accept nothing less than full victory. Good luck and let us all beseech the blessing of Almighty God upon this great and noble undertaking."

Airborne assaults went first, bombing the enemy defences on and behind the beaches, dumping thousands of tons of bombs on the German positions built into the cliffs and taking out some of the huge guns capable of shelling the advancing fleet. Troops were already aboard the ships, and the mighty armada moved slowly forward in the black night. A great fleet of transport aircraft flew overhead, carrying airborne troops, who parachuted into France, with weapons and equipment. French Resistance groups received the action message and began sabotaging German units and communications.

It was a great strategic triumph. The Germans were taken completely by surprise and caught off guard. It was unbelievable that the German High Command did not detect this vast sea and air armada bearing down on them. Rommel was in Germany celebrating his wife's birthday and many senior commanders were away from their posts.

As the landing craft neared the beaches, there was a great logjam of vessels, tossing in the surf—much confusion as troops began to disembark. Some, hampered by their heavy equipment, drowned in the deep water. Others were cut down by gunfire as they struggled towards the beach.

It was sheer horror—dreadful noise, planes roaring overhead, explosions, smoke, flames, screams. A horrifying experience for the courageous young men who had been brought up in peaceful lands, to be thrown onto those bloody beaches, to kill or be killed or possibly both. To see their dear friends being blown to bits or writhing in pain as the men still standing fought to the base of the cliffs beyond the beaches, making their way past their dead and dying comrades.

Yet, for all the terror and horror, the Allies landed and secured those beaches with much lighter casualties than the planners had feared and anticipated. The Allies lost 2,500 men, each one a tragic loss for their friends and loved ones and a high price to pay, but a much smaller number than expected.

Allied organization for D-Day was the greatest logistical achievement in modern warfare. England was bursting with military personnel, ships and supplies. Organizing troops, equipment and supplies in southern England was a monumental task. The assembling of this gigantic mass had to be carefully orchestrated. The Allies had already gained complete air superiority over northwest Europe, with the might of the Luftwaffe drastically reduced. Another important advantage was that the Allied intelligence-gathering was much superior to that of the Germans.

Operation Fortitude was the Allied deception plan. It was highly successful in keeping the Germans in doubt about when and where the invasion might take place.

The Battle for Northwest Europe was off to a brilliant start. However, the Germans were regrouping and fighting was heavy and ferocious as our troops fought to move inland. Roads were blocked with wreckage, tanks and vehicles. The sky was black with Allied bombers destroying German positions ahead of our advancing armies, blasting rail lines, bridges, fuel stocks and factories. Casualties were great and some units suffered severe losses. One hundred and fifty-six thousand troops were put ashore during the first 24 hours. Long and savage battles ensued through June and July. The going was heartbreaking, tough and costly, but the Allies slowly moved forward. By late July, Allies had nearly two million troops and a quarter-million vehicles in Normandy.

The Canadian forces encountered very stiff resistance at Caen. They fought heroically, often hand-to-hand skirmishes, and finally in early July, Caen was secured. Many towns and cities in Normandy took a dreadful pounding by heavy artillery and air bombardment. Carpiquet Airport and Falaise Gap and countless small towns along the way will long be remembered as places where our Canadian troops fought and died so courageously.

The Mulberry Docks was a great engineering feat. Not enough seems to have been written about this harbour that was conceived and constructed in Britain and actually towed across the Channel to the Arromanches Beach area. Fifty-eight older merchant ships were lined up, two miles offshore, shortly after D-Day, where they were scuttled and sunk to form a breakwater. More than a million tons of materials was necessary to build this port. Huge concrete caissons towed across the Channel were put into position at the end of the ships and sunk, forming a formidable concrete wall rising out of the depths. Curving, it made a very sheltered harbour. Piers were built out from shore inside this enclosure and ships could unload, regardless of the weather. The Royal Engineers, sometimes working under enemy fire, put in bridges and roadways to move men and supplies ashore. This harbour proved very advantageous to the Allies and contributed greatly to the eventual success of the Allied cause. Thousands of tons of equipment, fuel, food, personnel and military hospitals all arrived via the Mulberry Docks. Plans for "Mulberry" were a very well-guarded secret.

The Germans fought with desperation and tenacity. Their losses were horrendous, as Hitler overrode the advice of his generals and continued to insist that more and more divisions be committed to Normandy. His generals were beginning to realize that it was becoming a hopeless situation.

There was a wild storm at sea from June 19th to 21st, and 140,000 tons of Allied stores and ammunition were lost, en route to France.

It continued to be a bitter struggle, with each town and village taken by the Allies costing dearly. The Germans suffered 450,000 casualties in Normandy, with 40 divisions destroyed. Carnage and destruction was unbelievable and terrible. The combined military might of the Allied Forces proved too much for the enemy and the battle for Normandy was finally won.

NEWS CHRONICLE, Wednesday, June 7, 194

D-Day

Our Men Landed On A Beach Like This

Thousands of pictures of the French beaches were taken by the RAF before the invasion. This one is typical. It shows Germans running from the low-flying plane, but more important, it shows the nature of enemy defences below the high-water level. At high tide they are covered by water. Said Mr. Churchill the day before: "The obstacles which were constructed in the sea have not proved so difficult as was apprehended."

D-DAY

June 8th, 1944
Dearest Mother and Dad:

Well, D-Day has come and gone. We waited for it, impatiently, and then it snuck up on us quite unexpectedly, right on the heels of the entrance into Rome. Monday, we were all so excited about the news from Italy and more or less forgot about what we are really waiting for. Great excitement in the wards and throughout the hospital.

It was quiet when we went to bed, the night of June 5th, and I slept like a log and didn't hear the planes going out. Ruth and I have both been just waiting for the invasion news, and have been listening to the radio for months. I was halfway through my breakfast when Ruth finally looked up from her coffee and calmly said that things were under way.

Amazing how the whole tempo of life suddenly speeded up. Perhaps it was much the same at home—people walk more quickly, look as if they have a definite purpose and interest. Everyone wonders what is going on and how soon we will have news. Of course, everyone is worried about their own particular relatives or friends that may be in the big "Do".

I stayed and had supper with Trudy and we worked for a while after. She has taken the news of her fiancé's death remarkably well, but I hated to leave her alone.

The air show has been spectacular lately. Do wish you could see it. Some day I will be able to tell you more about it. It is thrilling to be in England now—we have not seen a great deal to date, but there is such excitement in the air. Gerry is probably over there somewhere. At least, I imagine that is where he is. Guess I won't hear anything from him for weeks.

Aileen is all packed and will leave on Saturday. Five other Corps members are also leaving, some heading home to have their babies.

The girls in the Maple Leaf clubs and Corps House have a great spirit of camaraderie—all work hard at their jobs but are ready to laugh and have fun, as well. As in any group, there are probably a few that find our way of life here difficult, but on the whole, all are so friendly and ready to help and do small favours for each other.

In the months leading up to D-Day, weddings began to take place, which was very exciting. Everyone pitched in. The kitchen staff looked after the food for the reception. Others decorated the lounges while friends loaned clothes to the bride and helped her with many details. The mother of one girl, in Toronto, went shopping for a wedding gown and veil to send to her daughter. The sales lady enquired why the bride was not there herself. On hearing that she was serving in England with the CRCC, the store manager was quickly contacted and the store, I think it was Eaton's, was very happy to present the dress and veil, also a bridesmaid's dress, as a gift. All was carefully packed and sent on its way. It is a beautiful gown—worn with pride by the bride who received it. Known as "The Dress", it has been loaned to close to twenty girls in the weeks that followed.

D-Day and the days following, as our troops press forward, are surely taking their toll in our ranks. After the initial landing, there are new widows every day. As the dreadful news comes in, it is a time of great sorrow and sadness. The girls have become very close and all know the husbands and fiancés. As the war moves ahead, we learn of more casualties each day. Yet with all the terrible grief, there is much bravery amongst the bereaved. Some are pregnant and plans will be made for them to

The troops climbing this gangway to board an LSI (Landing Ship, Infantry) at a port in Britain are now with the beachhead forces in France. Suspended from special davits and hidden by the gangway are landing craft in which the men went ashore.

return to Canada. Mrs. Lee is a great comfort to the girls during this tragic time in their young lives. There will be sadness, too, as the girls leave for home, hating to leave Corps House and the friends who have become so dear to them.

Canada's Weekly *is a magazine published over here, by Canadians, for Canadians, so has all our news, pictures, latest awards and decorations, also casualty lists. When it arrives every Thursday, Ruth, Aileen, Trudy and I pore over it.*

Much love to you both and Timmie. Lois

June 12th, 1944
Dearest Family:

So very much has happened in the last few days—guess you must be wondering what it is all about—getting my two cables. The first one, I phoned in at Basingstoke on Friday night. They made a mistake in the address and in the confusion, did not send it off until Monday. I got tired waiting for a reply, so sent another one from London. Then I called B-stoke and Mrs. Simon told me what had happened to the first one.

To go back to Friday afternoon, Mrs. Lee called me at the hospital about 5.00 pm, and asked if I was interested in welfare work. Of course, I was just dying to do it. She needed to know immediately, so I said, "Yes". Then she told me to report to London, bag and baggage, on Sunday. Aileen had gone home early, as she was packed and ready to leave. It was pouring rain, a real deluge, but I was in such a dither, I didn't realize it was even damp. I got home simply soaked, with water sloshing around in my shoes. It was utter confusion. Aileen had only a few minutes to get to the station, and there was I—all wet and so excited. Her taxi arrived and we got her into it, with all her luggage, and the engine died! However, the ancient driver cranked and cranked and finally they got under way. I got my trunk, dunnage bag and suitcases and started tossing things in. Ruth and Mrs. Simon were wonderful and helped so much. We took all my things downstairs to the conservatory and I packed there. Filled my trunk and my haversack with all the things I will take, then put the things I can't take in the dunnage bag and two suitcases. Also bought a mattress cover and sewed it up the middle, then I had two bags to hang my coats and suits in.

Mrs. Simon was so afraid I would be hungry and cooked the most super meals for my last ones. Hoyle said he really felt ill by the end of the weekend.

It seems like a dream that I have actually left Coombehurst. I really hated to leave, and would not have done so for any other reason than this opportunity. Mrs. Simon assured me that I will always have a home in England, as long as she is at Coombehurst.

It seemed awful to leave Hackwood—we had been so happy there—and everyone, with the excep-

tion of the two nasty "Limeys" we worked with, had been so kind to us. All the Sisters, doctors, the Matron and C.O. were so nice when I said goodbye. Really made me feel as if we had made a worthwhile contribution. Although many times I wondered if we were really doing very much to help. Colonel Botterell, the head surgeon, was especially nice, and also Colonel Harvey, the C.O. who kissed me and wished me luck. Made a quick trip around the wards and it was difficult saying goodbye to all the patients. I had a wonderful winter in Basingstoke, both at the hospital and Coombehurst—one I will always remember. It's a lovely part of England and when peace finally comes, you will have to come over and see all these special places.

The last month, things were a little quiet, although after such a gay winter, I was quite happy to lie about in the sun with Ruth and Aileen. It would not have been the same without Aileen, and it was better to leave while it was still wonderful.

The doctor, the Captain, Ruth and Hoyle were all there to help me pack—even Mary and Elsie, and Mother Hubbard and child came to see me off. I came rushing down the stairs at the last moment, breathless, only to find that the hem of my skirt was all hanging down in front. Mother Hubbard promptly got a needle and thread and tacked me together. Then Ruth and Captain Hedges took me to the station. My trunk had been sent Saturday, but I still had my knapsack, helmet, gas mask, also tennis racquet, bicycle and trench coat. Transport gals met me in London.

I know the cables I sent must have been very confusing. Mrs. Lee had said we should have parental consent to go to the continent. I could not wait beyond Sunday, and you did not receive either cable until early the next week. By then I was on my way, and you were both hoping I would stay at Hackwood. Thank you both so much for your cable sending love and encouragement. Will let you know as soon as we have any word of which hospital we will be with.

It is now June 15th, and we have arrived at No. 18 CGH in Colchester. Am with Laura Sharpe, Sheila Birks and Grace Rodgers, all of Montreal. It all happened so quickly. Neither Laura nor I knew that the other one had been called until we both got to London. It's funny, after all these months, because we had asked to be posted together in the first place. So everything has turned out perfectly. We are here with Prue Holbrook Craig from Ottawa. She has recently returned from Italy and is training us. Prue is a dear. Certainly knows a lot about the work we will be doing and can tell us so many things. She is a very smart, intelligent lady and has been wonderful to us.

We have a hut—the five of us. I am rooming with Sheila, who is a darling and lots of fun. Laura and Grace are right next door. This is not a luxurious place like Hackwood, but very pleasant. We arrived on Monday night for dinner. Prue met us at the station with a vehicle and brought us here, with all our gear. We all brought our bicycles—so will be able to bike around in our free time. It is a very friendly unit. Col. Abbott is the C.O. Some of the Sisters have been on exchange at Hackwood, so there are several familiar faces.

Tuesday there was a Mess dinner, and then a movie and party afterwards. Today Sheila and I had the day off, so we cycled to Dedham, about 12 miles away. We took a circle tour, so must have biked about 30 miles, but it was a lovely bright day and we had lunch in a quaint old pub.

It is a great experience, being in England now. We have seen so many things in the past few months. Things I will never forget and there has not been a dull moment. England is perfectly beautiful now. The rhododendrons are a picture and the roses simply glorious. Never have I seen such large blooms and so many heavenly colours. Sheila and I had a lovely day, just cycling along slowly through the quiet country lanes and seeing so many inter-

esting things. We came back through town, so I sent you a cable and also one to Grand-daddy Kelly for his birthday.

Please don't be too disappointed because I have left Coombehurst. I am terribly thrilled to have the opportunity to go abroad. Prue will be home soon and said she will contact you and drop in to see you and tell you all about everything. I am hoping to get back to Basingstoke before long. Promised Mrs. Simon I would do so if at all possible. She was absolutely wonderful to Aileen and me and I certainly won't forget all her kindness.

We are to be here two weeks, then back to London for an indefinite period until we get our posting. As soon as we know the number of the hospital we will be with, will let you know. We have been terribly busy. There are so many things for Prue to tell us and so much to learn in the limited time. We spend much time in the wards and are getting to know the patients here.

Please don't worry unnecessarily. I'll write and cable often, and keep in touch as much as possible. I am absolutely thrilled about being a Welfare Officer. It is a wonderful job and it is quite an honour to be chosen. Laura and I had never applied for it, although most of the others had. Now, instead of doing only handicrafts, we look after all the comforts—cigarettes, candy, magazines, shaving gear, etc., do the library, write letters for the ones unable to do so, read to them, do their shopping, send their cables, visit each new patient as they are admitted to see what they need, and visit each patient every day, trying to remember their names! It's terribly interesting, and we still look after the handicrafts, too.

Could you save old magazines? It doesn't matter how old, because the stories and articles are always good. Perhaps some of the family can save them for you, too. When I finally get an address, you could send some and they will be marvellous. In the field, we will not have as many books as here, so the magazines will be most welcome.

We are hoping to get a little leave when we return to London. If so, Laura and I will go to see the Langers in Kent for a couple of days, then Sheila will come down to Basingstoke with me for several days. However, we will have to wait to see what develops. Sheila went to London today—she just received word that her cousin was killed and his wife is one of our Corps girls. Saw in the Weekly that Joe Courtwright got it. It seems so dreadful, am afraid it is just the beginning of a very long list.

I had a lovely letter from Mrs. Reford, saying how much she appreciated the work Aileen and I had done at Hackwood. She is a charming person and was very good to us. Am sure she was aware of the problems we had with the miserable pair we worked with. Gratifying to know that the decent people did appreciate our efforts.

I will surely miss Aileen and hope she will be all right and that George will be safe. Also Infantry—they are always in the thick of battle. When he leaves, she is going to Somerset to stay with the wife of George's fellow officer. They will have a house so should be comfortable.

Please don't worry—I am doing the work I really love and want to do more than anything else.

Heaps of love to you both and all the family.
Lois

June 24th, 1944
Dearest Folks:

Our time in Colchester is almost at an end. The days are busy—we are on the go from morning to night. Instead of having weekends off—as we did in B-Stoke—we work the same hours as the Sisters, work all week, Sat. and Sun. included, and have a day off during the week and also Sunday morning or afternoon. Which is the way it should be, as the patients don't get a weekend off! May Beasley and Ann Savard are at a nearby hospital. Sheila and I biked over there this morning

We have been busy; there have been parties, then a movie twice a week, a couple of ball games. We have been out to dinner several times and tomorrow night we are going to a dance at a nearby American Mess. One evening, the four of us biked to a seaside town for dinner. Had heard about a restaurant there, famous for its steak dinners. It was a terrific meal. Excellent steak, nicely cooked, with a fried egg on top! Rather a new twist, but very good. There were new potatoes, fresh garden peas and carrots and we finished with strawberry tart. It was surely worth the bike ride. As we cycled along, the planes thundered overhead, incredible sight. Sky was black with them, heading out for the next strike.

Had a letter from Jack today. He is at sea again—for a while—but not for long, so perhaps I will see him again in London. Gerry is somewhere in France—as far as I know. When I hear of the American losses, I feel cold all over, thinking of Gerry and all his friends—the lads we went to parties with. Such a carefree group. However, no news is good news.

I forgot to mention that the pictures arrived today, taken at your Anniversary party. They are wonderful; I love them and will frame the one of you two, sitting together in the back garden. Felt as if I was there with you, too, seeing the pictures of all the family.

Please don't worry needlessly about me. I'm perfectly well and safe—being well looked after—very happy in my work—and with three exceedingly nice girls. We are anxious to get our posting, and know what hospital we will be with. We'll probably be in this country for a while yet.

Lots of hugs, Lois

June 28th, 1944
Dearest Mother and Dad:

A note to keep you up on the latest news on this side of the ocean. We are living at Corps House, for the time being. We returned from Colchester on Monday after a very pleasant two weeks. Sunday night was the dance at the American Bomber Base. A colossal party and great fun. Met a very nice lad from Detroit. They had a marvellous band. Sounded like one of the Big Bands back home. We had all sorts of delicacies—even real American hot dogs! It was a super ending to our time at No. 18.

We arrived back in London in a downpour and two Red Cross station wagons picked us up and we were soon at Corps House. Have spent the last two days at Headquarters, learning bookbinding. If our books fall apart, we will be able to repair them. You have no idea how many things I have learned since being with the Red Cross!

It was rather hectic, trying to do the bookbinding with a Buzz Bomb raid overhead. Looking out the window, we could see them coming, one at a time. Looks like a small plane with wings, no pilot but a motor that makes a distinctive buzz, then suddenly cuts out and the piece of mass destruction either glides down or falls immediately. As soon as we saw one approaching, we all ran for the hall and crouched there, listening and waiting for the tremendous explosion. Pretty scary! We had been warned to get away from windows in case there might be flying glass. There would be a respite and we all would return to the bookbinding, until we heard another ominous buzz. None of the rest came quite so close as the first one, but it surely must be nerve-wracking to live with that, day and night.

Some of your letters just caught up with me and you must have been very worried by my cables. So sorry, I did not explain very clearly. Things were in turmoil here, with Aileen leaving and I was dreading being alone, working with the Limeys. Then Mrs. Lee called and asked me about going Welfare. It was like a bolt from the blue. I had seen enough to know that welfare work in the hospitals is an essential job, and also realized that it would be a job that we Corps girls, and we alone, will be doing. That means a great deal, but aside from that, I want to go. We are needed and it's our job—to be done to the best of our ability. We are not going with the British Red Cross, as Joan Fraser and some others are doing. We will be with a Canadian hospital. Will be taken on strength as part of the unit and will be directly under the Matron—although we will be free to run our part of the show as we wish. It will be a fabulous experience and we are really fortunate to be able to go.

I have been selected to lead our group of four, so hope we can manage all right. It will be refreshing to be able to run it ourselves. Did I mention that there will be Sheila, Laura, and Mary MacDonald? Grace was transferred to another group. I could not have picked a better trio to work with. Today we got some of our equipment, even a portable typewriter. Looks as if we will not have much room for anything extra. I hated to pack away all my pretty clothes.

Had felt recently that Aileen and I were capable of doing more and a bigger job than we were doing at Hackwood. We worked hard enough and did all we could, but there was always the feeling that we were being held down and thwarted at every turn by that overbearing pair. But then, I have already mentioned that. Of course, living at Coombehurst and having such a gay time compensated for the frustration, and we didn't let it bother us, but when this opportunity came, and when Mrs. Stickney and Gen. Price asked me to lead the group, I surely did not hesitate.

Last evening, I had dinner with Colonel Underwood and Brigadier Lane, a friend of his. Then we all went to visit Sir Thomas and Lady Gardiner.

Charming couple and a beautiful home. They are longtime friends of Col. Underwood, seemed so happy to see him, and made me very welcome. First time I had seen him since he returned from Italy, and pleased to see him before I go.

Have just heard that our new address will be No. 12 Canadian General Hospital, so we hope to join them fairly soon, but it still may be quite a while before we move on.

Had a letter from Jack today, wanting me to go down to Bath this weekend; however, have already made plans to go to Basingstoke with Laura, and Mrs. Simon is expecting us. He does get to London frequently, so may see him here.

I do love to get your letters.

Much love, Lois

WELFARE OFFICERS

July 4th, 1944
Dearest Mother and Dad:

Well here we are, with our unit! Glad to settle in. We arrived yesterday in a wet drizzle. Hardly July weather, but surely a relief to get out of London. It is quite a bedlam there, with the Buzz Bombs and V-2s zooming in, day or night. Feel for the girls living there. They get so little sleep, having to retreat to the basement for much of the night.

Laura and I returned from B-stoke Sunday evening and got our packing done. Do wish you could see all our equipment. The Red Cross have fixed us up quite completely and have really done a noble job of looking after us ever since we have been over here.

Had a few problems getting here—lost our baggage when we were changing trains—finally found it but then we had missed the next train so had to wait a couple of hours for another one. I felt like a mother hen, trying to look after the girls and the baggage. We passed through the city where Margaret and Nora live. Perhaps I will be able to see them later. (The city mentioned is York.)

When we arrived, Marion Crawford met us. She is a friend of the Curriers. I did not recognize her at first, but she knew me. Guess she had been given my name. She is our Assistant Matron and has been very thoughtful and kind to us. We were too late for dinner, so she took us into the kitchen and we had a very good snack. It was especially nice to be met by someone I already knew. They did not have a room for us but squeezed us in, separately, with some of the Sisters. They were all very friendly and decent about it, having another person thrust into their already crowded rooms. It has all turned out

Team of Canadian Red Cross welfare officers with No. 12 Canadian General Hospital in July 1944, in Whitby, Yorkshire, mobilizing to go to the continent. Left to right: Lois MacDonald, Ottawa; Sheila Birks, Montreal; Mary Macdonald, Ottawa; and Laura Sharpe, Montreal.

very well, as it gives us a chance to get acquainted much more quickly.

We are living in an old resort hotel on top of a cliff, looking out to sea. Beautiful sand beach and can hardly wait to get my bathing suit out. Old part of town is a quaint fishing village. Wonderful time of year to be here. This seems to be a really super unit. The Sisters and M.O.s are all so friendly and am sure we will be very happy with them. As yet we have not been issued our battledress but hope to get it soon.

This is a glorious place. We have been swimming and sunbathing and generally enjoying life. Sightseeing, eating seafood—could not have chosen a prettier spot for a holiday. We have some lectures and we understand that route marches will begin soon. Our C.O., Col. Fraser, seems a fine man and has also made us feel at home.

It is now July 10th, and will add another note. Loving every minute of it. Have only been here a week but already we know what a super unit No. 12 is, and are very proud to be part of it. We are resting and waiting until needed. Am even enjoying the route marches. It is quite exhilarating to walk along the winding roads, beside the sea, breathing the cool sea air. We couldn't be in a nicer place. Our mobile food unit goes along with us, and we break for lunch in a pleasant spot.

Yesterday morning we all arose bright and early and went to church. I went with my three roommates, Brownie, Kempie and Jean, to a little Presbyterian church. It was a very nice service—much like at home. Then in the afternoon, two of the officers in the unit took Mary and me to a nearby village. We went up on the moors and walked for miles. Saw the Mallyon Spout and had tea in the hotel. Walked farther to a quaint old pub where we all had a glass of milk! Then back to the village hotel where we had a scrumptious dinner and caught the bus back to our hotel.

Tomorrow Mary and I are going on a picnic with four Sisters. We have found a very nice little restaurant on the waterfront—seafood—and Mary and I have become friends with one of the owners and went to her home for tea. The people here are so much more friendly than in the South. Several of them came up to us in church and asked us to visit them. Also, on the streets, everyone is very friendly—if you can understand the lingo. Arthur's accent, only much more so!

Now July 13th and will carry on. Two letters from you today, Mother, dated June 30th, and July 5th. Delighted to hear about Bill and Billie's wedding. Sounded like a perfect day. So glad they received my cable.

You asked about our status, etc. We are attached to the Army Medical Corps now, and their rules and regulations apply to us. All winter at Basingstoke, we were really civilians, as we lived out, but now we are actually part of the unit. My title is Sr. Welfare Officer. Use whichever you like on mail, however, Lieut. Red Cross will be fine.

We are having a lovely time here, swimming, going on picnics, riding, route marches and movies and parties. Seems a lazy life; however, we might as well enjoy our leisure now, as when we start to work, expect we will be very busy and work long hours.

Yesterday, our Precision Platoon went to a nearby town to take part in their local "Salute the Soldier" parade. I am in the platoon and guess we will be doing this frequently in various towns in the area. We were entertained to tea later. Some of our girls who were not marching came along and they overheard a British officer in the crowd remark, "Here comes Canada—with 21 pairs of the nicest silk stockings I've seen since before the war!"

Speaking of stockings, I could use some brown silk ones, like the Sisters wear. Just two or three pair, as we will be in battledress soon. Also, if you feel like knitting, Mother, I would love some khaki socks, just one or two pair, in three- or four-ply wool. We will be wearing boots and need the socks to go with them. They have issued us some but they are very heavy and so long. The length you make them for Dad would be just right.

Yesterday we had a lovely letter from Mrs. Lee. She gave us all the news of the Corps and will keep us posted as to their activities. We know that if we ever have problems or need anything, she is the main person we can count on in London.

So glad you got in touch with Mary's mother, and explained some of our work to her. She had been worried, too. Mary was so pleased when I told her you two had been in touch.

Monday, we went to tea at Mulgrave Castle—with the Marchioness of Normanby. A beautiful old place with a lovely garden and a broad stretch of grass in front, where we sat and looked out at the sea. They call it the quarterdeck. The interior of the castle was lovely. Not all in use, but their quarters were beautifully furnished.

More later,

Hugs and kisses, Lois

(We were stationed in Whitby, Yorkshire. It was a beautiful seaside resort with many hotels lining the cliffs above the broad beaches. There was a curving serpentine road leading down to the beach, and to the south, where the river flowed into the sea, was the Old Town, the fishing village with docks, fishing boats and gear, quaint little restaurants and pubs. On the cliff beyond were the ruins of the old Whitby Abbey. It must have been a magnificent building.)

Sheila, Laura & Grace
Colchester, Essex

Precision Squad
Whitby, Yorkshire

No. 12 CGH Inspection

Route March, Yorkshire

Noon break during Route March

Our Mess, Whitby

July 25th, 1944
Dearest Family:

We are getting to know many of the Sisters. They are younger than most of the ones at Hackwood. Peppy, interesting and exceedingly friendly. We are fortunate, having this opportunity to get acquainted with everyone before we start our work.

Today we went to a concert of the local Boy Scouts. Two of our Sisters organized it. Sister Osborne was the only woman Scoutmaster in Canada, so is really up on Scouting. They sang all sorts of Canadian songs and did skits that are familiar to us. All in a heavy Yorkshire accent, so you can imagine how it sounded. We were just in fits.

Another letter from Mrs. Lee today, with more sad news of the girls there. Mary Harrington's fiancé and Betty Morlock's husband have both been killed. Every day there are new names. Betty Morlock was our C.O. on the trip over; remember, I mentioned her often. Such a fine person. She left the Corps recently, expecting a baby. Now she will be heading home. So tragic.

Mail is coming very well. It is now July 27th, and the days just seem to roll into each other. We are still having picnics, route marches, lectures, parading in the various small towns, swimming and sunning on the beach. Yesterday, after our route march, we went down to the beach. It's really fun, playing in the breakers—quite cold but invigorating and I do love to bathe in the sea. There is an elevator that goes from the beach to the cliff, high above. Such luxury. They are so modern about some things—yet the plumbing and heating is often so primitive.

Sheila, Mary and I are going on another picnic this afternoon, with some of the Sisters. We will pick blueberries! I did not think they had all kinds of berries here, but they surely do. Gooseberries are a big favourite. Thorny things, but they do make excellent pie. Our meals are delicious here. Not quite like Coombehurst, with Mrs. Simon's wonderful cooking, but still very good. If you are wondering about what to send now, candy is always at the top of the list. Canned fruit and fruit juice sounds wonderful—bought a can opener in anticipation!

We had a Mess meeting, the first one since we have been here, and I was elected Vice-Secretary/Treasurer! It is all quite amusing to us, because one of the things instilled in us during training was that we would probably be invited to attend the Sisters' Mess meeting, but we must always remember that it is their Mess and we are present as guests; in other words, we should be seen but not heard. We went, intending to sit quietly and listen to the discussions, but take no active part. Then, first thing I knew, I was on the Executive! They have a system whereby there are five members on the Ex. And you hold office for three months as Vice, then three months Pres. Or Sec./Treas., whatever the office may be. There are close to 100 members.

A gesture like that illustrates the spirit of No. 12 more than anything else. They are the greatest group of girls and it was more or less their way of welcoming us Red Cross members and making us feel one of them. After the meeting, we had a rather informal reception to welcome the new Matron, Miss Paterson. She came to the unit shortly after we did.

The only thing that marred the day was the news that Mrs. Lee has been relieved of her duties as our Commandant. We all feel so badly about it. She did so much for those girls at Corps House, and waited on them hand and foot. We had sensed trouble in the past few months, but never thought it would come to this. It seems that a few of the girls didn't get along with her, probably the ones unhappy in their jobs. Bad news travels quickly, got to Toronto, and this happened. Such a shame, to think that she has done

Abbotsford
Home of Sir Walter Scott
Melrose, Scotland

No. 12 CGH stationed in resort hotel
Whitby, Yorkshire

such a wonderful job—with so little appreciation. However, these things happen and it is unfortunate. Miss Pepall, from Toronto, will take over and Mrs. Lee is going to work at another job in London.

It is August 4th and I will continue—we are still enjoying life by the sea. As the weeks roll by we realize more fully how fortunate we are to be with No. 12. Certainly a great group, with such camaraderie amongst the girls. Fun to be with them and one of them.

We now have our battledress and took some pictures in full regalia and will send them as soon as I get them. Hope you will be able to find my face in the mass of khaki and equipment. This is a good time to tell you a story that has been popular lately. It seems that two Brigadiers, one British and the other Canadian, were standing side by side, watching troops embark. A crowd of English nurses straggled up—some in blue, some in grey and red, others in khaki. The Canadian Brigadier looked at them and said to his English colleague, "I would hate to have that motley-looking crew taking care of me". A few minutes later, a platoon of Canadian Sisters marched up in precision order, in full web equipment. The English Brigadier surveyed them carefully and remarked, "By Jove, old man, I would rather die in peace than let those commandos tackle me!"

We have been having a busy time. Thursday, another picnic, up the river with some of the Sisters and medical officers. Beautiful day and great countryside. There was a party for the other ranks, so I went with one of the officers. We have a marvellous room for a dance. No doubt it was the hotel ballroom, and must have been beautiful in peacetime. Some day I hope to return to all these places. Wednesday night, I was in a bridge game. Had not played since coming over on the boat, so really enjoyed it. One evening, some of the senior officers that we had not gotten to know took the four of us and two of the Sisters to a nearby country pub.

Getting acquainted and remembering peoples' names is really part of our job, but everyone has made it very easy for us, and being in separate rooms, each with a different group of Sisters, has been helpful, too.

This is a delightful spot and we will certainly hate to leave. The swimming has been really wonderful. What a glorious place to have a summer vacation! However, we are all anxious to move on, to do something meaningful and constructive.

Much love to you both. Lois

August 10th, 1944
Dearest Mother and Dad:

Last Saturday we went on the bus, five of us, out on the moors, to pick bracken, etc., to decorate the Mess for the dance that evening. It was a warm bright day, so we wandered around, had tea in a little cottage, picked what we needed, then caught the bus home. We were each carrying armfuls of fern—guess we looked like camouflaged troops. The bus driver looked a bit dubious but finally let us on. As I mentioned before, we have a marvellous big ballroom, with chandeliers and mirrors. It looked quite festive when we got our haul of ferns and huge white daisies in place. Our swan song by the sea!

We passed close to Coombehurst recently. It was a case of being so near and yet so far! Did not have an opportunity to see Mrs. Simon, but did call her. Wish I had a movie camera or some way to record and picture all this. Am afraid that by the time I get home, I will have forgotten so many things. Life is so full and busy, with so many new experiences, it's difficult to say just what will make a lasting impression. I find it hard to keep a diary. Guess my letters home will have to suffice. This has been a fabulous year. It's almost a year since we left home, August 1943.

Have lived in various places—met so many interesting people—lived in rooms tiny and large. I wish you could see the place we are in now. An old estate, in the wilderness. A colossal place, beautiful scenery, very special. We have a lovely room looking out over the front entrance. Not exactly single rooms. There are 15 gals in ours! We all say we will never be able to live alone again. The weather has been incredible, so we have our meals out on the lawns and terraces. We use our Mess tins and sleep on our own camp cots now. They are quite comfortable—very sturdy and well built. This is a heavenly spot. Only drawback is the ablutions—really primitive. The bathtubs are huge affairs, with high walls all around them. You almost have to be a commando to get in and out. Then the outdoor plumbing is quite something. An eight-holer—you are never alone.

It's really an education to see an army unit move. Has been a revelation to me. Everything is done with such organization and so systematically. We have absolutely everything we need to live quite comfortably, and yet in an amazingly short time—everything can be picked up and stowed away, and we move on, bag and baggage, to set up camp, just as speedily, elsewhere. We even have a dog, Skip, a little fox terrier. He travels right with us and has become a member of the unit.

I must tell you about a spot we visited recently. It is an American camp and is quite spectacular. Like something you might read about or dream about but seldom see. A tremendous place—being in it, it was hard to realize its full extent. Just like a very well-run summer camp—everything done on such a monumental scale, and so lavishly. We lived in a tent for five, Laura, Mary and I, and Flora and Goody. There were many American nurses, British nurses, ATS, CWAC, American Red Cross, etc. We met many of the Yankee gals and they were a great group. Also chatted with the American Red Cross members and exchanged ideas, etc. The whole set-

up was like a movie. There was a public address system throughout the camp, and all notices and orders were given out that way.

There were hot and cold showers, well-kept ablutions and latrines. We were on U.S. rations, so had many goodies. There were different movies every night and other diversions. The Yankees really do know how to live. Everything was so clean and orderly. We used our Mess tins to eat, and then dipped our utensils and Mess tins into a series of vats of boiling soapy water and disinfectant, then the final one, clear boiling water. It was all done so easily and efficiently. I was really impressed. This is a marvellous experience and every once in a while I realize that I am really here—that it's me, Lois, here, seeing and doing all these things! And I would not miss it for anything!

We are surely well looked after—so you need never worry about me. Our medical officers are great and see that everything is done for us. Also, the other ranks are a wonderful lot and do so many things, readily and cheerfully.

Just heard that Moira's husband, Dick Logie, has been killed in France. Poor darling must be devastated. She was just leaving for home to have their baby. You asked about Gerry. He is over here, too, although I have not seen him, as the U.S. troops are in a different sector. Last letter, he was still all right; however, you never know.

More later, Much love, Lois

ONWARD TO FRANCE

August 18th, 1944
Dearest Mother and Dad:

As you have probably guessed, we are now in France. Have been here for about four days but have not had a minute to write.

Landing in England last summer was a tremendous thrill, but coming across the Channel, seeing all the boats with their barrage balloons overhead, the hordes of planes, and knowing that we were actually going to be on the same continent with the enemy—was a feeling all its own. Don't remember if I told you about the trip across or not. We left the swish American camp and drove to the docks in lorries. Thousands had preceded us, but the people lined the route and cheered and waved as we passed in our tin hats and packs. We all sang "O Canada", and threw the remains of our English money to the children. Wish you could have seen them scrambling for it.

We boarded our Liberty ship in lovely weather, with our barrage balloon flying high, and spent most of the time on the deck. Moved out quickly into the Channel. The Captain needed some help with extra typing, so the Matron referred him to us, and we did it for one of the Ship's Officers. He asked me to sit at his table for dinner, which was very pleasant.

It was getting late, approaching midnight, when we finally bedded down in the ship's hold, wrapped in rough, scratchy, grey army blankets, and woke up to see the shore of France ahead. It looked truly beautiful as we sailed in. It was surely thrilling and made one especially proud to be part of the great Allied Force. They have done a magnificent job—beyond anything you could ever imagine. Waiting for D-Day, everyone was impatient, wondering if we would ever invade, then, to see the job that has been accomplished, the equipment and the great organizing and careful planning that must have been necessary to make it all possible, you soon realize that it was all done so efficiently in an incredibly short time. The Mulberry Docks were something to see. To think that they built them, then towed them all the way across the Channel. It was quite a feat.

We were obliged to climb down the net ladders. A little scary, with the boat bobbing up and down; however, the medical officers were positioned on either side all the way down, leaving a strip in the middle for us to descend, in full gear, hanging on for dear life. They gave us a hand and encouraged the timid ones. We came inland in lorries. It was hot and dusty but still glorious countryside—much like Canada. It almost seemed as if we were coming home. The part we saw first was not badly damaged—it was hard to believe that this was really war-torn France. Of course, the dust was thick from the lack of rain and heavy traffic. The fields were pretty well chewed up, but it looked like the scenery up the Gatineau. You would hate the dust, Dad. We drove along through tall Lombardy poplar trees, in stately rows on either side of the roads. Passed through towns and villages, seeing names on signposts that had become familiar to us in the past few weeks on the news broadcasts.

Finally, we saw a Canadian hospital sign, and turned into a huge field jammed with many colossal tents. One of our hospitals is set up and working here. We know so many of the Sisters, and also our Red Cross girls. Betty Maw and her group are here. Also Sister Lois Malone, who used to visit at Coombehurst, and so many others that I knew at Hackwood. Just like Old Home Week. Great to talk with them all and find out just what is going on.

We are living in tents—at present in some huge ones—because we are not established to work yet.

It's an experience to live in a tent with 39 other women. You are certainly never lonely! Good thing they are such a wonderful crowd, and we do have many laughs. It is like a huge summer camp. Everyone looks fat, healthy and tanned. France seems to be the land of sunshine. Living in England, I had forgotten how wonderful it is to have summer days of long unbroken sunshine. England is a veritable garden, especially the South, and I shall always love the southern counties, particularly Hampshire—but France is like home—we even drive on the same side of the road!

Now August 19th, exactly a year since we left home, and what a year it has been! Will continue—the first morning we were here, we contacted Col. McKenna, our Overseas Commissioner, and found out about our supplies, etc. He is extremely nice—is from Montreal and will help us a lot. We went to the work tent and saw the girls and went to the wards with them. Will help them as much as we can. There is a fair-sized town not far away, and we go there occasionally. One day it was a Catholic holy day, so all the shops were closed and everyone was all dressed up. This town has not been damaged much, so the people go on as before. They are mostly women and children, and even in their shabby clothes, they manage to look chic and achieve an air of smartness. Their clothes fit, they are petite and carry themselves well and impart a feeling of nonchalance. (This town was Bayeux.)

Most of the women wear black. Don't know if they are in mourning or just prefer it, although it looks pretty hot these bright August days. They wear large black hats with long black veils trailing down their backs. That day, we really saw them at their dressiest. All the fancy extreme hats—with such high crowns and drooping brims. Some were felt, some checked taffeta and other brightly coloured materials. They seem to have a certain touch that is different from England.

The children were a picture. Of course, we did see them in their Sunday best, but they were sweet. Little girls with black hair and eyes, nice complexions and beautifully dressed, with little pink or white dresses, flowers in their hair and crocheted gloves on their little hands. The tiny boys were in darling knitted suits; all have big dark eyes and curly hair. The little boys, seven and eight, were in long black pants and white silk blouses and white silk gloves. The people, especially the children, looked well-nourished, tanned and healthy.

That day, the shops were all closed, but there seemed to be quite a few things in the windows, although we cannot buy anything as it is reserved for the civilian population. I had my eye on some pink lace undies—they would look great under my battle rompers!

(Two of my older granddaughters, both in their early twenties, first Erin, then Christy, have travelled in Europe. They have surprised and pleased me by each taking time and trouble to depart from their planned itineraries to make pilgrimages to Normandy to see the beaches where our valiant troops landed, to visit the Canadian cemeteries and the Canadian War Museum in Bayeux. Both felt it a very moving and poignant experience. It made me very proud that they each had the desire and motivation to visit Normandy.)

We went to another city—one taken by the Americans, a few weeks ago. It was a case of complete and utter devastation. Really a heartbreaking sight. You may have seen snatches of it on a newsreel at the time. A completely dead city—in reality, a pile of rubble—with dust inches thick all over everything. It was not possible to tell what the heaps of broken masonry had been. Not a scrap of colour anywhere, not a green leaf or blade of grass. Nothing but grey dust and the dank foul odour of death. Will be forever in my memory. (the city was St. Lo, in the Cherbourg Peninsula.)

Also visited another city—one taken by the Canadians, not long ago. It, too, is badly beaten up (as the Yankee lads say), really smashed, but does not have the same hopeless dead look of the first one we saw. (This city was Caen.) The French people are beginning to return to their homes—if there is anything left. The centre and heart of the place is completely wrecked, but in the midst of all this ruin stands one restaurant or brasserie, as they are called. It must have been lovely, really a swish place. Has been damaged but not badly, operating as NAFFI canteen. There is a movie showing currently, and it is a rest spot for the troops coming back from the front lines. A place where they can sit down and have a meal and relax for an hour or two. It is a huge place, done in marble and modernistic circular booths, once well-upholstered, but now a bit shabby and worn. Walls covered with huge mirrors and a stage with a grand piano. Now, instead of a French musician, there is either a Canadian or Limey soldier at the keyboard, beating it out.

The boys look dirty, tired and covered with dust and grime. We spoke with many of the Canadian lads, asked about different people we knew and talked of home. Also met the French woman who runs the place with her two daughters, about 14 and 15 years old. One of the Sisters with us is French, so is able to converse with her. She told us many interesting things about the occupation and their life then. We wondered how they feel about us coming to liberate them, but smashing their homes in the attempt. She was most effusive, said that they are thrilled that we are here and that they can rebuild their city, now that they have their freedom.

We have seen much of the countryside, and it is exciting to go through all these places that have been in the news so much in the past few weeks, where our troops fought so valiantly and at such great cost. We saw evidence of recent battles, burned-out tanks, dead farm animals rotting. Fields chewed up, trees scorched and shrubbery flattened. We saw an airfield that the Canadians took recently (Carpiquet) where tank battles took place, towns that must have been the scene of hand-to-hand skirmishes, with snipers everywhere. Tiny graveyards here and there by the roadside, with their rows of white crosses—some with a tin hat on top. It's all like a dream, or perhaps I should say, a nightmare. Sometimes I can hardly believe that we are really here, witnessing all this. So many heart-rending, horrible sights—but everywhere you are aware of the power and amazing resources of the Allied Forces, their fighting spirit and will to finish this struggle properly. We are more proud than ever to be Canadian. It is especially exciting to be part of the great Allied Expeditionary Force, led by General Dwight D. Eisenhower. We wear that patch with great pride.

There are many amusing aspects to our life here. It's a bit primitive at times, but quite an experience. The girls are a super bunch, such good sports, and you really need a sense of humour. Our latrines are a long way from our tent. Another ten-holer, and we sit back to back. No roof, and just some burlap stretched around the perimeter, about five feet high, drooping in spots. Small planes fly low, dip overhead and am sure the pilots are convulsed with laughter. After so much sunshine, we had several rainy days and the dust turned to mud. An epidemic of the Normandy Glide struck most of us, and we were a sorry-looking group, slipping and sliding in the mud trying to run for the latrines.

Potable water is in very short supply. We each get one very small canvas bucket of water every day. This is for drinking, washing ourselves, brushing teeth, etc., so there was nothing left for laundry. We heard that there was a village pump about two miles away, so Laura and I started off to find it. We met a little French boy—something you might see in a picture. He was about 9 or 10. Wore a little tunic, much as I wore at O.L.C., great wooden shoes, and a bunch of flowers in his hand. I asked in halting French where we might find some water to wash our clothes. He beamed, gave us each some flowers and took us to the pump. We wash out our khaki shirts, etc., take them back to our tent and hang them on the nearest tree to dry. Of course, ironing is out of the question, so as soon as the shirt is dry, we put it on, wrinkles, crinkles and all, and head out for the evening party.

Mary can converse quite fluently with the people, so is a big help to us. They really do appreciate it if you can speak with them in their own language. They are much easier to understand than the French at home. They speak more slowly and distinctly, without slurring the words together. I can understand practically everything they say, and am able to talk with them a little, too.

We have been visiting at a nearby American Mess and they have a French chef—with an amazing history. Mary and I talk with him and Mary translates for the Yankee lads—because they had been depending on sign language when addressing him, and some of the meals, although delicious, did not bear much resemblance to what they were expecting.

Our first batch of mail arrived yesterday, the first in over ten days. In answer to your question, Dad, the financial situation is fine. We are paid every two weeks by the Army Paymaster. We get 700 francs, or 1,400 francs per month. About $35, and as in England, we have very little to spend it on. We pay Mess fees but they are very small, and in an emergency, the Red Cross will cash a cheque for us.

I am still trying to get used to French money, and being involved with the Mess Treasury, have to figure it out quickly. I had just reached the point where I knew what something should cost in shillings and pounds, without mentally figuring it back to dollars, and now I have to start over again.

Have written to Major Coulter, Dad, as you suggested, about supplying us with magazines. Thank you so much for looking into it for us. That will be a great help, if he will supply us.

Had a letter from Mr. Jobson, saying that Arthur was reported missing. I feel so badly—he is such a sweet lad and Wyn, his wife, a darling. However, seem to have a feeling that he is safe somewhere. Wrote back to them, to see if I could try to get information for them from over here, because we are in direct contact with the British Red Cross re POWs. Much love, Lois

August 22nd, 1944
Dearest Family:

I saw Bill Wood the other day. He was the chap who was with me at Harvey's Investiture. Was so surprised to see him and very glad, too. He had come in here with another lad to see one of the Sisters, had no idea I was here, then saw me walking to the Mess tent. He looked awfully tired—has been here since D-Day, so has seen a good deal of action. There seems to be little left of his outfit. Nairn Boyd from Winchester—remember, he was quite a track star a few years ago—was killed, also his brother. Nairn had been in Hackwood for a month or so in the winter and I had gotten to know him through Bill. Such a nice chap, and one of Bill's best friends, so he feels pretty badly about that. He looked so sad as he told me of losing many friends.

Was talking to some Cameron Highlanders recently and they said that both Harrison Bennett and his brother Ron are gone, too. How devastating for these families back home to lose not one, but two sons. I find it hard to take in when I hear they are gone. Am sure I am storing up a great flood of tears and some day it will burst forth. These are some of Canada's very finest young men, and once again, they are being killed in Europe. It's quite strange, being here in France—not many miles away, bitter battles are being fought, and here we sit, in bathing suits, in the bright sunshine, writing letters home. We are anxious to get settled in our location and start to work, but in the meantime, we are told to get as much rest as possible.

Sheila's brother, Drum, was here the other evening. He is married to Muriel Scobie from Ottawa. He had only about an hour here, then returned to the front, but she was so excited to see him. We see so many familiar faces over here. Much more so than in England. Guess it is because we are concentrated in a fairly small area. Laura was delighted that you got in touch with her family in Montreal—and I am sure they were pleased, too. Yesterday afternoon, Mary and I and our Matron and one from another CGH had tea with Colonel McKenna at Red Cross HQ. He had not met Matron Paterson. It was very nice.

Have met some fine young American lads. They seem to be an exceptionally nice group. Three of them have been taking me out. They come over here and then we usually go to the château, their rest home that I told you about. Don is from Chicago, Bob from Springfield, Ohio, and Keith from Kansas.

There are Canadians in the vicinity, too. We are going to their Mess this weekend. Tomorrow, expect to see more of the country, the part the Yankees took first. Life is so completely different over here than in England. I will always be very grateful for my year there. It's truly beautiful—so many diverse areas. The South, so green and beautiful, then the coastline with its rugged rocky cliffs and smooth white beaches below. Yorkshire, with its wild beauty on the moors. Then Essex and those counties with their gorgeous flowers. England is lovely and truly a garden but I would never feel at home there—perhaps it's because the majority of the people fail to understand us, and continue to regard us as colonials. While France, with its wide-open spaces and rugged beauty, is much like home.

I started to tell you about doing our laundry and washing our hair at the village pump, but somehow got sidetracked. The other day, Mary, Laura and I went to the pump to wash our hair. It is just at the side of the road and a little drain flows by. You carry your own basin down there, then get down on your hands and knees and dunk your head into the ice-cold pump water. We were all working away, with our heads all lathered up with shampoo, quite oblivious to the surroundings. Suddenly, we looked up and there were 14 or 15 British Tommies standing quietly by, watching us. They had come to fill their large water containers. So when we got ready to rinse, one would step forward with a great can of water and carefully pour it over us. Such service! It was really pretty funny and I wanted to laugh, but they were being so helpful and were so serious about it all.

One thing about being here: everyone is always ready to help you, give you a lift or share whatever they have quite happily. Everyone quickly learns the art of scrounging and you realize that if there is something to be had, you take it, or someone else will. I came home the other day with six beautiful percale sheets, gift of an American lad—also chocolates, cigarettes, fruit juice and an orange! Mary acquired a blanket and a gorgeous box of American chocolates. Laura had more canned fruit and even a can of flea powder! Which, by the way, is most useful.

We have a standing invitation to go to the U.S. pilots' rest home nearby, so go many evenings. There is a different group of pilots every night and they are great fellows, all young and full of fun. It's a lovely old château—used to belong to a French count, then was taken over by a German general. It is in excellent condition—still has the French books in the bookcases and pictures of the children of the French family on the walls. There is a badminton court outside and billiards and Ping-Pong. We usually go over about 8.30 pm and they always bring us home at midnight. It is the closest thing to home I have seen since leaving Coombehurst. They have a radio and piano so we can dance and usually have food. Also, take turns slipping into their marvellous marble bathroom and taking a quick bath in the lovely tub with all that wonderful hot water. It's a little bit of heaven for us. It is surprising, there is a little French town on the way to the château and it is completely levelled—a pile of rubble—then, just around the corner, not 25 yds. away, is this lovely peaceful spot, untouched by war. The spacious home, with its smooth lawns and green trees and even a fat, sleek donkey grazing in the meadow.

We went to a ball game, Laura and I with Bud Hoffman and another chap. Bud is our Educational Officer and has been extremely good to us. He works with our groups and is always so helpful. Have been to various American Messes and it is fun. Saturday evening we went to a party with some friends of Sue Edwards and Margie Ambrose, two of our Corps members here. They had a wonderful band—best music I have heard since Gerry's Infantry band in Basingstoke. Party was in an old school, with German writing on the walls. It must sound like a round of festivities. Actually, it is not—there are so many lads and each one only gets to an occasional party. When they are slogging away, in so much danger, they need a little relaxation. They're all doing a magnificent job.

It is now August 24th, and I will continue. We really have been having a busy time. Have been able to travel around and have seen quite a bit of this part of France. Once we start to work, we will be working long hours, without much time off, so might as well make the most of the time now. The days are bright and hot, just like summer at home. Yesterday, we went on a picnic with Bob, my friend in the Army Air Corps, and two of his buddies. We had the most gorgeous food. They provided it all. It was rations in boxes, but after the stodgy diet we have been having, it was pretty exciting, opening the various boxes and cans. We are on British rations, so have had a steady run of rice, dried peas, greasy canned bacon, bully beef, trifle, bread pudding and lumpy custard!

We have driven for miles, past Bayeux, Tilly, Caen, Carpiquet, Carentan, Isigny, Valognes, St. Lo, Cherbourg and many other towns along the way. The day we went to Cherbourg was the day news broke about Paris being liberated. It's easy to see that Paris is truly the heart of France. The whole spirit of the people seemed to lift. They smiled and waved with renewed vim and vigour. Everywhere, they told us the news. The streets were filled with flags and banners—and driving back, through the battered towns and villages, it gave us a thrill to see how everyone reacted. We saw some German prisoners here and there, a sorry, dejected lot, sullen too. Crowds sang the "Marseillaise" and everywhere, one was conscious of a great wave of jubilation sweeping across the country.

Got a smart new shirt in an American shop. Flannel and very well cut. Wish I had bought two. Will do so next time I have a chance. Khaki, of course. They have no epaulets and they are necessary; however, it has an exceptionally long tail, so I will chop off a piece and make epaulets. Please don't worry. We are being very well looked after and are probably safer here than in London, dodging the doodlebugs!

So much love to you and all the family,
Lois

Our canvas home
Bayeux, Normandy

Normandy Hotel
Deauville

D-Day Dodgers
No. 12 CGH Ball Team Bayeux

Noon break
Route to Belgium

Troop carrier
Betty, Ruth, Pearl and Laura

REMEMBERING DIEPPE

By late August, the Allies were advancing on all fronts. Leading Canadian troops linked up with the Americans below Rouen, August 25th, 1944. The first Canadian regiment to do this was the 12th Manitoba Dragoons, an armoured car long-range reconnaissance unit. They had rushed east, liberating towns and villages as they went.

Canadian troops were given the job of clearing the "Rocket Coast" where many of the V-1 and V-2 bomb sites were located. As many as 300 V-1 sites were found as the German troops fell back. The take-over of these launch pads brought quick relief to London and southern England, which had endured continuing day and night raids from these unmanned monsters for months. The people of London and the south counties were lavish in their praise for the Canadian regiments who liberated this area from the Seine to the Leopold Canal, and in doing so, terminated the terrible ordeal of the flying bombs.

These bomb sites were ingenious. Each site had a steel launching track about 150 feet long, rising on an angle of about 40 degrees, through an opening cut in the trees. Surrounding the site were heavy concrete buildings storing the bombs. Many of these sites were heavily damaged as the French Resistance group had passed very precise information re their locations to England; hence very accurate bombing had been carried out.

General Crerar, remembering Dieppe and the valiant effort of some of the 2nd Division regiments who took part in that disastrous raid two years earlier, ordered the 2nd Division to proceed to Dieppe. The Division advanced rapidly, expecting a fight, and were ready, but instead, the German garrisons had fled, blasting bridges as they withdrew.

For the men who had been there two years before and had survived that desperate bloody battle, this was surely the war's sweetest victory!

The people of Dieppe recognized and remembered the 2nd Division with their dark blue arm patches, and gave them a tumultuous welcome. There were tears of joy, a great display of affection for the heroic warriors who had tried so hard to free their town two years earlier. Flags waved, wine flowed, and there was singing and dancing in the streets.

A fitting completion to the Dieppe Raid—a Memorial Service was held at the cemetery on the hill where the French people had buried the Canadian dead after the dreadful savage encounter in 1942. The 2nd Division solemnly paid tribute to their fallen comrades. Dieppe was taken without a shot being fired!

Much has been written and discussed about the Dieppe Raid—should it have taken place and what did it accomplish? Although very costly in the loss of precious lives, it seems to have been pretty well accepted that many worthwhile lessons were learned during that ill-fated raid, leading to successful planning for landings in North Africa, Sicily, Italy, and the all-important D-Day Landing in France.

The main lessons that were learned:

- the need to make the landing on a beach and not try to storm a very well-defended port
- much more support should be provided for the Infantry by heavy guns of the offshore fleet
- the absolute need for a safe docking area to be built as soon as possible—hence, the famous Mulberry Docks
- the need for complete secrecy about plans for a proposed landing, plus much more.

It really gave the military planners a basis to start with, to realize the military might that would be necessary and to think of every last detail, leaving nothing to chance.

The Canadian Force of 5,000 in that raid came mainly from Windsor, Toronto, Hamilton, Winnipeg, Calgary, Regina and Montreal. Much sorrow in these places as news arrived of the 667 dead, 218 Missing, 1,894 POWs and 592 wounded; 1,619 made it safely back to England.

Probably thousands of British, Canadian and U.S. lives were saved in later landings because of Dieppe. Although disastrous and costly in lives lost, the Dieppe Raid has shone brightly through the amazingly successful landings that followed.

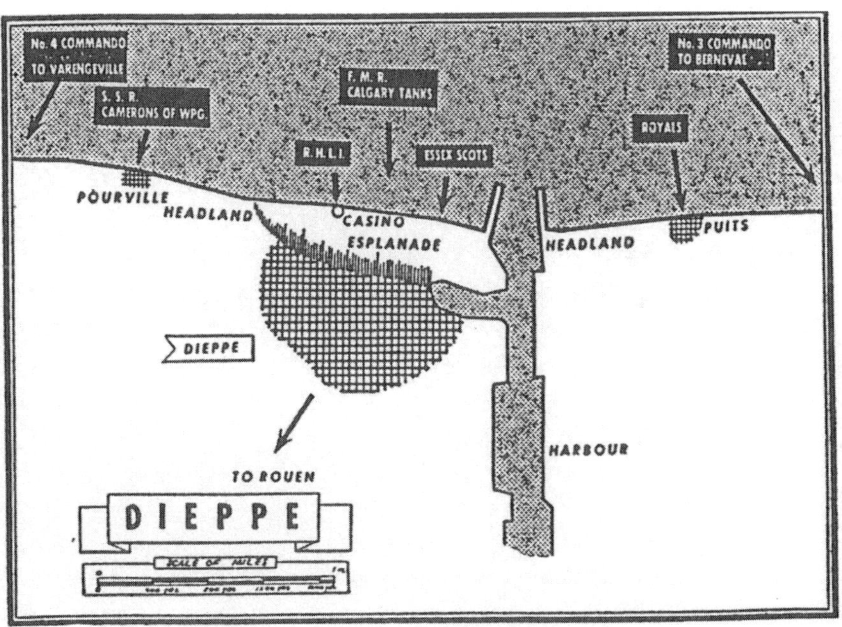

NORMANDY

August 26, 1944
Dearest Family:

We went to the dance at the RCAF Mess Friday night. It was a lovely party. The nicest we have been to yet. They had gone to so much trouble—had even arranged a dance floor in a marquee tent. It was made of boards, laid side by side on the ground, covered with cocoa matting. Made the smoothest, springiest floor. They had found odd flags and pennants for decorations and Bob Hyndman from Ottawa had done some excellent drawings. The food was scrumptious. They had beautifully iced cakes with tiny Spitfires on top.

Air Marshall Breadner was there and I had a pleasant chat with him, catching up on their family news. Ages since we were neighbours on Fourth Ave. He asked to be remembered to you.

Boxes are arriving very well, and we all thank you so much. The fruit and juice is great. Also the chocolate bars and hot chocolate. Boxes from home meant a lot before, but now, when we are more or less camping and our meals are not good, they mean a great deal more. We can make tea, hot chocolate, or soup quite easily, but anything beyond that is more difficult.

Saturday night we went to a British Mess party. Six of us were invited. It was a lovely place. An old château in a good state of repair, much as the French family had left it. They had an excellent band, which was a pleasant surprise. We danced on the open porch under the stars, a very pretty setting. My only regret seeing these places is that I did not see them in the years before the war, when life was happy and pleasant in France. The food was delicious, all so attractively served. We were the only Canadian girls there, so were something of a novelty. I met a very nice lad in Ordnance Corps. Young and handsome, the nicest Englishman I have met for quite a while. He is most interesting and is an interior decorator in peacetime. Is coming to take me out on Wednesday. We do lead an exciting life, meeting so many people, all types—usually British, Canadian or American. It amazes me how three nationalities who are basically the same, speak the same language, and have much the same beliefs and customs, can be so totally different.

Sunday morning, I went to see Bill Wood. He is burned but is quite all right. I promised to write to his mother to reassure her, as he is afraid she will be unduly worried. As I came out of the tent where Bill is, I bumped into two Cameron Highlanders and one was Wiley Sharpe! He had been over at another Canadian hospital and someone told him I was here, so he and his friend, a lad from Montreal, came looking for me. We had a wonderful chat and caught up on mutual Ottawa friends. He and cousin Bill were such close friends through school and he was so interested to hear that Bill is married, and all about Billie.

Went to an American Mess for dinner and it was very special. It was Sunday. A white tablecloth on the table. The food was marvellous—I was almost afraid to touch it in case it wasn't real! There were five U.S. lads and they invited five of us. We topped it all off with real American coffee. Quite a shock to our systems after a steady diet of rice and dried peas!

Did I tell you that we had a look at France from above? It was my first flight and it was really thrilling. There is something new and different every minute. The exciting part was seeing other aircraft whiz past us. We were up for about 45 minutes. Didn't expect to have my first flip over France!

This war has given us a chance to get to know the Americans—they are a friendly and generous people. They do things so well and really look after their troops, making sure they are comfortable, in decent living quarters, and well fed, with a proper diet. We all need to be thankful that they entered the war when they did, with their vast resources and endless supplies. As we drive through the countryside, we see acres and acres piled high with U.S. supplies and equipment. Their extensive airstrips and huge, well-run camps are surely a credit to them, and an example and inspiration for the rest of us.

It is now September 3, 1944, the fifth anniversary of the war. It was just a year ago today that we landed in Liverpool. I remember how excited I was, setting foot on English soil. It has been a strange and wonderful year, and I feel I have learned a lot.

Friday night, we went to an RAF party. Their Mess is in the middle of an apple orchard and they had a huge bonfire. We all sat around and drank beer or cocoa. I still have not acquired a taste for beer, but the cocoa was delicious! It was a beautiful moonlit night and made me think of Gauvreau Lake and our many bonfires there. I can understand why cousin Bill has such an opinion of the RAF, and after that evening, I can surely agree with him. They were certainly not the most hospitable crowd I have met.

Then Saturday was our unit anniversary. Just a year since No. 12 was formed in Canada. We had a celebration. It began with a field day. You may be sure, the weather was unfavourable—it usually is for those affairs. Rain, on and off, all day. There were races for the men, also three-legged and sack races for the Sisters. Then the classic of the day, a baseball game played by us. Two teams of Sisters: one was the "D-Day Dodgers" and the other, the "Trotting Twelfth". Each team had a suitable yell and bounded out on the field in the most amazing outfits. The D.D.D. s wore great big bath towels as veils, with our hair completely covered—right down over our foreheads. We carried canvas water buck-

ets to catch the ball and each one had a crazy name. The others were all dressed up with their canvas basins on their heads, tied on with great red bows under their chins. One gal wore long red underwear and another a German helmet! It was quite a game and pretty funny. I was a D.D. Dodger and we did have fun. The afternoon was a great success; then we had a cocktail party and dinner at seven. Later, a singsong, then a dance. It was purely a unit affair, the first one since we left Whitby.

French money is the flimsiest stuff, just like play money or Monopoly money. We have to use our own toilet paper, so usually carry it in our pocket. The other day, one of the girls walked into the latrine, dug into her pocket, pulled out a crumpled piece of paper, used it, then realized it was a hundred franc note!

Much love to you both and my dear doggie. Lois

September 7th, 1944
Dearest Family:

This time we have seen another and more exciting part of France. I was thrilled when I saw London, even more so when I saw Edinburgh, but Paris! Surely the pièce de résistance.

It is really beautiful—so modern and clean—wide tree-lined boulevards and so much colour. Such a gay, happy place—certainly gives no evidence of being so recently occupied. I was with Laura and Flora and think I may say that we were the first Canadian girls to enter the city. We arrived—in an American ambulance. We drove in and there was Paris set up on a hill—we passed through a beautiful residential district, wide clean streets, large leafy trees and modern architecture. It was just about 6.00 pm as we drove towards the Arc de Triomphe—quite a marvellous sight, majestic and stately in the evening sunset. We saw the Eiffel Tower, Place de l'Opéra, the Rue Rivoli, Champs-Elysées, Avenue de la Grande-Armée, Place de la Concorde, etc. It's hard to describe just how you feel seeing these places for the first time, when you have read about them for so long. To be there so soon after the liberation, was especially thrilling. Paris has remained intact and lovely. Recognized as a jewel in Europe, it was spared the ruthless bombing and devastation that so many other marvellous old cities endured.

What a fantastic reception! Every time we slowed, people mobbed our vehicle. Adults and children shouted and waved, climbed on the running boards and clutched our hands. They all smiled and threw flowers, with tears running down their cheeks. We were part of a never-ending parade of military vehicles pouring into Paris. They all asked what and who we were, and seemed thrilled to learn that we were Canadian.

Everyone was beautifully dressed—the place was a myriad of colour, women so smart and chic. Amazing hairdos, the fanciest shoes and such extreme hats, earrings and a distinct aroma of marvellous perfume. Everyone rides a bicycle and we were told that there are over a million bikes on the streets at all times. The shop windows were exciting and unusual. Everywhere there were flags and banners in red, white and blue. Even the flower shops carried out the patriotic colour scheme, with blue delphiniums, white daisies and scarlet poppies.

We stayed in a lovely old hotel on the Rue de la Paix! That was very exciting, as I thought of that old song, "At a Perfume Counter . . ." Our very good friend, the Education Officer who was already established in Paris, came to our assistance and got us installed in the hotel. He was quite amazed to see us and warned us not to walk around after dark as there were still a few thousand snipers at large. We had a lovely suite with a beautiful bathroom, so spent much of the night splashing in and out of the tub! The following day we had an opportunity to window-shop and explore the wonderful store,

Galeries Lafayette. You could spend days wandering around there, just looking. There are cosmetics galore—everything, absolutely everything! It's certainly difficult to believe that it was an occupied city. The dresses, hats and shoes on display are really gorgeous, and the lingerie! It just broke our hearts that we did not have more time. However, we hope to come back some day, soon.

We drove around for ages and got a good idea of the city. Everything is just as it must have been in peacetime. In the Rue de la Paix and Place Vendôme district are all the famous names of the fashion houses. The hotel was quite luxurious; after our crowded tent, it was a little bit of heaven. The waiters in the dining room were in the traditional long-tailed coats, and everywhere, all seemed truly glad to see Americans and Canadians. Our Canada badges caused quite a stir. It is all an experience I would not miss for anything. To see these places now, under these conditions and circumstances, more or less on our own, is surely an adventure. Everywhere there were big signs: "Honour to our Liberators". That meant the Yankees, but the Canadians have been in there, also.

Later, will tell you more about the whole trip but I was so intrigued with Paris that I just had to write about it first. I wanted to get in there early and see it all, and we certainly did.

We had dinner in an American Mess in Versailles, where the peace treaty was signed in 1918. General Bradley was at another table. We also went to Orly Airport. It had been in German hands until quite recently, is now American and they are fast repairing it. We had gone up the Maple Leaf "UP" route partway, then followed the famous "RED BALL" route, but came back a different way. Visited Liseux, the French holy city. It is pretty badly shot up, but the shrine, which is on the outskirts of town on a hill, was untouched. It's quite beautiful—a wonderful piece of architecture. Brother André's Shrine in Montreal was patterned on the one at Liseux, although this one really seems to stand out more. Perhaps because it is on top of a hill. We came through so many familiar names on the way home. Some towns were badly damaged, others untouched. It was surely a memorable trip and one we will never forget. Perhaps leave in Paris—we can dream!

September 10th, 1944
Dearest Ones:

Here it is Sunday, again. When in Basingstoke, I knew when the weekends rolled around but now, the weeks are not divided at all—just one day after another. We have been staying close to camp after our long trip. Thursday night we went to an English Mess. It was quite a nice party—very good food but horrible punch. They make it with Calvados, a French concoction, and I cannot figure out why anyone would drink it. Not sure what it is about the Limey officers, a certain air of arrogance and superiority. We feel more at ease with Canadians or Americans.

Friday was a lazy day. It rained so we just stayed in. There is never a dull moment in our tent. It's really fun. The girls are a riot—especially when someone returns from a shopping trip. All crowd around to see the loot. Then everyone screams as they drag out each bottle of perfume. We all try to outdo each other, getting fancier bottles.

Yesterday, we went scrounging—the food here gets monotonous, so occasionally we go out to see what we can find. It was a gorgeous afternoon, so we roamed around the countryside, armed with some cigarettes and a couple of chocolate bars and soap, and gathered up a few eggs, tomatoes and lettuce. We had some canned rations that American friends had given us, so the hungry Canucks will eat again! It's really not as bad as it sounds, but just the dreadful sameness of the meals, with never anything fresh. No fruit or vegetables. However, my boxes will soon arrive; all the girls receive stuff from home and we pool it and five or six of us have picnic suppers. We vow that when we all get home, we will live on salad, steak, vegetables, ice cream and fruit!

Must tell you about our recent ball game. We of No. 12 have a girls' team, again called the D-Day Dodgers. I am in the field, and Saturday we played the nurses of No. 16 CGH. It was quite a game. They finally won 18-15. And we will have a return match on Monday. It was really a scream. The girls from 16 were very good—quite professional. They knew all the rules, etc., while we floundered around like the bunch of amateurs we were. We had no proper shoes but were wearing either our rubber boots or high leather ones. I fell flat on my face, twice, right in the mud. Do wish you could see some of the games. We are really getting organized for Monday, being coached and getting proper shoes. The rest of the unit turns out and cheers and laughs hysterically.

There are so many little things that happen. Funny things that I wish I could tell you about. The other day, we hitched a ride to a neighbouring town. Flora and I were sitting in the back of an American truck, no roof on it, and suddenly, it poured rain. There were seven or eight French refugees with us, and they were all characters. We huddled under a tarpaulin, and the others were strewn around, trying to keep dry. One man had a bicycle on the truck, and he stood for ages in the pouring rain, holding the bike. He had open sandals, and was standing in a couple of inches of water. He also wore a black rain cape with hood, and it floated out behind him. He looked just like Winged Mercury, standing firmly, clutching his bicycle and chewing frantically on some gum we had given him, as he stared straight ahead. Flora and I were most amused. Another man was a member of the Underground—very nice and well-educated. Said that before the war, he had two cars, and now he is thumbing rides. The Bosch took everything. They were awfully hungry, so the young American lad driving the truck passed back a box of rations and a huge loaf of black bread. Flora and I tore it up, opened some of the cans, and put meat and cheese between chunks of bread and handed it around—all this done under the tarp, with the rain coming down in torrents. There we sat, and munched great chunks of black bread, too, looking as bedraggled as the rest. If it had not been so funny, we might have noticed the rain, or the fact that we were sitting on a couple of gasoline cans that bounced all over.

We are going to Deauville on Wednesday. It's a big Canadian Leave Centre and we are all having an opportunity to spend a few days there. Twelve girls go at a time and stay for three days. I'm certainly looking forward to it. To live in a hotel for a while, with white tablecloths, etc. Seeing Paris even briefly was just a taste of it all. Will write again, probably from Deauville, and tell you all about it.

Heaps of Love, Lois

September 17th, 1944
Dearest Family:

Hello again! Mail has been coming very well. The box of magazines arrived today and I am thrilled with it. Just the kind we will need and the patients will love them. Will guard that box carefully and take it with us.

We had a fabulous time in Deauville. Laura and I went—fifteen of us altogether. It's really a heavenly spot. Right on the coast and known as France's second Monte Carlo. Now it is a Canadian Leave Centre! How did we manage to get that plum? We went Wednesday morning and returned Friday evening. Stayed in the Normandy Hotel, a perfectly beautiful place. Typically French architecture. We had a lovely room. Twin beds, the furniture white, wallpaper deep blue and white, with rose carpet and flowered floor-length drapes. The French windows opened onto a little balcony, overlooking the prettiest courtyard, full of flowers and pear trees. It was all so clean and modern. An inviting bathroom and comfortable chairs.

The most luxurious hotel. Huge lobby—marble and beautifully decorated. A marvellous dining room with large windows looking out to sea. I guess we all appreciated it even more after living under canvas for weeks. The casino was just in the next block. It was colossal. It housed a gorgeous theatre. We saw the Canadian Army Show there one evening. There were several ballrooms, each one lovelier than the last, with gleaming dance floors, mirrored walls and glittering chandeliers. We had a dance one night with a fantastic orchestra. The bars were surely something to see—much chrome, so colourful and attractive. The games rooms were upstairs but were closed. Would have been fun to see the roulette wheels, etc.

From the deck we could see the warships shelling Le Havre and the fires were burning there. Hard to imagine in the midst of all this luxury that war was so close—just across the bay. The front of the casino looked out over the sea, a beautiful white beach, tennis courts, a formal garden with trim hedges, then a huge terrace with beautifully made garden chairs, each with different coloured canvas. They were rockers and so solid-looking. You would love them, Dad.

Thursday, we went to Rouen. It must have been a lovely city with fine modern buildings, but it, too, is smashed up. We had lunch there at the Hotel Dieppe and looked through the shops. Of course, after seeing Paris, other stores seem bare and rather uninteresting. In one swish dress store, they brought out their pre-war stock—what was left of it—and showed us dresses, negligées, housecoats, etc. Absolutely beautiful things, ridiculous prices, but all were carefully cut and exquisitely made.

We had marvellous meals at our hotel. It's just army rations, but they have French chefs and they certainly manage to disguise and camouflage the regular issue of bully beef, dried peas and rice. Delicious French pastries and even cream puffs. I was in seventh heaven!

The night that we saw the army show in the casino theatre, there was quite a large civilian audience. Before the show started, while the lights were still on, the F.F.I. women (they are the Free French) came in, rounded up 29 collaborators, and dragged them, kicking and screaming, from the theatre. You never know just what you may see.

Yesterday, we had a picnic with our medical officers. There were about 70 of us. It was a clear sunny day and we left about 2.00 pm and walked several miles to a wonderful green meadow, beside a stream, just at the bottom of a little waterfall. We played volleyball, then swam. It was a cool and refreshing pool below the falls. Finished with baseball, then had supper, a delicious hot meal. Our cooks were there and had it all prepared. Even steak. We sat around after until transport arrived to take us back to the Officers' Lines. We stayed for a movie. Our unit is a great group, such good sports, and we do have fun together. Officers' tents are in a field a mile or so from ours.

We have a new scheme. Every night there is transportation to a nearby base laundry where we can have showers. It's really an amazing place. It is in two tents, joined together. The first tent is the dressing room, then you walk into the other one. There is a canvas floor and overhead are numerous pipes, running parallel and about 24 inches apart. Each pipe has a spray nozzle on it, about every 2 ft. So forty of us, all shapes and sizes, go in and each stand under a nozzle. The water is turned on by a main switch and is supposed to be regulated at the correct temperature. It is quite a scene, with all of us wearing only a bar of soap, slipping and sliding on the slightly sloping

Bombers on Next Strike

St. Lo., Cherbourg Peninsula
One of the main streets

Rouen
City in France

More destruction in French cities

floor. If you drop your bar of soap, you might as well forget it, as it slides quickly out of reach.

Tomorrow we are playing ball with a nearby American unit. Their girls have invited us to lunch, then we will have the game in the afternoon. We are all looking forward to it. They are extremely nice girls and it's fun to get to know them. Suddenly, I have an extra job, as the Mess Secretary/Treasurer is leaving the unit and I have been her assistant so now, I'm it. There will be an assistant, I hope. We are still in the same spot, but should move fairly soon.

Did I tell you that Gerry is back in England? He was wounded about two weeks ago and went back by air ambulance. I didn't hear for some time, and wondered if he was all right. Then letters came in a bunch. He is in an American hospital and quite OK again, so will probably be back over here before long. I never did see him because he was away up front with General Patton, and Gen. Patton tears ahead like a whirlwind. Gerry got out of the hospital for a few hours and went to Basingstoke and called in at Coombehurst. Mrs. Simon was quite amazed to see him, but was delighted, too, and insisted that he stay to dinner. We had heard that his outfit had been pretty well cut up, and I guess it was true, because most of the lads I knew, his fellow officers, have been killed or wounded.

Mac, who had such a fun line of chatter, in good old Brooklynese, Bill, the cute little Southerner who told me about his kid sisters back home and gave me some of the fudge they sent him. Neeley, another lad, who always looked sleepy but loved a good time and was usually the life of the party. They were such a gay, carefree lot. It's so hard to believe that they are all really gone. Gerry said he went to some of the pubs we used to visit but it was pretty depressing when everyone enquired about the other lads. Being here, as we are, and rather far away from it all, we seem many miles from the war, but every once in a while, something really brings it home to me.

The other day, a young Canadian came in to see Flora. He was from Winnipeg, and knew her family. He had been here since D-Day and had many stories to tell. They have seen so many grim and horrible sights, these very young men, and most of them have aged years in the past few months. He had passed a British and Canadian cemetery coming here, so went in to see if any of his men were buried there, and he saw his own brother's grave! It must have been a dreadful shock, as he had no idea he was even missing.

On different occasions, we've heard tales of the brave and heroic deeds done by the "Maquis", the French underground group, in the past five long years. It's almost unbelievable and incredible, the things they accomplished. They had little to lose and much to gain, so they took all sorts of risks. There was one young girl with a fair knowledge of English, so she listened to the BBC every day, knowing that it would mean her life if she were caught, translated the news, and passed it on so they could know what was going on. We met another French girl who had watched the Germans laying mines, taken careful note of where they were put, and then when the Allies arrived, the Maquis was able to help them clear the mine fields. These are only a few of the lesser tales, many stories of sheer heroism and bravery will never be told, but are buried in the broken rubble of these French cities. It certainly makes you think and realize that they had their share of grit and determination to carry on their amazing organization, wondering and waiting for us to come.

To get back to today, we went to play ball with the Yankee girls. It was pretty funny. We drove in, the D-Day Dodgers, and there was a huge mob, about 6 deep all around the base lines. G.I.s from all over the Cherbourg Peninsula! We were slightly abashed, but played. It was really fun and very close, but we finally won 6-2. Then our boys played theirs, and they won, so we split it. Then we had a delightful supper. The girls were all so friendly and good to us. Mary and I met the Red Cross, enjoyed chatting with them. In fact, we were so busy chatting that we suddenly realized that it was after 7.30, when our transport was to leave. Three of the Sisters were with us, and we all dashed out of the tent, but they had left without us. There we were, 20 miles from home. However, the Yanks were very nice and quickly drove us home. It was a wonderful day. They are coming here next week for a return match so we will try to see that they enjoy it.

Life is surely full and busy. Quite a mix of emotions as we see the battle damage and hear of friends lost. It all seems a dream world and perhaps we will wake up in our beds at home! But it is real and we know that the intense and savage fighting is going on not too many miles ahead of us. Losses have been heavy and it seems such a waste of so many fine young lives. We are anxious to move up, get our hospital set up and be able to do something worthwhile. Please don't worry as the hospitals are usually positioned in fairly secure areas. We expect to move very soon. Will keep you posted.

Much love,
Lois

September 24th, 1944
Dearest Mother and Dad:

Here it is Sunday afternoon and we are at Deauville again. It is certainly a glorious place. We left early yesterday morning and arrived in time for lunch. It's a three-hour lorry ride, dodging in and out of convoys amid the dust, but once we get here, all feel it is well worth the trip. The drive is always fun. Everyone sings and jokes and it is so interesting, driving through the countryside. Laura did not come this time, so I have a single room, in a suite with Flora and Goody and Betty and Ruth. We have the three bedrooms and bath and an attractive sitting room.

Betty and I had dinner dates with two Canadian lads—Duke of York Hussars—just back from the front. These boys have surely seen action, although reticent to mention much, but from the things they say, so casually, it is really grim up there. The Canadian forces are certainly doing a magnificent job. Everywhere they have faced the toughest opposition, but they are fighting soldiers and plenty tough, almost ruthless.

The whole set-up here is beautiful. Lavishly decorated and such luxury. It was here at the Normandy Hotel that the Duke and Duchess of Windsor used to stay. We took pictures on the terrace by the sea this morning, so will send them home.

I must tell you what some of the girls did at noon. The meals are excellent. Dinner at night is five or six courses. Lunch is very good, too. Usually several courses, with a very good dessert. Some of the girls were still hungry when they finished, so whipped upstairs, put on their hats, came back and sat at another table, then started all over again! We were amused and jealous because we did not think of it. We pay 30 francs a day to stay here and that covers meals, too. About 75 cents a day.

Did I ever tell you about losing my hat? We wear khaki berets with Red Cross pins on them, and one night, at a British Mess, it was quite dark in the hall where we left our coats and hats. When we were leaving, I got my coat and the hat that seemed to belong to it, and we drove home. I did not wear my hat, just carried it. In the morning, I looked for my chapeau—there was a huge big pancake of a beret, edged in leather, with an RAOC badge on it! I nearly had a fit and tried frantically to get my hat back, but in the meantime, that group had moved up with my hat, so there was nothing to do but put a Red Cross

Badge on the beret I got in exchange, and wear it. So, here I am, trudging across France and western Europe in some poor old Brigadier's hat! I can just imagine him, with mine perched on top of his head, Red Cross badge gleaming.

Mrs. Simon mentioned Gerry arriving there. Said he looked terribly tired, thin and ill. Was returning to the hospital for surgery to remove a bullet from his chest. He never told me anything about that, so I just assumed he was fine. She has asked him to spend his leave at Coombehurst, to recuperate. She is a dear soul, so kind and thoughtful, does everything so efficiently, yet unobtrusively, without gushing or making a fuss. Do hope he will go there. She will surely look after him, feed him well and get him back on his feet. Those boys have been through so much, first in North Africa and now, on the continent. The Infantry groups have taken it on the chin. I do hope they will ship him home to Oregon when he recovers.

Hugs and kisses, Lois

TRANSPORT – Canadian Red Cross Corps volunteer drivers qualified in driving and maintenance of motor vehicles and in First Aid – serving on call to the Armed Forces, Military Hospitals, United Kingdom Technical Mission and Red Cross Services including Blood Donors Clinics.

NURSING AUXILIARY (V.A.D.) Canadian Red Cross Corps, serving in civilian and military hospitals and First Aid Posts, voluntarily assisting the nursing profession in their work of mercy.

OFFICE ADMINISTRATION and FOOD ADMINISTRATION, Canadian Red Cross Corps. Office Administration members serve in Auxiliary War Services, Military Hospitals, First Aid Posts and elsewhere where their expert assistance is requested. Tribute is also paid in this painting to Food Administration. Food Administration members are trained in dietetics and nutrition, ready for emergency service to the public in the event of bombing or disaster.

The "BLUE SMOCK" RED CROSS WORKER is the symbol of service of thousands of Canadian women who knit, sew, make surgical dressings, and hospital supplies, pack Prisoner of War parcels and serve in many other ways our soldiers, sailors, airmen, and suffering . . .

Canadian Neurological and Plastic Surgery Hospital
No. 1
Basingstoke, England

Hackwood Park, location of the hospital in the background

Memlinc Palace Hotel
Canadian General Hospital No. 12
Bruges, Belgium
(now a bank, in the year 2000)

Market Square in Bruges
where Nursing Sisters' Mess was located.
Nursing Sisters' Mess

Crawsfordsburn Inn near Belfast, Ireland
Mrs. Cooper, at the doorway, revisited the Inn in 2000.

BELGIUM

September 30th
Dearest Mother and Dad:

Since my last letter, we have come a long way, to the land of Leopold. It was a marvellous trip, but more about that later. We had a fantastic weekend in Deauville, then Tuesday, we entertained the American girls at baseball. We had brought back fresh greens, tomatoes, etc. It rained all morning, so we thought they would not come; however, about 2.30 pm their trucks pulled in. We quickly rounded up a team and got started. We won again, then their G.I.s played our O.R.s, then the officers played, but it was getting later and we were all hungry, and their game was called after the third inning. We had a very nice supper. Quite super. First we served beer, and they were thrilled as that seems to be something they don't have. We had the salad items we had bought, plus potato salad, cabbage salad and cold meat, then pie and coffee. We think they are so lucky to have such great meals, then they come to our place and go into raptures about everything we have for them.

Our American friends entertained for us the following evening, our last one there. We went down to the beach and watched the ships. It was perfectly beautiful. We were on top of a cliff, looking over a broad smooth stretch of beach with foamy breakers thundering in. Out beyond was just like fairyland. All the ships lying at anchor were lit up. It's a long time since I've seen so many lights. It was quite exciting, just to stand there and watch them. Also, to see the amphibious Jeeps coming in across the water, then driving up on the beach! We returned to their château, and after dancing and Ping-Pong, adjourned to the kitchen for a late snack of bacon, eggs, etc. It really was our breakfast, as we were pulling out at the crack of dawn.

We have been very fortunate to have such an opportunity to see so much of France. Motoring across country, as we did, was wonderful. Loved the whole trip. We thought it would be exhausting as we ride in lorries, not the most comfortable mode of travel, but we took it in stages, so it broke the monotony and gave us a chance to rest and get cleaned up in-between. We spent one night in an erstwhile Bosch hospital—rather grim place, but interesting. Beautifully camouflaged. We saw Flying Bomb sites—great long runways—they are the demons that do so much damage and scared me so in London. We saw the Canadian Memorial at Thiepval and many other noted landmarks from the last war. Then on into Belgium, truly the promised land. Everywhere, we saw fruit and vegetables, and even more amazing, ice cream! Ruth Corr and I were sitting together and she likes ice cream as much as I do, so every time we saw a sign, "Glacée", we practically leapt out of the truck.

A wonderful agricultural land—everything so green and verdant. Flat, smooth fields, strong healthy crops and huge cattle and horses, grazing in the fields. The country looks so prosperous, with large, well-kept farm houses, no fences anywhere. That rather impressed me. At home, our farming districts are a mass of motley nondescript fences. Glorious flowers, rows of them in every hue in the rainbow. People are well-dressed, look happy and cheerful. Hard to believe they were so recently occupied! As we drove through the towns and villages we got a tremendous ovation. We were in the first lorry, really the Commodore of the Convoy. It was quite exciting as they all waved and cheered. Perhaps we were the first women in khaki that they have seen. Every time we stopped, they rushed forward with grapes, apples, pears, etc. In fact, one woman heaved an apple so enthusiastically, and with such gusto, that she hit Pearl right on the nose and caused a first-class nosebleed!

All looks so festive and gay. Flags, banners and streamers in profusion. Red, yellow and black instead of the inevitable red, white and blue. Of course, they have the Union Jack and Old Glory draped everywhere, too, but their own colours do predominate. I wish you could see the windows in the houses. Spotlessly clean, with beautiful curtains, all sorts, with lace, fringe, etc., some draped, some straight, but all so neat and clean. Really catches the eye. It is a very clean and wholesome-looking country.

We drove through what is to be our town to the outskirts, to a monstrous, forbidding-looking building which had been a Home for Delinquent Girls, then a German hospital, and now, to be our No. 12 CGH. It is three stories high, built in a triangle surrounding two courtyards. Enclosed by a high wall. We moved in, and we ladies, all one hundred of us, set up our cots in a tremendous room. We were there for almost a week, then the Sisters' Mess was moved to a very comfortable old hotel in the Main Square downtown. We understand that this is one of the very oldest cities in Europe. Very historic. Many canals. At present the Army Corps of Engineers are hard at work, putting in temporary pontoon bridges to replace the lovely old bridges that the retreating German troops had scuttled as they left.

(Our town was Bruges, known as one of the oldest cities in Europe. It was first established in the 8th century on the Zwin River. The town developed around an old fortress and having access to the sea, became a trading centre. The Dukes of Flandres settled there and by the 13th century, it was a world port. The Dukes of Burgundy took up residence and were responsible for the truly magnificent buildings in the ornate Gothic and, later, Baroque styles. It is still recognized across Europe for its ancient and priceless architecture. The Belfrey, situated in the Market, or Main, Square and many other marvellous old buildings were erected in the 1200s. Our Sisters' Mess was located in the Memlinc Palace

Hotel in the Market Square, so we were surrounded by the historic architecture of this beautiful little city—but in the midst of a war, we rarely took time to appreciate its magnificence.

(In September of '98, I did return briefly to Bruges. It was completely inundated with tourists marching along, shoulder to shoulder and heel to toe through the narrow cobblestone streets and swarming through the Squares. There were horse-drawn carriages everywhere. Tour boats clogging the canals. On previous visits to Europe with Jack, we had not gone to Belgium. Somehow, I did not want to go back, knowing we could never recapture the life we lived there. However, by 1998 and on my own, I did return and found our building, no longer the Memlinc Hotel, but now a bank, with an entirely different facade on the ground floor. I was delighted to see Bruges again, but did have a deep feeling of melancholy as the memories flooded back.)

The shop windows are a dream. As we flew by, we all craned our necks and gazed at fruit, vegetables, gorgeous bottles of perfume and crazy, extreme hats. Our town is very interesting. We are enjoying our hotel, and exploring the place. The hospital is being set up and we will work soon.

Ruth and I headed right for an ice cream parlour. We found a nice one and rushed in and ordered fruit sundaes. It was much like a milk bar at home. We stood at the counter and sailed into them—such delicacies—not even taking time to speak to each other. When we were halfway through, and able to pause, we enquired how much it was, and got out our money. It was then that we learned, much to our embarrassment, that they would not accept French money. I thought for a horrible moment that we would be washing dishes, but two RCAF lads came to our rescue and changed our money for us.

We wandered around our first day, mostly window-shopping. Stores full of lovely things. Lace and magnificent crystal, seem quite reasonable. Food is expensive. Ruth and I spied another place that had ice cream, so in we dashed. Betty and Laura said they could not face another one so soon, so they continued to shop. In the store, they made such a fuss over us, fed us chocolates, and gave us each a huge sundae. I had caramel this time. It was a tall glass and perfectly delicious. When we got to the bottom, they whisked away the glasses and filled them again. We were both beginning to feel quite satisfied, but couldn't hurt their feelings, so waded through to the bottom again, then beat a hasty retreat before they thrust another one in front of us.

We stepped out onto the sidewalk and someone pushed bunches of pink roses into our hands, "Pour nos libérateurs". We didn't feel much like liberators, but there is no use spoiling their fun. The afternoon went on; as we trailed around, everyone gazing in curiosity at our high boots and battle rompers. All the civilians looked so smart in their bright colours. In the evening we saw a Bing Crosby movie. Beautiful wide soft seats, just like easy chairs, with a great aisle in front to stretch out your legs. Then we went back to our hotel to eat "les pâtisseries" that we bought in the afternoon.

It's now October 11th. I am afraid there has been a gap in the correspondence. Have just not had a minute to myself. A word about our set-up. Our hotel is about two miles from the hospital. Laura and I have a pretty room. Not large but with pink wallpaper, twin beds, blue taffeta spreads, a basin with running water, two easy chairs, a cupboard with full-length mirror, small desk, two bedside tables, two large windows. The bathroom is away down the hall; at least it is not across a field!

We have a large bright dining room and a very attractive main lounge. We are working very hard, long hours, seven days a week; however, after our long summer vacation, we are really delighted to be finally doing something useful. We rush out in the morning, catch the 7.00 am truck to the hospital, or walk if we happen to miss it! Then we get back to the Mess about 7.30 pm, have dinner, then go out on a date, or fall into bed. Have been here about a week and haven't even had a chance to unpack my knapsack, to say nothing of the trunk and bedroll.

We have two rooms at the hospital for our Red Cross activities. They are side by side, neither very large, but serve our purpose. One we use as our supply centre and general office, and the other one is to be a lounge and recreation room for the Up patients. So far we have had little time to do much work on it. We hope to make curtains, cover the chairs, etc. We have scrounged a certain amount of furniture. We have had bookcases made, have a gramophone and records, dart board and various other games. Pretty vases full of flowers, and we are trying to find a radio. Have acquired cups and when we get properly organized will have tea or hot chocolate available in the afternoon. At present, we are too busy elsewhere to do much work on it, but little by little, we will get it going. Laura, Sheila and Mary are all great workers and we get along so well together.

(Our hospital was in Saint-Andres, a suburb of Bruges.)

Mary has been on another job, so the three of us have been carrying on without her, which makes much more work. To give you an idea what we do, we have baskets and visit the wards daily. I found a tea wagon, so wheel my wares around on that. We are on the lookout for wagons for Laura and Sheila. It is a 1,200-bed hospital, and filling up quickly. At present we each look after the needs of about 300 patients, so it keeps us on the jump. We keep them supplied with shaving kits, toothbrush and paste, comb and mirror, hankies, note paper, envelopes, pencils, air letters, cigarettes, gum, pipes, tobacco, cloth bags to hold their toilet articles, razor blades, matches, stamps, playing cards, games, books, magazines, newspapers, etc., and carry ink and lighter fluid. Also write their letters, collect their mail, do their shopping. We buy everything from fruit and cream puffs for them to perfume, stockings and even wooden shoes for their girlfriends. It's certainly a full-time job, but a very pleasant and satisfying one. They are the nicest lads, all so quiet and gentlemanly, and so very appreciative of every little thing we do for them

Time really flies and I must get to bed. There have been numerous parties and we have seen much of the surrounding countryside. There is a Canadian regiment at Dehanne-sur-mer, and we go to their Mess most evenings. The Manitoba Dragoons—they are a fine group, and five of us usually go: our neighbours Ruth, Betty and Pearl, with Laura and I. The Manitobas have liberated much of this area, including Bruges. Usually we are dog-tired by evening and it would be easier to crawl into bed; however, we realize that the young fellows we dance with have been on patrol and in battle all day, so really look forward to a little relaxation and fun. Also, it keeps our spirits up or we could drown in sorrow.

Heaps of love,
Lois

THE LEOPOLD CANAL
BATTLE OF THE SCHELDE ESTUARY

The ports of Le Havre, Boulogne and Calais had been secured; then the Canadian Army had the difficult job of taking control of the Leopold Canal. Part of the German 15th Army was positioned there, determined to make a stand.

The Canadian 4th Division, aided by Polish troops, had advanced up the French coast and into Belgium, liberating towns and cities along the way. The Manitoba Dragoons had occupied Ostende and the seaside resort towns on the Belgian coast. They had also freed the ancient city of Bruges.

This was accomplished by mid-September. Fighting was intense and the Canadians faced stiff opposition to cross the Leopold Canal, as it was covered by machine guns, heavy artillery and mortars. There were many casualties but the Allied Force finally gained their objective, securing both sides of the canal.

It became apparent that the great Port of Antwerp was necessary to the Allies to keep supplies flowing to the advancing Armies for the final trek into Germany. The Port of Antwerp had been captured by a British Division early in September, but to be completely useful, it was necessary to clear the 45-mile estuary, which was still in German hands.

This assignment fell to the Canadians and it was a tough one. The Germans had fortified the entrance to the estuary heavily and were determined to defend it. This was Dutch Polders country, very low, below sea level in places, some of it flooded, marshy and wet, with 15-foot dykes in many areas. The weather was dreadful, extremely cold, with rain and sleet. General Crerar had become ill and returned to England, so his command was assumed by Lieutenant General Guy Simonds.

By October 6, 1944, the plan was ready. Lieutenant General Simonds ordered the advance. The 2nd, 3rd and 4th Canadian Divisions were there, also the Poles and a British Division, so they were able to attack in strength. Our troops were faced with this flat, muddy and often flooded land—difficult terrain for armoured cars and tanks. Troops waded knee-deep in mud and water, soaked to the skin. It was bitterly cold. German garrisons were stationed all through the Schelde system. It was tough, intense fighting, hand-to-hand skirmishes as the Germans were captured or driven from the area.

It was here in Bruges on September 27th, 1944, that No. 12 CGH arrived, set up and quickly realized that we were operating as a casualty clearing station rather than a general hospital. Patients flooded in directly from the battlefields. Our first patients were from the Leopold Canal, and then from the Schelde Estuary. We were a 1,200-bed hospital and were soon filled to overflowing, with cots in the halls.

We all worked twelve-hour shifts, seven days a week. This taxing schedule went on for weeks and everyone just kept going. The Matron asked for one of our Red Cross group to assist in the operating room, doing clerical work. We sent Mary, expecting to get her back in a week or so, but she became so valuable to them, she was there until after the end of war!

Needless to say, Sheila, Laura and I carried on, doing the work of four. We had two surgical theatres going day and night. There were three operating tables in one room and four in the other. In those dreadful days during the Schelde struggle, 1,860 surgeries were performed in ten days. Medical staff worked in shifts around the clock, spelling each other off as the casualties continued to pour in.

We helped where we could, with the stretcher cases on the floor, waiting for surgery. Untying soaking boots, giving tea if they were able to have it, doing whatever was necessary and generally trying to cheer them.

This pace kept up through October, and on November 1st, a successful assault landing was made by sea on Walcheren Island. This action finally brought the bloody, muddy struggle for the Schelde Estuary to completion.

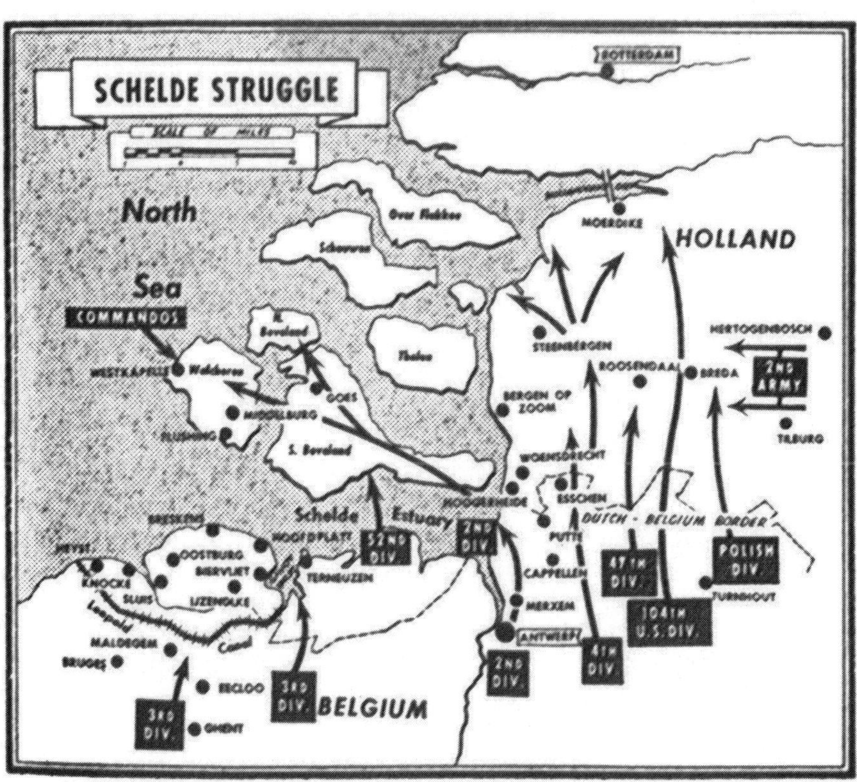

October 15th, 1944
Dearest Family:

This will be a hasty note, but all time permits. Do wish I could sit down and write about all the things as I was able to all summer. So many interesting and amusing incidents. Perhaps I will have a chance some evening this week. Parcel 42 arrived safely and was indeed welcome. All previous ones accounted for, too, and we are eagerly awaiting the others. One thing we can use is candy. The Red Cross does not supply it on the continent and all the boys crave it. We save and scrounge bars here and there for the ones that really beg for it. The four of us are suggesting to our families if you will send candy and nuts this year, instead of personal Christmas gifts—because our Christmas this year will be in the wards, and we want to do as much as possible for the patients. As it is a 1,200-bed hospital, we have to start preparing early. There will be fruit, too, as the civilian population in Bruges have formed a club and bring in grapes and apples daily, and we distribute them.

I suppose you heard Aileen Corkett's devastating news. I did not know about it until yesterday when I had a note from Mrs. Simon. I was absolutely shocked. Poor Aileen must be heartbroken. Mrs. Simon had called the girl Aileen is living with in Liphook, and she and Ruth will go to see Aileen as soon as she feels like seeing them. It is so very hard to believe. It was only a few weeks ago that George returned to his regiment in Italy, and somehow or other, I never thought of him getting it. He was such a great fellow, and was always so good to me.

We are having a full and busy life. Work all day and there are many parties, too. Mostly Canadian, and it's really a treat to be with Canucks again. They are such nice lads—really the finest are over here. Before I left Canada, I thought the English were just about tops, and still have much respect for the ordi-

nary people who have carried on through thick and thin, but have been disillusioned and disappointed by the so called "upper crust". Guess it is a good thing to travel and see people in their own land and atmosphere. Certainly gives you a different slant on things, and again I'll say how glad and proud I am to be Canadian. The Yanks are a pretty nice lot, too, but the British officers—many of them are arrogant and often rude and insulting. It is disappointing.

Just wrote to Joan McCarthy at the Met Red Cross, asking them to send us candy. If anyone wants to know what to send me, or any groups or societies are looking for a new venture, please tell them to ship candy to No. 12. Preferably chocolate bars, hard candies or toffees or caramels. Also gum is very scarce and the men all ask for it. It seems so hard not to be able to give them what they want, when all they ask for—when they come in dirty, tired and wounded—is a stick of gum or a piece of chocolate.

It is so good to be busy again. We are really working hard, on our feet and running for twelve hours a day. We never did get Mary back. They asked for one of us to do clerical work in the operating room, so we sent Mary, expecting to get her back after a few days, but she is still there, and probably will remain there while they are so busy. Consequently, the three of us are doing the work of four, with the hospital running close to capacity—we each have close to 400 patients to visit daily. It is a wonderful job and I would not change places with anyone for the world. The boys are really super, never a word of complaint, and they always have a joke or a smile for us. There is little we can do for them, after the sacrifices they have made, but they are so appreciative and almost embarrass us.

Surely do miss you both.
Much love, Lois

Nursing Sisters' Mess
Memlinc Palace Hotel
Canadian General Hospital
Bruges, Belgium
(now a bank, in the year 2000)

November 10th, 1944
Dearest Family:

We are taking a half-day off a week now, and I had this afternoon, and I had a lovely time, shopping. Came home and put on my high boots, so I could take my shoes to the shoemaker. The heels are badly run down. Finally found him and tried to make him understand what I wanted. You see, these people speak Flemish, with only a vague knowledge of French, and mine is rather vague, too, so you can imagine what kind of a conversation we had.

Then I bumped into one of our medical officers. He was buying a radio and at that point, I was pricing gramophones to see if the Red Cross funds could stand to purchase one. We have only one and it is rather inadequate in a hospital of that size. However, we went to another music shop where our M.O. had already priced the portable gramophones. They were roughly $75.00. I explained that it was for the patients in the hope that we would get a slight cut—so the two shopkeepers went into a huddle and decided to give me the machine—for nothing! I was really floored, but they insisted, so that was that, and it will be enjoyed so much.

It is November 13, and life goes on as usual at the hospital. These first weeks we have been operating as a casualty clearing station, with the battle wounded coming straight to our hospital, caked in mud and blood. Convoys continue to come in with the wounded. "Admitting" keeps us posted as to when a new group is due so we can have one of us there, day or night, to greet them with whatever goodies we can muster. Other groups leave, either headed back to England, to hospitals there, or if recovered, back to join their regiments. Some of the boys are terribly injured, and are in a special ward. So sad to see them, so severely hurt. They are usually sent off to England as soon as they are strong enough to travel. The first weeks we were working, the patients came in so quickly, many needing immediate surgery, so their stretchers were placed on the floor, outside the O.R., and doctors went from one to the other, assessing their wounds and taking the most urgent cases first. We visited them too, doing what we could, trying to cheer them. The medical staff worked long and hard, doing their best for each lad.

Sunday, several Manitoba Dragoons arrived back from Holland. They came in just at noon, looking bedraggled and hungry. It was Laura's afternoon off, so she took them back to our Mess for lunch. Then they went out to their old stomping ground—they arranged with Momma (the pubkeeper's wife) to have a party for us in the evening. They picked us up after work, then we went on to De Haan. When we arrived, Momma had a huge supper all prepared. When the regiment was there, we were there many evenings. Belgian homes have many family pictures displayed, and Momma had hers in full view. In the centre, a large picture of the Dragoons, surrounded by her loved ones, so she considers the regiment part of her family!

Tonight, Laura, Sheila and I went to a civilian home. Extremely nice people and they are so eager to entertain us. We had a beautiful dinner and a very pleasant time. They come to the hospital every week with fruit, have a most attractive place, somewhat similar to a Canadian home, and are most charming. One of the daughters, Yolande, comes to the hospital frequently to visit a patient. The Belgian girls are quite vivacious and beautifully dressed. The family speak French with a very limited knowledge of English, so we all wave our hands, nod and smile, a lot!

Everyone here has been discussing the Ralston resignation over the conscription issue. It's strange—I really had not given it much thought, but like everyone else, felt it was high time the Zombies were shipped over here. Then this morning I spoke with a little Canadian Despatch Rider. The cutest lad, and he had a lot on the ball. He had cracked up on his motor bike no less than 12 times, and broken various bones. Looks like an irresponsible kid, but he had done a lot of serious thinking. He was leaving for England and I went to say goodbye to him. He said that for five years now the Canadian Army has been overseas, all purely voluntary—and we are proud of that record and of the people who have made it possible. We are all here because we believe in the same things and because we have chosen to come. We have much in common and one purpose in mind. To force the Zombies to join us would spoil that record and feeling of pride. Without total conscription of manpower, Canada's war effort is just about the finest in the world. His theory was, conscript the Zombies, if absolutely necessary, but let them serve in the Far East, not bring them over here at this late date to be mixed with our volunteer Army, just when victory is in sight. There is a lot of truth and good sense in what he said. There is a great deal of pride and fellow-feeling in our Army, and much of that would be lost if men were forced to come over, without those ideals and sense of duty and love of country. I have fully appreciated Canada's war effort since I've been away. For the size of our population, we can be justly proud. Perhaps you need to be outside a country to see it in proper perspective.

We meet so many boys—oodles of them—laugh and joke with them, or talk quite seriously. Know them so well, sometimes without even knowing their last name. When they leave, it's like losing a very dear friend. One little lad who was leaving today looked so pathetic and lonely. I asked if there was anything he wanted to take with him. He said, very shyly, "Just a kiss"! So off he went to England, with a smear of lipstick on his cheek.

Many patients I met in Basingstoke have come in here, too. It's a thrill to see them again. Just before I left Hackwood, there was a little curly-

headed blond—we called him "Junior" and he called me "Grandma". Today, the door opened and a mischievous baby face looked in and said "Hi, Grandma!" There was Junior, a veteran of Italy and now, Holland.

It's suddenly very late and we do have to get up so early to catch that 7.00 am truck every day, so must hop into bed.

Heaps of love, Lois

NO. 12
CANADIAN GENERAL HOSPITAL

Nov. 15th, 1944
Dearest Mother and Dad:

Laura and I spent a quiet evening at home, and a Saturday night, too. Sister Shea came bouncing up to say that my cousin was downstairs looking for me. After much persuasion, went down and there was Hans Geggie. A cousin of a cousin! Was delighted to see him; he looks extremely well, tanned and healthy. He is with a field dressing station not far away, had no idea I was here until tonight, when he went into a bar and was speaking with a little Belgian girl I know. In the conversation, she said she knew one of the Canadian Sisters and mentioned me. That is the third time we have seen each other over here. First day in London, bumped into him in the Park Lane Hotel, then another time, he was driving a Jeep into Hackwood and almost ran over me on my bike. Each time we have had a great chat and catch up on family news. He must have had a few exciting days when he joined British Commandos for a Holland landing. It sounded pretty scary.

Gerry is back in action again—up front with General Patton. Have not seen him, as the Americans are in their own sector. Hear from him often. He did stay with Mrs. Simon for a few days and enjoyed being there. It's a thrill to see the planes in the sky now. We were so used to them in England, and in France, but rather forgot about them here in Belgium. However, now it is rather special when we stand in the Main Town Square, with many civilians all gazing skyward.

Boxes continue to roll in. Box 68 came in 9 days! Must have taken wings. The candy will be simply wonderful. Think we will really be able to make it a good

Canadian General Hospital
Saint-Andres, Bruges, Belgium
1944-1945

Christmas, thanks to your efforts. Had a note from Joan McCarthy of the Met, saying they had shipped us 35 lbs. of candy, too, so that is marvellous. It was exciting to receive the boxes last year in Basingstoke, but there, it didn't mean nearly as much as now. I am afraid my letters have been few and far between, but will do better from now on. The first few weeks here were absolutely hectic. We worked long hours and had a gay social life, too. It has eased up a bit now. Although there are still several dates a week

Our Dragoon friends arrived back yesterday for a three-day visit. Three of them came, so Pearl, Ruth and I will have a busy few days. We are all having our day off tomorrow so will go away somewhere for the day. This was Laura's day off and how I hated to crawl out of bed in the chill, dark dawn while she snoozed on peacefully.

Today was one for the books—with the Dragoon friends still here, suddenly, my friend from the other armoured regiment appeared. He is in a different part of Holland, but had a couple of days off and had driven for hours in an open Jeep. Had not seen either of them for a month, then they both arrived on the same day. There isn't any justice! We went back to the Mess and got Laura and she entertained Blake. We all went off to the Cosy Corner for the evening. Had a very pleasant time and the absolute highlight—we each had two fried eggs! Am sure I'll dream of them all night, and for many months to come. Blake had to leave this morning. It was a shame it happened that way; however, he may have an opportunity to come back again.

Had a lovely letter from Aileen Corkett today. She is surely a brick and certainly has what it takes. She has applied for passage home, and in the meantime, will divide her time between Devon and Basingstoke. No, George's people are Canadian and live in Brampton, Ontario. She said that George was killed instantly—had only been in action again for two days and was in the thick of hot and heavy bat-

tle. He had led his company in two successful attacks and then they were to cross the river north of Ricini. His Company was the 2nd to cross and he gained his objective. He was the only officer left in his Company, and then he got it. I will send Aileen's letter to you. In the midst of all the strife and turmoil at home over the Zombie question—her letter stands alone, and makes all the bickering seem small and petty. To us, the Zombie issue is not very important. If they don't want to come—we certainly don't want them. They would not be good soldiers and don't deserve to be part of our Canadian Army. I feel so badly about all the fine young men who have been lost and just had to get this off my chest.

The Dragoons stayed until Friday, and we all had a great few days. Had dinner in their hotel several times and they came to our Mess various times. We danced at the Cosy Corner and also in the Mess. Thursday, we went out to the coastal towns for the day. We have had very little opportunity to explore our own town. Thursday was our first day off in two months.

Laura and I and two of the medical officers went to a Belgian home last night for dinner. They are charming people and have a beautiful home, tastefully furnished. There were the parents, two daughters, one about 20 and the other 13, also a son about 19 and the granny. The so-called "society" of the town all speak French while the working class use Flemish. We can understand each other quite well and they do have the good grace not to laugh at our French.

We had a delicious dinner and it is different, you must have at least 3 servings of everything. The maid came around with the soup tureen—gorgeous cream soup, with parsley. We ladled it into our soup plates, and enjoyed it. Then back she came with a fresh tureen of steaming soup. I said, "No, thank you", but they all looked quite hurt and said, "But you must". So nothing to do but fill up the dish again. When she appeared the third time, I began to think that soup was all we were going to have. However, it was very good, so we all ladled it out again. Then she appeared with a great platter of sliced cold rare roast beef and watercress, French-fried potatoes and a creamed vegetable that looked like leeks but tasted like asparagus.

Laura and I grinned at each other and started again. Then back she came, with a fresh platter of meat, another heaping bowl of the fries and more of the strange vegetable. Far be it from us to insult them, so filled our plates. Then the maid appeared again, with the third round of meat and vegetables. We drew a deep breath and helped ourselves. By this time, I thought that dinner must only be two courses, but, no, on came dessert. A very good apple pudding with crust on top. Again, there were three rounds—each time, a fresh pudding. By this time, it was 10.00 pm. so we struggled into the living room for coffee. We played card games and they showed us snaps, taken skiing in Switzerland. We were so enthusiastic that Monsieur dashed away and came back lugging a huge pair of skis. Really beautiful, steeled edges and cable harnesses, but covered in dust and cobwebs. It was a most enjoyable evening. Although I could hardly keep my eyes open after all that food.

Enclosed is a little poem that one of the patients wrote and gave me. Thought you might like to see it. They are all so appreciative of every little thing, really embarrass us sometimes. Also, we get such effusive letters from wives and mothers—some that we write to, and others that have had letters from respective husbands and sons.

Much Love, Lois

OUR "SUNSHINE RAY"

Our Daily Ray of Sunshine
Is the "Sister" who comes through
With cigarettes and magazines
And sometimes, gum to chew.

Her cheery words and lovely smile
Are part of her stock in trade,
And many a weary soldier
How happy she has made.

We watch for her eagerly
In the middle of a lonely day
To change our books and magazines
And "dream" of words she'll say.

Her voice is sweet and vibrant
And makes us think of home
Of Sweetheart, Wife or Mother,
While we are so alone.

So now my story's ended
And if you doubt it true
Just take particular notice
The next time she comes through.

November 28th, 1944
Dearest Mother and Dad:

Had a nice letter from the Ottawa Kiwanis Club, saying that they have sent gum and will keep on sending it. You must have really spread the word and it is wonderful. Everyone has responded so wholeheartedly to our appeal and we are thrilled. Did I tell you that the hospital is building us a recreation hut? We are so excited about it, as our present Red Cross Room is pretty small, and only big enough for an office. It's always full of Up patients and they are just jammed in. It is mainly for the

Red Cross, but the padres will use it for devotional services and the K. of C. for some of their activities. The hut will be marvellous and should be finished in plenty of time for Xmas. The local people have been very kind, Mrs.Vander Hostadt, in particular. They are going to provide a tree, complete with decorations, for every ward, and a big tree for our hut. We will use our decorations for a tree in our office and the rest for the hut.

We are planning to have a party for the boys on Christmas Eve afternoon. We will save some of our fruit cake, candy and anything special we can find. Will ask a few Belgian girls in to help us and to entertain the lads. Then in the evening, we will have carol singing for them, and Christmas morning we will deliver their presents. The Red Cross will provide stockings. They are hand-knitted socks, with the second sock rolled up inside and other goodies tucked in. The socks are very nice and always a hit with the patients. Then all the candy, gum and cigarettes we have accumulated. Plus, crates of fruit from the locals, so we should have plenty to hand out.

There will be a dance in our Mess Christmas night, so are looking forward to that. Life is pretty full and fun. Sunday night we all went to the Belgian Ball—to celebrate the liberation. It was strictly Belgian, and quite the funniest social function we have attended. Really a mob scene. They jitterbug in the most amazing manner. Jump up and down, with elbows flying in all directions. We danced everything from the Bumps-a-daisy to the Lambeth Walk, then the Heputchi, which is the local dance rage at present, and were completely exhausted before the evening was half over. We danced with many Belgians and tried to communicate, but Flemish is a little difficult! Thought it was a good opportunity to break in my shoes!

Two of our transport drivers came in today. They had both come over on the boat with us, so it was very good to see them again. They are both driving ambulances for the British Red Cross, and stationed about eight miles from here; they will come back on their day off and perhaps we can spend a little time together. Theirs is a tough assignment—driving in the Blackout on strange roads, sometimes without a map, with four serious stretcher cases on board.

This has been a wonderful day. My day off, and I have had the laziest, most luxurious time. Kennedy, our batman, brought my breakfast in about 9.30. If you have been able to scrounge an egg, you write your name on it and how you wish it cooked and leave it in the kitchen the previous day. We are able to get a few eggs and some other goodies from some of the civilian group working in the hospital. There are several Belgian men, clad in wooden shoes, whose job it is to wash the hall floors. The building is in a triangle, so they just keep going, round and round—never finish.

Had lunch with Matron Paterson, and went shopping with her. There are always many things to get for the patients. They always want fountain pens, Christmas and birthday cards, Brilliantine, etc., and always perfume and lace hankies for their wives and girlfriends. I got a darling little dress for cousin Kay's baby, Janie. Do hope it will fit her. It's quite large, so she can grow into it.

Found a Ping-Pong club, went in, and first thing I knew, they were giving me a table for the hospital. The people are really very kind—you have only to mention something and they will produce it. On to the gramophone store to pick up one of our machines that was being repaired. They play them all day long, so the springs don't last. We always seem to have one in being fixed.

Dick Dymond, from the badminton club, is a patient. Has a wound in one leg, but should be OK soon. He became a Rifleman overnight, with little or no training. I believe he was in Ordnance, then shoved in as a reinforcement. He is very game about it all, and hoping to get back to his regiment soon. He said that when he left, they could see Germany! It's really a shame, putting these chaps in the front line without training, when the Zombies have had so much time, effort and money spent and wasted, training them.

It is now December 6th, and I have been in bed yesterday and today with a cold. It's not serious but I hate to go around the wards, sneezing at everyone. There was not a bed available in the hospital, so am in my own room and it is really much nicer. Poor Laura has been rushed off her feet. Sheila was admitted to the hospital earlier in the week with laryngitis, so Laura has been doing the whole hospital herself. Ruth loaned her two Up patients to replace Sheila and me. They are two husky Sergeants; they each put on a Red Cross armband and rushed around the wards.

To the casual observer, our job looks like a picnic. They only see us in the wards, going bed to bed, chatting with the patients, and may be inclined to think that we have a pretty soft job. Well, the two Sergeants certainly have a different idea after doing our work for two days. Laura said that when they finished up tonight, after going strong from 7.30 am until 7.00 pm, they were a sorry-looking sight. They both had headaches, and circles under their eyes and they staggered back to their wards to collapse on their beds. We are quite used to it and can climb the stairs 20 times a day without noticing it. No matter how many things you take with you, someone is bound to ask for something you haven't got. Laura said they got along fine, although some of the patients took a dim view of it and sent in a requisition for Red Cross girls!

I laughed today. One of the Sisters came dashing up and handed me three letters. There was one for me, one for Laura and one for Ruth. They were from the Dragoons and I could not imagine where they had come from. She said she was walking along the street, and a tank came roaring up, stopped abruptly, a lad climbed out, asked if she was from No. 12, and handed her the letters. Said he would be passing through on the return trip and would stop at the hospital for replies!

Sunday, we were invited to a supper party at a Belgian home with several of our medical officers. We were supposed to be there at 5.30, but by time we all finished our work and got there, it was nearer 7.30. The civilians seem to think we can drop everything and dash out when they entertain. It was all very charming and enjoyable. It's really a scream, they are definitely interested in the M.O.s, with an eye to the future for their daughters. We were no sooner in the door than "Mama" inquired if the officers were married or single. Of course, they all promptly produced snaps of their families at home, so soon settled that, and I think "Mama" was bitterly disappointed.

We have finally discovered why our supplies take so very long to get to us. Unfortunately, everything has to come through the British Red Cross and they are pretty hopeless. Piles of supplies have been in Brussels for over a month and they just have not bothered to unpack them. They say they cannot get anyone to do it! It's perfectly ridiculous—our driver went in there the other day, and the British workers were all sitting around, drawing cartoons for their own amusement! I don't know who they think unpacks our crates—we do it ourselves, with the aid of a few patients. The first few weeks we were here, the three of us waded through crates of stuff, with toothpaste all over everything and half the cigarettes mildewed and mouldy. I just wish some of those snooty Brits could have been in on that episode.

I must sound really browned off, but it is infuriating to think of everyone at home contributing to the Red Cross, in perfectly good faith, and thinking the stuff is going directly to their boys, and there it is, sitting in a warehouse because some of them are too lazy to unpack it. The last crate of cigarettes we received were so dried out that all the tobacco fell out as we were distributing them. I wouldn't mind if it was their own stuff they were hoarding, but it is a pool, made up of British, Canadian and American goods, and unfortunately, it was placed in their hands.

Today, we had no supplies. I had called our HQ in Brussels yesterday and they promised faithfully to send them today. We could not do our rounds until after lunch, so went in to town and bought a lot of coloured paper. Then we had the stuff you sent, also silver paper and cellophane off the cigarettes. Have been saving it for weeks. We took it to various wards and got the boys all started making Xmas decorations. By the afternoon it was really amazing what they were able to do with the little bit of material on hand. Some of them are very artistic and clever. One lad is a commercial artist and he led the way; they turned out some very attractive designs.

Mrs. Simon wrote and Aileen has a baby girl, called Anne. Mrs. Simon and Ruth were going to see her as soon as she is out of hospital. She will go to Canada as soon as Anne is old enough to travel. Most of the single Sisters who used to visit at Coombehurst have left Hackwood. The married Sisters and Red Cross Personnel are not eligible for service on the continent.

Enough for now, Your loving daughter.
Lois

December 10th, 1944
Dearest Mother and Dad:

Here I am, a patient myself. Nothing serious, feel fine, but completely lost my voice. At breakfast, the Matron was at the same table, asked me a question and when I could not utter a reply, she sent me off to the hospital. Just came in this morning, had no intention of doing so, and came quite unprepared. However, Goody, who is in charge of this ward, fitted me out in some hospital pyjamas. Am sure they must be size 44. The sleeves fall right down over my hands, anything but glamorous! Mary went home at noon and got my things, so I'm fully equipped now.

I wish you could see my room. A great high ceiling. Must have been a Nun's cell; however, it is quite bright, with a huge barred window and a great heavy door. The walls are pale green, halfway up, then a bright pink, with swastikas scratched all over. There is a British officer next door and he knocks on the wall frequently. The walls are at least 18 feet thick; his fist must be black and blue.

Still sitting here and being waited on. Expect to go home tomorrow. The orderlies have been wonderful, dashing in with tea, coffee or cocoa and biscuits. Guess what I had today before lunch? One of the Sisters came in and asked if I would like some champagne as an appetizer. Something to pep up my appetite. As if mine needs any encouragement! I though she was kidding, but a few minutes later, she came back with a mugful of the stuff. Liberated goods, but very fine all the same. If they keep that up, they will have everyone swinging lead!

Did I tell you about the Belgian Red Cross and one of their members, Dominique? He is a little fellow, doesn't reach up to my shoulder and has been haunting me. It seems that there are 20 radios that have been liberated and we can have them if Dominique will release them. For some silly reason, it seemed to hinge on me attending a Belgian party with him! In the interest of getting the radios for the wards before Xmas, I agreed to go, and bring a can of salmon! He was calling for me about 7.30 pm, so I got to the front door, and there he stood, in the pitch black, with two bicycles! The party was six or seven miles and there was no way I was going to ride a bike over here, in the dark. It was one thing to go a short distance in England, but this was totally different. Am afraid I lied and told him I couldn't ride. Just then, our transport rolled up with 30 Sisters coming off shift. They climbed out, looked at me and my little friend, and all had a good chuckle. I left him to wheel the two bikes away and even forgot to give him the salmon! Returned to our room and Laura was amazed to see me back so soon, and laughed hysterically when she heard the story. Dominique was very forgiving and did arrive with the 20 radios a few days later. The only fly in the ointment—most of the radios needed some repair and possibly new tubes.

Our electricians worked on them but Friday, about 2.00 pm, our quartermaster decided that a certain number of tubes were required. It was necessary to go to Brussels to obtain them, and I was elected. We wanted the lads to have the radios operating for Christmas, so it was important to leave immediately. It was 5.00 pm when we got there, then to Red Cross HQ to get the money and authority to purchase the tubes. Neither the driver nor I had any idea where to go. I had a list of eight different types of tubes, so we found a radio shop and they sent us to the Mazda factory. We went to U.S. Army HQ and found out how to get there. After much difficulty, struggling around in the Blackout, finally found it. They had two of the tubes we wanted and the manager phoned a retail store up town. They had another two we needed, so they stayed open until we got there. Then back to our Red Cross HQ and gave them the rest of the list and they promised to try to get them the following day and send them to us.

All in all, it was a hectic trip—we could not get anything to eat, and it was dark and cold and close to 10.30 pm when I finally got home. The Battle of the Bulge has been raging and we were stopped by military police who explained that the Germans had broken through and some of them were wearing American uniforms and could be in this area. We had no idea we were so close to the action! Here we were, on a mission to obtain radio tubes! We were not to stop for anyone, but to drive right through to Bruges as quickly as possible. The driver took the advice and we fairly flew to Bruges. He used to be a jockey and had ridden in the Kentucky Derby and the Santa Anita Handicap, so kept me amused with tales of Sea Biscuit and War Admiral.

However, the trip was not in vain, as we got the radios all connected and had one in every ward by Christmas.

I imagine you have snow by now, and how pretty everything must be.

Much love to all, Lois

CHRISTMAS 1944

December 27th, 1944
Dearest Family:

Christmas has come and gone and it was extra special.

Sunday we had a luncheon for some of the Up patients. It was in the new recreation hut and we entertained 70 lads. The church service was in there until 11.30 am and the boys were coming at noon, so you can imagine how we rushed. The Sgt. Major had found tables for us, and we got sheets for table-cloths. We had snowballs for centrepieces. They had big red bows on top and sprigs of holly. They were hollow and we filled them with packs of cigarettes, with long red streamers on them running to each place. We used those Xmas serviettes you sent and had little coloured boxes of candy at each place.

We started with tomato juice and Ritz biscuits, then a steak dinner, and later, pie for dessert. Then chocolates, fudge, etc. from our boxes. We asked eight of the prettiest Belgian girls we know to wait on tables. Also, the Colonel gave us enough champagne for everyone, so I think they enjoyed it, and got such a kick out of popping the corks! We also had a little boy playing the accordion. One of the lads got up and made the nicest speech to thank the Red Cross girls, and I said a very few words, too.

Just in the middle of it, our Auxiliary Officer appeared and said that he was holding a concert and needed to have the place by 2.00 pm. He had it planned two weeks before, but didn't have the brains to mention it or move it up an hour. We told the boys what had happened—we were finished—so they pitched in and helped. The dishes fairly flew off the tables, cloths disappeared. They folded the tables, swept out the hut and set up the benches, all in the flash of an eye. Then brought in the dishwater and three husky Sgts. rolled up their sleeves and started washing the crockery. It was funny because we were doing the dishes on the stage, and the boys began to file in to see the concert. I turned around and we had an audience of at least 300, watching us clean up. The lads got a big kick out of seeing the Sgts. working so hard.

We still had our ward work to do, so we rushed around and finished that, then home to get ready for our Mess dinner at 5.30. It was delightful. Turkey with all the trimmings. The usual toasts, then we all proceeded to the lounge for a singsong. We really enjoyed it. It was the first official Mess dinner since we joined the unit. The first time the Sisters wore their blue uniforms with veils, and they looked so nice.

Then Jack (Belgian friend) had invited me to his home for Christmas dinner. I could not go because of the Mess dinner, but they insisted that I must come for dessert. It was a lovely dinner party. They turned out the lights and brought in the plum pudding in flames. It was quite an evening, with much wine and dancing. Then, at midnight, champagne was served and we all wished everyone a Merry Christmas.

Christmas morning came very early. Laura and I struggled out of bed and growled Merry Christmas at each other, then off to the hospital to get things started for the day. Then got into our blue smocks. First time we have worn them since we left England. At 9.30 am, about 30 Sisters and the four of us went on a tour of all the wards, singing carols. It was really quite moving to go into the wards; each of us went and sat by a different lad and we sang a couple of well-known carols (I have such a lovely voice!).

All the girls looked so nice in blue and the wards are just a picture. Also, the radios going certainly pepped things up

When we finished, we rushed back to the Red Cross Room, hoping against hope that the Santa Claus costume had arrived. I must go back a few days to explain this. About two weeks ago, I went into one of the department stores to see if they would lend us a Santa suit. They said "yes", and asked me to call for it the Saturday before Christmas. I did so, and it was all wrapped up in a huge box, so lugged it home and opened it. You can imagine how I felt when it turned out to be a St. Nicholas suit. In this country, this is a long red velvet cape, trimmed with ermine, a high red hat and a huge staff. More like a priest than Santa. We needed to see it modelled, asked Kennedy to put it on. Also had a great white beard, and wig. He looked pretty funny. We had a good laugh, but realized that we needed a real Santa suit.

One of the Sisters had made a Santa Suit for the children's party, so we contacted her quickly to see if we could borrow it. She had loaned it to a nearby British Naval Base and they had neglected to return it. After much frantic phoning on Xmas Eve and Xmas morning, they finally brought it back. After the carols, the costume had still not arrived, but Kennedy had it at our Mess. We got it and rushed it to the lad who was to wear it, only to discover that the trousers were missing! The final straw, almost. Santa had to have red pants. After some quick reconnoitering, we discovered that the hospital screens were just about the right shade of red. Needless to say, there is now one less screen, and Santa was properly clad. After quickly stripping the screen, we cut pants and used the sewing machine in the Operating Room to sew them up.

Many of the patients had asked for a blonde for Christmas. We were determined they should have one. There are two Sergeant patients who are very good pals. One was Santa, so we dressed the other one up as a girl. He wore Sheila's plaid skirt and my pale green sweater. It is a real Sloppy Joe that I bought from Laura in England. We had rented a wig. It was just perfect. Parted in the middle, blonde, long and glamorous. We tied a big yellow bow on top and made up his face. He wore a pair of my lisle stockings and his own running shoes. He was a real sweater girl, shape and everything. We had to stop for repairs every little while because Santa's stomach kept slipping (he was well padded with pillows). "Gertrude's" shape slipped, too!

They were a scream. Santa had a great sack over his back, filled with Xmas stockings from the Red Cross. We visited every ward, Santa and Gertrude leaping around, and the boys were just in fits. Laura, Sheila, Mary and I laughed so hard we were bordering on hysteria. We had 1,000 stockings, and it was very close, only a few left. They were very nice and the lads were delighted with them. We distributed all the other goodies, candy, gum, fruit. Everywhere, there was Christmas cheer, champagne flowed freely. After the first few stops, we fairly floated through the wards. Johnny Forsythe, former swimming coach at the Toronto Granite Club, was helping us, and he said he was sure my feet barely touched the ground all afternoon and I wore an ecstatic smile. Johnny and Red loaded reserve stockings on stretchers and wheeled them around for us.

It was a very busy afternoon, as it is a big hospital to cover. Santa and Gertrude were getting awfully warm and tired, but they were such good sports, and kept going. Santa's costume was beginning to disintegrate, but before he entered each ward, he would straighten up, brace himself, rush in with bells clanging and bellow, "Merry Christmas, boys". "Gertrude" used almost a whole tube of Laura's lipstick, as she wished so many people a Merry Christmas!

There was such a gay and festive atmosphere around the hospital. Everyone was smiling, laughing and completely happy. Various wards had parties and almost every lad said it was the very best Christmas since they left home. For many of them, it was their fifth or sixth Christmas away from home! They had their Christmas dinner at noon, and we had another one, too. Also, they all had candy, beer and champagne. There was never a dull moment. When we finished with the Santa routine, we all went back to our own wards to spend a little time in each one. By 6.00 pm we were pretty well exhausted, after being on the go since 6.00 am. One of our Colonels invited us in for a drink.

Then he took us to the service the POWs were having in their ward. That was one of the most amazing and emotional experiences. When we entered, the ward was in darkness, except for candles on the tree and other candles to break the gloom. It is impossible to describe the things you think and feel, sitting there, listening to our carols, also prayers and music, being sung in German. Then one of the prisoners spoke and their own German M.O. translated for us. They paid a great tribute to the Canadians, said they had received the very best medical skill and attention, and that nowhere else, under the circumstances, could they have spent such a happy Christmas, as prisoners of war.

I hate the Germans thoroughly, as a race, even more when I think of the thousands of our own boys who have been killed or badly wounded, but somehow, on Christmas, looking at all those Germans sitting quietly in their beds, singing and thinking of their homes and families, it was impossible to hate anyone! I couldn't help but think that these fellows, the majority, ordinary soldiers, fighting for their country and the things they are taught to believe in, don't like or want this war any more than we do. And you begin to wonder just how and where it all started. A power-mad maniac like Hitler, with a hard-core group around him. Many less than truthful and dangerous politicians in his country and many of the other countries, too. A lot of false prop-

aganda everywhere. Now I realize that some of the stuff we were told and read was probably untrue, too. Being there with the POWs was something I would not have missed, but we certainly came away with mixed feelings.

The Dragoons arrived and we had a wonderful evening. A very good party, just our own unit and friends, so everyone knew everyone. A very Merry Christmas. It was truly the most wonderful Christmas possible; being in that hospital and seeing the boys so happy and full of fun was surely a privilege.

And they really appreciated it all so much. All day today and yesterday they have told us how wonderful it all was. We enjoyed it just as much as they did. Many of the patients left today. Hate to see them go. However, the incoming convoys will start arriving and others will take their place.

There is one young lad, small, with red hair and freckles. We call him Red. He tells the most amazing tales and at first we thought it was just a line, but strangely enough, seems it is all quite true. He is only 17 now, and has been at sea since he was 11. He was in the American Merchant Navy and also in ours. At 16, he held the rank of Chief Petty Officer. He has quite a collection of ribbons and medals. One of the lads found a couple of write-ups about him in an American paper, so he has had rather a spectacular career at a very young age. Now he is headed home because someone checked his birthdate.

Two new Red Cross girls joined us today. Sylvia Smellie and Audrey Calhoun. They were with No. 20 CGH and will be attached to this unit for a while. We will be able to find plenty for them to do. Mary has worked part-time with us lately, but it will be great to have them to help out.

I missed you very much at Christmas, but fortunately, we were just too busy to have time to be homesick.

Very much love to you both,
Lois

Santa and Gertrude disheveled
after ward visits

Market Square in Bruges
where Mess was located.
This picture was taken in the year 2000.

THE ARDENNES AND BATTLE OF THE BULGE

In mid-September 1944, Adolf Hitler decided to stage an all-out offensive attack through the Ardennes Forest. Three months later on December 16th, this attack was launched with 20 German Divisions, including seven crack Panzer units, against four U.S. Divisions. The U.S. units were sorely outnumbered in an unequal encounter, meeting the German Tiger and Panther tanks without support of their own armoured units. The U.S. troops stood their ground as best they could but suffered very heavy losses.

It had been a complete surprise and shock to the Allies, with their superior intelligence and air reconnaissance resources. They had completely missed the huge buildup of men and armour poised against them. It defied all military reasoning—for Germany to launch this huge operation through the thick forest in mid-winter. The Allies did not realize that Hitler had forced his ill-conceived plan on his generals, much against their experienced judgement.

The U.S. was slow to respond, not grasping the full significance of the situation. U.S. generals were hesitant to change their plans in their push towards Germany, but Eisenhower prevailed, and great numbers of reinforcements were re-routed to the Ardennes area. In the winter weather it took a while to get there. Germans had broken through U.S. defence, hence, the Battle of the Bulge.

Two German armies were advancing, one to the north and the other in the south, heading for Antwerp and Brussels. It was some of the bitterest fighting of the war.

The Battle for Bastogne was savage. Two of General Patton's corps from Third Army arrived and bolstered the beleaguered U.S. troops.

By December 23rd, the fog and cloud cleared and the Allied air power came on in great strength.

Battles raged all through Christmas week. General Patton was in charge against the south part of the German thrust and Montgomery in command in the north, directing U.S. troops, with U.S. General Collins directing battlefield tactics. By December 26th, German units began to flag. Tanks ran dry of fuel and ammunition was in short supply. It was the turning point in the Battle of the Bulge and the end of Germany's last major offensive.

The Allies had received a huge shock, thinking that Germany was not capable of delivering this last desperate blow. In this battle 600,000 Americans fought, with 19,000 killed. The British, who entered in the final days, lost 1,400 men. Germany put forward half a million men, including old men and very young boys, losing approximately 100,000 of them. It was a very costly episode for all, with so many lives lost. It also caused the Allies to lose at least six weeks in their march to Berlin.

Anglo-American relations hit a new low with the arrogance of British General Montgomery, who was insulting and very critical of the U.S. generals. His statement to the world that the British had saved the U.S. Army caused deep resentment and was surely untrue and uncalled for.

In the Battle for the Ardennes against the top Panzer Divisions of Germany, the U.S. certainly proved that they were a true fighting force and worthy opponents against heavy odds.

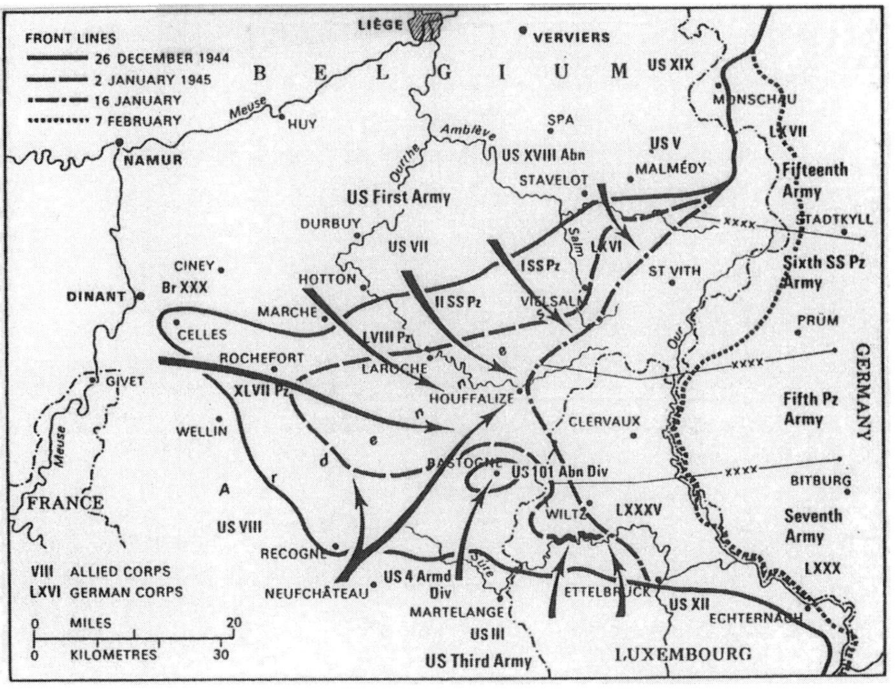

The Allies now proceeded to crush the German "bulge." The battle for Bastogne was the scene of some of the bitterest fighting of the war.

NEW YEAR'S EVE

January 2nd, 1945
Dearest Family:

Laura and I were hoping to go away for New Year's to spend it with the regiment, but couldn't go together and leave Sheila alone to do all the work. However, when the two extra gals arrived, it removed that obstacle. Permission was refused at first, then, just when we gave up hope, 48's were granted over New Year's weekend for six Sisters. We were among the lucky ones.

It was a fabulous weekend. We left Sunday morning and went to Brussels. Transport had not been granted so we went to Ghent in the mail vehicle, then to the Canadian Leave Centre. There was a staff car just leaving for Brussels, so they took us right to the hotel. Ian and Jack were waiting and we headed to Holland. Bright and sunny but very cold.

As we rolled along in the car, we gazed at the countryside. A little bleak at this time of year. Very flat, and covered with a thin layer of snow. Every pond and flooded field was well frozen over and just black with skaters. They wear strange wooden skates, clamped unto their wooden shoes.

Holland looks much like Belgium. Little by little, I'm beginning to realize that people and places are pretty much the same the world over. I always imagined Holland as a quaint romantic land, where everything was painted blue and white—masses of windmills, tulips and daffodils. All in national garb, orange skirts, snowy white blouses and aprons and caps. Definitely not so!

There was not much destruction where we were. A flat, dreary land. Modern architecture. Straight smooth highways, and everywhere, the inevitable canals and dikes. The highways are filled with military traffic. Instead of the familiar red, yellow and black of Belgium, everywhere there were great orange banners and pictures of Queen Wilhelmina and the rest of the Dutch Royal Family.

Store windows rather bare, in comparison to the other lands. Nowhere did we see the great quantities of lace, perfume, souvenirs and trinkets so familiar and common in France and especially in Belgium. The Dutch are a more stolid race and don't seem to manufacture the bright flashy junk jewellery, exquisite lace and lovely crystal found in Belgium. The people looked shabby, cold, thin and undernourished. Not the round jolly people one would expect to find in the Nederland. Of course, we were in a poor section of the country and at the very worst time of year. Many poor souls had been near starvation during the occupation.

It was a long drive and we finally arrived. They have a perfectly beautiful Mess. It, too, is a commandeered hotel—quite luxurious and comfortable. That is their HQ, so very lavish. Laura and I were certainly the honoured guests. The only English-speaking gals there—so you can imagine what kind of a reception we received.

It was such a thrill seeing all the lads. We know most of their friends and they all made such a fuss over us. The other girls at the party were all civilians that they had invited. Only a few spoke English, and they were all in long flowing evening dresses. War-torn Holland on New Year's Eve!

It was a wonderful party. The Mess was beautifully decorated, The music was great. There was plenty of good food and champagne. We welcomed the New Year in the time-honoured fashion, singing "Auld Lang Syne" and throwing coloured streamers. It was quite a concession for us to be guests of the Mess. And everyone from the Colonel to the batmen showered attention on us.

New Year's Day was bright, clear and cold. We struggled to our feet at noon. It was Open House in the Mess; many of the officers from the various squadrons dropped in to pay their respects. It was a very merry place. All the others arrived, and it was much like the days in De Haan. Quite an experience, and certainly a wonderful 48, spending it with the Dragoons. It was almost too good to be true. We intended to leave on New Year's Day but we had permission to be away until Tuesday noon—so Colonel Black insisted we stay until Tuesday morning.

It's now Tuesday afternoon and we are safely back in our hotel. They brought us home this morning. It was truly a wonderful New Year's. Never expected to spend it in Holland, practically at the front, but it was very special. Some of them had come in right from patrols and most hadn't seen Canadian girls for quite a while. One rather quiet chap just sat in a corner and looked at us for ages. Then he asked shyly where I got my silk stockings. I said that my parents sent them from home. He said so seriously, "Well, thank your Mother and Dad for me, my morale has gone up one hundred percent!"

The Huns celebrated the New Year in great style. All along their side of the front, they fired all sorts of stuff into the air—just like the 4th of July. The Huns, too, had dropped propaganda leaflets, wishing us all a Happy Christmas. I don't think I will ever understand it. Then I remember we are fighting for the freedom of the Western World, and it is very precious!

All my Christmas gifts are just what I need, and the stockings are really beautiful. I certainly appreciate them. Nice stockings and perfume are the only way we can dress up at all. We all stick to one perfume and it seems to become part of your personality. Mine is Tabu and if I forget to put it on, the patients are sure to notice. I have such an urge lately to wear civvies. We have worn nothing but khaki since last June, and get very tired of it.

Did I mention that we are to have leave in England? In the spring. We are so excited about it and can hardly wait to get going. We didn't realize how much we missed things, like the London shows, etc. I am anxious to return to Coombehurst for a few days. The months we lived there seem just like a dream. After we left England and came over here, Coombehurst, Corps House and The Warren, in Kent, all seemed so far away and unreal. While in England, Basingstoke was home, but since we left, we think of home as Canada, and England is part of a dream world.

This 48 has been wonderful. Laura and I were both pretty tired as we have worked long hours, day after day, without much time off, so this was a very welcome break and now we are ready to start again tomorrow, with renewed vim and vigour.

Thursday, we had a tea and reception in our Mess for the local civilians. It was from 4.00 until 6.00 pm. They were expected to drop in, say, "How do you do", have tea and cakes, and depart. However, no such luck. Great mobs practically stormed the place. By ten minutes past four, you could hardly squeeze in the front door, and everyone stayed until well after 6.00 pm. An exhausting episode, but we have done our duty by the local civilians, so now can relax for the rest of our stay.

We have received some beautiful boxes. Everything has been wonderful and all have been so good to us. Had a great box from the Met today. Quite a variety and two cartons of clover honey.

We had a delectable New Year's dinner with the Dragoons. Turkey, even cranberry sauce. It's a strange life over here. You really have to be here to appreciate it fully. To see the humour in various situations and the very different set of values.

You just cannot imagine how casual and nonchalant everyone is. With the regiment, life is gay and happy. The lads think the world of each other and are quite sure that their outfit is the finest in the whole Army. A Buzz Bomb flits overhead and someone will say, "There goes the 5.00 pm Special! Have another boiled sweet!" Someone called in from an outlying post and said casually, "Seventy Jerry aircraft just went over—heading in your direction—Happy New Year!"

Much love to you both and the very happiest New Year. I am sure we will be home in '45. We were planning it today. Hope we can go in the summer, perhaps August, so we can lie on the deck in the sun! Fun to think about it.

Hugs and kisses. Lois

(All these years later, I am amused by that wish to lie on the deck! With 7,000 troops crammed onto that ship, on deck we walked in a solid mass. No room to stretch out!)

January 6th, 1945
Dearest Mother and Dad:

So sorry you were so worried at Christmas. The news must have sounded pretty grim at home. It was the Battle of the Bulge and we really hear very little war news. Not much news of any kind. Not the way we listened to the BBC when at Coombehurst—especially when we were waiting to hear of the invasion! I sent a cable home as soon as your letters came and I realized how concerned you were. When we came to Bruges we were pretty close to the front, but now, it's more back-line, so absolutely no need to worry.

(It was a pretty tense period leading up to Christmas as we were on an alert to pack and move on very short notice while we were busy trying to make it festive for the 1,200 patients. Of course, we did not mention it in letters home! Fortunately, it never came to that.)

We had such a perfect Christmas—so gay and happy. We felt that it was a satisfactory and successful day at the hospital. We were so tired and the only time we felt the least bit blue and lonesome was when we got up to our room after such a long hectic day, after supper Christmas night, and thought the fellows were not going to make it for our Christmas dance. However, that thought was soon dispelled when they rolled in about 9.00 pm. So it was a completely happy Christmas. Have already told you about New Year's. Spending it with the regiment was simply marvellous. We were the special guests of their Colonel, so were the spoiled and pampered pair.

Laura has been in the hospital with an infected foot. I surely do miss her, both on the job and as a roommate. Our neighbours, Betty, Ruth and Pearl, are all on night duty, so hardly see them, either. Have been in for six nights in a row. First time that has happened since landing in France!

Laura is home and Ruth just came in for a chat. We laughed so hard about the Bayeux days when we were wallowing in the mud and dust, scrounging American rations and sightseeing. We certainly have many amusing memories. And sad ones. We just heard that Johnny, the young U.S. pilot who took us flying, has been killed. He was the nicest lad and very young. Every time we hear of another friend lost, it is a sad blow.

Remind me to tell you in detail about the days in Bayeux, our trip to Paris, also Omaha Beach and all the other places we visited. The Americans surely were good to us. Whenever we wanted anything, we never hesitated to go to their Information Officer or military HQ. They were always so obliging and nothing was too much trouble. Besides that, they practically fed us for six weeks.

It's a long day. We are up shortly after six to get dressed, go down to breakfast— being on the 4th floor, with no elevator, we try to take everything we need for the day with us down the stairs. We catch the truck at 7.00 am to the hospital, so are on the job soon after we arrive, then, home about 7.00 pm, with about half an hour for lunch. And yet, the days simply fly by. Never seems to be enough time to do all the things we plan.

Some of the patients left today. I hate to see them go. After they have been here for a few weeks, each one is like a personal friend. One chap, a friend of Phil Hooper, a very nice young fellow, had been married to an American nurse and she was killed in Bataan. He looked so sad, telling me. It's amazing the stories we hear—all so fantastic—but true.

Our supplies came in today. They are coming through a little better. There is a British Red Cross driver who sometimes delivers the stuff. He came last week and again today. So when he arrived today, with our complete order, looking quite pleased with himself, we said we were very glad to get the supplies and hoped he would make a weekly trip and keep us well stocked up, as we had been pretty discouraged before when we kept running out of everything. He looked quite indignant and said, "Well, we've turned over a new leaf—we have done much better in the New Year—why, we haven't missed a week yet!" This being only the 12th of January!

With Audrey and Sylvia, we have more time to do the things we have been planning. It's the kind of job that the more time you have, the more you are able to do.

We have been busy getting the hut organized, and starting handicrafts in the wards, and the usual welfare work. We have very limited handicraft supplies here. In England we had an abundance of leather, twine, felt, embroidery, tapestry, etc. Here it is a case of make do and mend. We had a little stuff from the Red Cross, but it was soon all used, so since, we have been improvising. The boys are so eager to do it and certainly don't need to be coaxed.

We have very nice wool and knitting needles, so have about twenty lads knitting madly. It's pretty funny to go into a ward and see big husky fellows, real tough guys, placidly knitting away. I started one chap on a scarf yesterday, with 60 stitches. Today, he had over 100, and no idea where they came from!

We have no felt for toy animals, so have the most colourful assortment of creatures made from curtain fabric, green flowered stuff that Laura's mother sent. Also blue and white checked ones (covers from Jerry mattresses), and the most startling yellow ducks—made from old Jerry sheets that we dyed yellow. Some of the civilians are collecting scraps of dress fabric and will bring it in tomorrow, while local hat shops are giving us scraps of felt to appliqué little figures on belts made of old Jerry sacking. Also making attractive tablemats out of same Jerry sacking.

Here it is January 17th, and I will continue.

Have had curtains made for the hut out of same blue and white mattress covers, and have them tied back with big red bows. Have the Ping-Pong table set up and dart boards in place, and various other games. We will serve tea every afternoon, and have bingo and other games some afternoons.

I really wish you could see the hospital and meet the boys. They are a great group—really tops. It takes me hours to get through the wards because I get to know them, and have to stop, talk, admire their latest pictures from home, read bits from their letters, watch card tricks, etc. You certainly learn a lot about people, and get to understand different types. There are very few, really none, that are hard to get along with. All are so appreciative and willing to help us.

There is one very cute lad, called Maxie. He is Danish—left Denmark about four years ago—sailed with the Merchant Marine to Canada. It was New Year's Eve, and in the midst of celebrating, he missed his ship and it sailed without him. He joined the Canadian Army, unable to speak much English. He speaks it now like a native, with the most amazing Southern drawl. I thought he was right from the southern States. He is thin, tall and blond, with a young appealing face and bright, intelligent eyes. He calls me "Miss Lois" and sits, by the hour, in the Red Cross Room, sewing a green flowered elephant. Says he would not dare take it back to the ward because the other fellows would laugh.

Another lad is a typical Irish Canadian, "Gunner O'Hara", with flashing black eyes and always in the middle of a good argument. Pretends to be belligerent and tough, and belittles all our efforts, but, in reality, does a thousand odd jobs for us—before we even think to ask. Tomorrow is his birthday, so we are making up a box for him and having him in for tea.

Then there is Peter who, at the age of 19, has lost a leg. He is one of the bravest kids I've ever seen. Is completely and unselfishly interested in everything that goes on around him. He is very thin, with huge dark eyes and a pale eager face. Each thing he accomplishes is sort of a moral victory. The other day he sat up in a chair for the first time, and the whole ward rejoiced.

The lads come and go; every day there are new faces. It's hard to remember names, but somehow, many of them stand out in our memory. Today, one of our unit boys had a birthday, so we had a cake for him. Our own unit boys are a fine bunch, and really look after the Sisters. The drivers, the cooks, the orderlies, the batmen, the boys in the post office, the orderly room, the Q.M. stores, the lab, the dispensary, the dental clinic, etc. are all so very good to us, and really friends to Laura, Sheila and me. They do countless little things for us.

I hope you like to hear about all this—I could write pages about them all. There is one Dutchman who was in a motor accident and unable to notify his wife. We have mailed numerous letters for him but without avail, because he has not had a reply. He seems to expect me to conjure some letters out of thin air, and is quite disappointed when I am unable to produce mail for him. He said to one of the other lads, "The Red Cross Sister—she is goot for the cigarettes, goot for the books, magazines and gum—but letters—no goot!"

We seem to have nicknames for many of them. We have "Curly-Top", "Glamour Boy", "Pic", "Dreamy Eyes", "Baby Snooks", "Dopey", "Terry" (who always says "Stay away closer, Sister, and let me smell your s-cent!"), and so many others. Some of them are quiet and shy—but most, with very little encouragement, will tell us all about themselves, and bring out countless pictures of girlfriends or family. When we finish our own wards, we try to visit as many others as possible, and just chat. We have a little more time, now that we have Sylvia. Audrey does the handicrafts and we help with that when we can.

I think the final Xmas parcel arrived today. Mrs. Clark's, with her wonderful shortbread and other good things. All the others seemed to come safely. Had boxes from you, all the aunts, Kay and Ebbie, McCuaigs in Edmonton, Chalmers Church, Ottawa Red Cross, Met Red Cross, and Met. Div., where I worked, the Daltons and the Gregorys, cigs from the Ottawa Waterworks, and a lovely box from Helen McCrady, my old roommate. All arrived safely and in excellent condition, so I was extremely lucky. I surely do appreciate all the time and effort that went into the packing and mailing of all those boxes. Have been working on my thank-you notes and will try to finish them in the next couple of days.

Time to get to bed. Morning comes so soon! So much love to you both. Lois.

January 22, 1945
Dearest Family:

Here I am again. Your last letter, written on the 11th, came today, Mother, so that was pretty good service. So glad you received my cable quickly and are reassured that we are all fine. So very sorry you worried so much, especially when we had such a wonderful Christmas and New Year's. Do hope that by now you have received letters telling all about it.

Saturday, Jack (Belgian friend) came home from Brussels, where he is at university, and we went to a civilian dance in one of the local hotels. He is a nice lad, and learning English quite rapidly. He must think we Canadians are a little strange. I came down the stairs and he was waiting in the lobby for me. I was all spruced up and thought I looked all right. There were three of our medical officers standing there, too. They took one look at Jack, realized I was going out with a Belgian civilian, so, all three made a flying dive for me. One straightened my tie, another fixed my collar and the third rearranged my hairdo, then turned me around carefully, nodded approval, and walked away. I think we Canadians amaze them, and small wonder. It was a very good party. We know many Belgian families now, also many of our M.O.s and Sisters were there.

Now January 28th.

Parcels continue to roll in. Don't think any have been lost, which is a pretty good record. It's so wonderful to get candy, magazines and books for the hospital. It does your heart good as we welcome incoming convoys—and some of the boys have not had candy for ages—to be able to give them a Neilson Jersey Milk Bar (strictly Canadian) and really a treat. Their faces surely light up. I just wrote to Claire Farley. She had written to ask for the name of a lad who never receives parcels. Good of her to want to do it, and I immediately thought of Maxie, and am sure there is no one who would appreciate it more. Told her about him, his history and sent her his address, so it will be a thrill for him if, suddenly, he receives a parcel.

I do wish you could meet these lads. Our Army is made up of a pretty fine type of man. Every single one a volunteer, here because he wants to be. There are the occasional few who are fed up, the lead-swingers and the ones who have definitely had enough blood and thunder, whose single thought is home and fast. Some have been away for over five years, and that is a long, long time, a large chunk out of your life. On the whole, they are enthusiastic, fearless and tough, but underneath it all, are kind, gentle, lovable and always full of fun. They embarrass us with their gratitude for such small things we do for them, and are always so willing to help us.

So often, there are ex-patients coming back to visit. Even the Limeys come back in droves! Today, being Sunday, at least twenty boys who had been discharged in the last few weeks came miles to visit at the hospital. It's a blessing we now have the hut, so much more room to entertain them as our Red Cross Room is quite small.

You would love "Blackie"—he is very young, has snapping black eyes, jet-black hair and dark skin. Full of vim and vigour. Being flat on his back has really bothered him. Now he is knitting a sweater! Seems like a dead-end kid, but looks almost angelic, propped up on white pillows, knitting so peacefully. I play rummy with him whenever I have a chance. Today he told me about one night when he and his fellow troopers were out on patrol in Holland. There were Jerry planes strafing the place, and suddenly, through the darkness, a Dutchman appeared, quite frantic—his wife was about to have a baby. One of the boys went off with him to try to find a doctor, and the other three went into the house. They managed to bring the baby into the world, long before the doctor arrived. Blackie said it was really something, to see one of his pals, a huge rough figure in his muddy battledress and large clumsy hands, holding the tiny baby girl!

A few words about us. Life is still very busy. Sylvia and Audrey are looking after the handicrafts, so Laura, Sheila and I are still doing the welfare work. We each have about 350 patients to visit every day, see if there is anything they need or want, and if so, try to get it for them, whenever possible, and believe me, they can ask for the darndest things!

Had hoped that Dragoons would get here this past weekend; however, due to circumstances on the war front, all their leaves were cancelled.

An old Ottawa friend called, said he was passing through here on his way home and could I find him a place to stay overnight? Telephone conversations over here are never very satisfactory, so I presumed he was calling from Holland and that home meant Canada or England. When he finally arrived, about 10.00 pm, I discovered that he had called from France, and home meant deep in the heart of Holland! It is funny; over here, if you live in a place for a month or more, you quite naturally refer to it as home. Last winter, Coombehurst was home, but now it is the Memlinc Palace Hotel! Had arranged for a place for him to stay and we sent his driver out to the hospital. The next morning, my day off, we went shopping for lace for his wife Bertie. She is the dietician in our hospital in Basingstoke, and a dear friend. He left for northern Holland in the teeth of a blinding blizzard.

Our leaves in England have all been cancelled; however, it may be lifted before we are eligible for ours. Will be nicer to be there a little later, when the weather is warmer.

One of the patients I like a great deal left today. He is Frankie Hamilton, the one who wrote those pieces of poetry. He had no idea he would be going so soon, then I was walking along the corridor this morning, and he was lying on a stretcher, waiting for air evacuation. We always stand at the door and see them off. Received a large shipment of woollen goods, so now are able to give them mitts, scarves, balaclavas, socks or sweaters, and they are certainly a blessing. It is very cold now, with quite a bit of snow. The most severe winter in Belgium for years. Many of them, going back to the front, have lost everything, are issued new outfits, but never the extra accessories.

Mrs. Simon said that she and Ruth had been to see Aileen Corkett, and that baby Anne is quite adorable. So tragic she has lost George. These fine young men, taken in their prime, when they had so much to live for. Such a shame! Such a waste!

You should see me, all decked out in white gown and mask, to enter the Diphtheria Ward. Must look like a creature from Mars. As I had a negative reaction, am one of the personnel allowed in. I get a truly warm welcome as the fellows in there are so tired of being in isolation.

January is just about over, and with it, my term of office as Mess Secretary/Treasurer and believe me, that was a super headache. Had no idea what was involved when I took it over. We were dealing in English money, then French and on to Belgian, all of which made it more confusing. As we have never operated a bar in the Sisters' Mess, but are each allowed a monthly quota of liquor, I was designated to purchase it. Which meant I was dealing with two hundred bottles of liquor and whatever champagne or wine was available. Had a Corporal assigned to assist, but it was ultimately my responsibility to get to the source and get it before it was all snapped up, or the most popular items taken. One month, I was a little late, and all that was left was Irish whiskey and not a top brand. Coming from a non-drinking family, I was clueless, and returned with the truck well laden with the Irish. I was surely in the doghouse that week. Some of them barely spoke to me for a few days. Along with my Red Cross job, it was certainly an extra load. It is with great relief that I turn it over to the next unsuspecting soul!

This is my night to be Orderly Joe. So here I sit, in the front hall, to answer the phone and door. Then dash to the first, second, etc., or fifth floor to look for the desired gals. No doubt this letter will be full of interruptions. Being on the Executive, we were always exempt from orderly duties, so this is my first attempt.

This was the craziest day at the hospital—all the patients seemed to be completely wacky. Some days are like that—everyone is full of fun. The climax was when I went into one small ward with four "Dip" patients. One young lad is about 19—I call him "Honey Child"—with bright blue eyes and a blond brush cut. Am sure he has never been teased before and the other lads kid him unmercifully. He doesn't realize he should just ignore them, but bites every time. The result is just bedlam. Today, when I went in, they said that "Junior" had learned to hypnotize people, and asked me to sit on a chair. Of course, I had to see the latest gag, so sat down and gazed at "Honey Child" who, for once, looked very serious and intelligent. He muttered strange lingo, and I was intrigued. In the meantime, his chum had crept up behind me and lit a match that was stuck with chewing gum, to the bottom of my chair, directly under the seat, which was made of very thin plywood. Enough said. I flew about a foot off the chair and the "hot seat" was a complete success. Anything for a laugh. They get cabin fever, being quarantined for so long.

Tomorrow is our Mess dance. Ruth and I are hoping that our Dragoon friends will be able to get down here for it. Communications have been poor of late, so we are hoping for the best.

Oh, I must tell you. About six weeks ago, I began to get fed up with this eternal khaki uniform. Now that the Sisters are wearing their blues for dress occasions, thought it would be an excellent idea if we were able to wear the official blue Mess dress, designed by Red Cross for the V.A.D. section. I wrote to Miss Pepall in London and put the suggestion forward, stating the need of a dress-up outfit for welfare officers and the numerous advantages. Imagine our surprise and delight when yesterday, a letter came, saying that Toronto had been consulted and not only approved, but had ordered and already forwarded the said Mess dresses to Mary, Laura, Sheila and me. They were writing to Betty Maw in Brussels, asking her to contact the other welfare girls to see if any of them would like to have the dresses. We are thrilled and just waiting for them to arrive. It will be such a treat to be able to wear another colour once in a while, and to wear a different and clean outfit when we go to a party, rather than the same grubby old khaki that we have been scruffing around in all day.

Another thing, Sylvia left us this morning.

Much love and a hug for Timmie.

LIFE IN BRUGES

February 11th, 1945
Dearest Family:

The end of another glorious weekend. We had no idea if the fellows would make it to our party on Friday, due to the new Canadian drive. Four of them did come, just as we were finishing dinner. They went in to eat, while we rushed upstairs to dress. Just as we got into our room, the lights went off and we were all in total darkness. Days of Bayeux, when we so often struggled around in the dark, trying to apply lipstick etc. We could not remember where our lantern was as it was so long since we had used it. After crawling around on our hands and knees, finally located it. The lights came on again about nine o'clock. It's a scream, living in a residence like this with one hundred girls; the lights never fail to go out when we are all getting ready for a special party. The very worst place to be in the Blackout is in the bathtub—no window in the bathroom and a long, very dark corridor back to our room. When the lights go out you can hear everyone scream at once, then muttered curses. Ruth, Betty and Pearl are right next door. We usually go to the same parties, so chat back and forth through the wall.

We all had a great time in spite of a few negatives. Our floor is full of hills and bumps and the liquor ran out in the middle of the evening. We were all happy to see the Dragoons and the eight of us always have such fun together. They had come 150 miles by Jeep, so it was quite a trip. We had all asked for Saturday off. They came for lunch, then we all crowded into the Jeep, eight of us, and went to De Haan. It is a lovely seaside resort. Really beautiful. It was the first time we had ever seen it in daylight. One by one, we emerged from the jeep—much to the amusement of the local bystanders. "Momma" gave us a very warm wel-

come, at their old hotel. Asked us into her own suite and brought out a very special bottle of wine. Again, we saw the large picture of the Manitoba Dragoons, in the midst of all her family pictures.

The homes and hotels of De Haan are so attractive. Clean and modern-looking. Beautiful architecture. It would be a marvellous place to return for a holiday in peacetime. We went back to the Mess for dinner, then all back into the Jeep, to the Cosy Corner for the evening.

Was so thrilled to hear about Aunty Jean's baby, and dying to hear more about it. Dad just mentioned that it had arrived and might be called after me, so I gather it must be a girl!

Heard from Gerry and he is going home to Oregon for thirty days' furlough. He was quite surprised and excited. A new scheme the U.S. have started and he was called for one of the first groups, so just packed and left. I had a note written from France, about two weeks ago, guess he must be home by now. He seemed really thrilled and well he might. They have surely been through a long, tough siege. Of Gerry's friends, all the ones we knew in England, only Rack and Bill are left. The Yankee casualties will be terrific when this and the Burma campaign are over. I don't think anyone will ever again be able to doubt the power and strength, as well as the will, guts and determination, of America. Americans are frank, warm and friendly, willing to accept an individual for their own worth. These Europeans have charming, polished manners, but are apt to be insincere and keep us on our guard. Perhaps I am quite wrong, and becoming too cynical. I do know that many are happy to have us here, but, you see, as far as these people are concerned, the war is over, and they are back at university, etc., while our boys are still making the sacrifices. One has only to travel through the Cherbourg Peninsula and across Normandy to Paris—see the great U.S. and Canadian cemeteries, to realize that each of our victories was very dearly bought.

We have a new Red Cross Overseas Commissioner in London now, Colonel Frost. His predecessor was a charming man, well liked by all, but didn't have the punch and drive for that job. We really need someone able to stand up and fight for what they need, dealing with the Army, and especially the British Red Cross.

I was in one of the "Dip" wards today, where the boys are all such screwballs. They have been cooped up so long, they are just bouncing around, full of energy and hardly knowing what to do next. One of them had a big net affair over his head, and was pretending it was a catcher's mask. Another lad was the pitcher and was throwing a can of cigarettes across the room. I decided that they needed a batter, so grabbed a great card-board box of "Bingo", the only thing close at hand, and took a mighty swing at the flying missile. The box of Bingo flew out of my hands and sailed across the room. Of course the contents scattered in all directions. There were literally hundreds of little round wooden chips for the Bingo. You should have seen it. The boys all ducked. I think they thought it was mortar or shrapnel again. They nearly died laughing. Guess they think I am just as wacky as they are.

Now Feb. 15th. Your letter came today, Mother, with news of Lois Anne. I was very thrilled and truly flattered, to think that Jean and Ted would call her after me. Also awed and pleased at the prospect of being Godmother. Tomorrow is my day off, so will see if I can find a suitable gift for the new godchild. Sent Jean and Ted a cable.

Letter from Dragoons today and they got back safely and are in action again. The Canadians are doing extremely well, aren't they? There are a few Canadian regiments who will go down in history; as a matter of fact, it is hard to choose. Regina Rifles, Winnipegs, South Albertas, Can. Scots, North Novas and North Shores, Chaudières, Lake Sups, H.L.I. and the Calgarys, Royals, Algonquins, Black Watch and

Camerons, Patricias, and of course the Dragoons and the Hussars, and many others. These names are all so familiar to us and I am sure we will never be able to forget them. It will seem funny to be in civilian life again—away from all this military jargon, pride in regiments and special lingo. Each outfit has their own individual set of slang. It's quite confusing. The North Novas have the strangest expressions. You really have to be trained to it, to understand it at all. Laura and I hadn't the foggiest notion what the Dragoons were talking about, although now we have picked up most of their expressions.

Laura and Sheila are both off on Saturday. I will be alone, as Sylvia and Audrey have both left us now. Have rounded up two patients to help me. Blackie, the belligerent little Yugoslav, is a compulsive worker. Always a big help. He learned to knit beautifully and now is doing an intricate piece of needlepoint, just like a professional. Jerry is also going to help. Tall and dark, only nineteen—was expelled from school for socking the principal, to avenge a wrong done to his beloved twin brother. He was seventeen at the time, so ran away and joined the army. It's a shame—these kids have not had a chance to grow up slowly, but instead have been pushed around and become grown-up and sophisticated overnight. Only now, they begin to realize that they have missed something very special and pretty important. Jerry sits by the hour and tells us about his home, his mother and twin brother, who is running the family farm in Southern Ontario. Just listening to Jerry, you can realize that they must be pretty fine people. Do hope you are not bored, hearing about all these boys, but they are our main interest, so our first topic of conversation.

Then there is Johnny, who draws cartoons. Really a character. An American from sunny California. Married and divorced before he was twenty—lived in many parts of the U.S. and Canada, then joined the Canadian Army before Pearl Harbour, so is really one of us. He thinks Sheila is quite wonderful—sits and watches her, with bright eyes just dancing.

Did I mention that we are to have two weddings in our group? Ruby Barnes, one of the Sisters, is to be married in mid-March to an Auxiliary Services officer. The ceremony will be in a little English church here in town, and the reception in our Mess. Colonel Fraser will give her away. We are all excited about having a bride in our midst.

The other is Tish Simon. She is engaged to one of our own unit boys. He is an orderly, so all is not so easy. It's really a shame—she can't have a unit wedding because he is an Other Rank (OR). That is quite a touchy point with all the Sisters. Here we are, in a foreign country, away from home, and not allowed to go out with our own unit boys, or any OR's, but on the contrary, encouraged to go out with any Belgique or foreigner that no one knows a thing about. Also, our boys, instead of being able to take any of us out once in a while, or ask us to their parties, have no one to associate with but the Belgian lassies. We wonder how many of these same little lassies were going out with Germans not so very many months ago.

Must sound as if I am on my soapbox again, but it does make us wonder just what this democracy is that we hear so much about. Makes it a bit of a farce, when we are not allowed to associate with our own Other Ranks, some back from the front, who have willingly risked their necks for Canada. It all smacks of England and their never forgotten class distinctions—but in a life and death struggle such as this, there is hardly room for such small, petty rules and regulations.

Last evening we went to a party at the Canadian Convalescent Depot. It is not far away and we sometimes see someone we know.

Well, enough for now, Time for bed.
Heaps of love,
Lois

February 18th, 1945
Dear Ones:

Here it is Sunday afternoon, and I am off for half a day. Laura and Sheila returned from Brussels this morning. I was alone Saturday, as I mentioned, but Blackie and Gerry both showed up first thing in the morning, as they had promised. They each took a wagon, completely equipped with all the things we distribute, and rushed off to the wards. They worked all day, except for a short break at noon. They were a great help and both looked a little weary by 5 pm. Then Chuck, the Sgt. who had been Santa at Christmas, dropped in. He is no longer a patient, but came in for a visit as he was in the vicinity. We walked into town together, and I got to the Mess in time for dinner.

Jack, a Belgian friend, was home for the week-end; he came over, and we went to a movie. Saw Pygmalion. *It must be five or six years since I saw it before, and I really appreciated it much more this time. Perhaps living in England helped, because the characters were absolutely typical. We visited several of the local cafés in true Saturday night style, then went back to Jack's home. His family are very nice and have been extremely kind to me.*

Sunday, we just give out cigarettes, candy and gum. It saves a lot of time and enables us to get off for half the day. Makes it a little special for them, because it is the only time we are able to give them candy and gum. Supplies are coming through quite well—since the New Year—and that is quite a relief.

Laura and Sheila had a lovely time in Brussels, and I was glad they were able to go. They brought me a beautiful bottle of Tabu, my favourite perfume, and a new charm for my bracelet. It's a tiny silver figure of the "Little boy of Brussels", a replica of the age-old statue in the Main Square there. They were working the afternoon shift, so about 2.30 pm, I was finished and getting ready to leave. Frankie

Gallow, the little lad that does the cartoons, came in with his hat on, so I asked him to wait until I got my coat on, and I would walk into town with him. He said that would be great and waited patiently until I was ready. He failed to tell me that he had fourteen friends—in fact, most of the Up patients in the Dip ward, who are allowed out for two hours every day. It was quite a spectacle—I sailed out the front gate, just like the commodore ship in a convoy, or a Mother Duck with a huge flock, surrounded by fifteen lads, loping along, in those dreadful blue hospital suits that they have to wear. Just then, a transport of Sisters came up the drive and they all leaned out of the truck and had a good laugh. I won't live that down in a hurry.

Now February 25th. Betty Maw had come from our Brussels HQ, and stayed overnight with us. She had my bed and I went in next door with Betty and Ruth, as Pearl was sick in hospital. Saturday was my day off and I was going to Ostende for the day, so Betty drove me, as she was going to another Canadian hospital and had to pass that way. I was meeting an English engineer, John. Got there in time for coffee at their Officers' Club. Then we went to the officers' shop, as I needed a new tie. It's the British officers' shop, and me being Canadian and Red Cross, they would not let me in. I was quite provoked and felt like some sort of a foreigner, standing on the outside, looking in. John, who is a decent sort, was furious and quite ashamed of his fellow countrymen, so waltzed in to get me the tie. Finally had to get a British Nursing Sister to buy it for him. Such a lot of confusion and red tape to purchase a 4-franc tie. Roughly ten cents.

To get back to today, we met two of his friends for lunch, then went to see Snow White. *The fun began when he went to get the car to drive me home. Someone had snagged the battery, so he had to trail around and find another one. He arrived back at the club, well covered in grease and grime.*

I went out to get in the car, so no one would steal it while he went in to wash. There were great plate glass windows in the Club Lounge, looking out to the street, with quite a rapt audience. I tried to get into the passenger side of the vehicle—it was a gin-buggy—but the door handle had disappeared, so clambered in over the driver's seat, and got tangled up in the gearshift. Then John came out but by that time the engine had stalled, so he got out the crank, without success. Then we collared some hefty Canadians passing by. They helped John push while I put it in gear and we soon got rolling. He jumped in and took over and we headed for home. Then, I remembered my parcels, still back in the Club! Back we went again—much to the amusement of our audience in the window. By the time I retrieved the parcels, the car had stalled again, and John had broken his braces trying to crank it. We finally got home at 7.30. The British and the Belgians can be nice and fun to go out with, but it would be such a thrill to move to a Canadian sector. We have heard that this town may become a Yankee Leave Centre. Just a rumour, but we are all hoping it is true.

We drew for our leave in England. Sheila is second and I am third of about 35 that want to go. I may change with someone else who is anxious to go soon, as I would prefer to go a little later, when the weather will be warmer.

Also received boxes 84 and 85 and the 5 lb. box of Lowney chocolates. Absolutely wonderful. Took it to the hospital and passed it around among the boys who had just come in from the new push. They were all delighted.

Much love,
Lois

March 1st, 1945
Dearest Mother and Dad:

One of the Sisters was anxious to go on leave to England as soon as possible, so switched with her, and now I won't be going until late in April. Am really just as glad, because England will be lovely then, warm enough for suits and dresses. Also, it will give me time to think about it and plan to see a few friends. I'm hoping cousin Bill will be able to get down from Scotland. We fly from Brussels, so it will be quite exciting.

So many of the patients have left. They come and go so quickly. It's funny—some I remember quite clearly, and will always remember, but others, their faces and personalities are just a jumble in my memory. Often they drop in, if they are nearby, and it is difficult trying to remember which is which. Blackie and Jerry have both left. Also Smitty and Frankie, but they are all at the Convalescent Depot, so come back on Sundays to visit.

Now Sunday evening and I am in bed at 7.30 pm. Just came home from the hospital and climbed into bed. It's just like our first days here, running to capacity again. Patience with our English cousins is wearing pretty thin. When our boys are not in fierce and active battle, you can stand being pushed around and insulted at every turn by the Limeys, who sit safely and comfortably in the towns that our troops have liberated, but when our troops are taking the brunt of the offensive, and we see just what is happening to our courageous Canadians, it's pretty difficult to understand the English attitude. I have met a few charming British officers, but they are definitely in the minority. It's hard to understand what their problem is. Whether it is jealousy or that they just dislike us as a nation, but it is always the same, in business or socially—they are either condescending, arrogant or downright insulting. If there is a Canadian present, they toss uncalled-for insult after insult, about our backward primitive land, lack of culture and background, and always the term "Colonials".

Even the more intelligent and supposedly educated class behave in the same rude manner. I was at dinner at Jack's (Belgian) home recently, where there was an English Major present. As soon as he spotted my Canada badges, I was in for it. To my mind, much as I have come to dislike his kind, I believe that while we are in a foreign country, we should at least try to preserve the appearance of a united front. The insults and slurs flew thick and fast, and each time I tried unsuccessfully to change the subject—but no, he just kept it up, until I reminded him that we were both dinner guests and it was hardly the time or place to stage a civil war. Fortunately, our hosts, with their limited knowledge of English, missed most of his nasty remarks. It's rather sad, because we all went to England with the highest regard for the English people, and the ordinary people we met were very kind. It seems to be this group of officers, who probably attended Eton or similar schools and universities, who seem to feel quite superior. When an invitation comes for a group of Sisters to go to a function at an English Mess, no one will sign up any more. The Belgians are quite aware of the English arrogance, and no longer refer to the "Liberation" as they did when the Canadian regiments were in their towns, but now call it the "British Occupation". It is unfortunate that a certain class can create this ill feeling.

Perhaps it is jealousy, stemming from the fact that young British women are so intent on snaring a Canadian or American husband and a whole new life in America that they simply throw themselves at our North American troops. With the seemingly lower moral standard over here, there seems much promiscuity. Also, the English officers seem to have the feeling that we "Colonial" ladies in uniform are easy prey. Hence the nasty attitude when they are rebuffed.

A letter came from the Dragoons today. They are in Germany now, and I guess the going is pretty tough. Some of the fellows who come in, that we write letters for, say, "I haven't had a chance to write to my wife for the last three weeks—will you please explain to her". This is Sunday, so many of the boys will return, to visit, and also for the chicken dinner! It's always a thrill to see them—only heartbreaking to know what they are going into as they return to their regiments. The time simply flies and it is really a privilege to be here and work amongst our Canadian lads. We get such a big kick out of them all. There is certainly never a dull moment.

Tuesday night I went to the Unit Men's Dance and it was certainly fun. One of the Medical Officers took me. Our unit boys are all tops and have been especially good to Laura, Sheila and me. They had even issued a special invitation to the "3 Red Cross girls" for their party, but we were not allowed to accept. I went with Sammy (M.O.). He was a good sport about it and held down a spot at the bar while I tripped the light fantastic with the unit boys.

I felt badly that Laura and Sheila couldn't have gone, also. The committee decided to ask us, so they wrote out a formal invitation and one of the orderlies presented it to the Matron, explaining that they wanted us to come to their party because they appreciated the way we had worked around the hospital, especially at Christmas. It was very thoughtful of them and we were all anxious to go.

Wednesday, Laura and I caught the noon train to Ghent. Bud and Ken met us. Bud was a former patient, and Ken, a friend of his that I had met several times. They took us to the Officers' Club. Marvellous to have Canadians in the area again. The Club is fabulous. Do wish you could see it. Beautiful, luxurious building, tastefully decorated, and has such a quiet dignified atmosphere. This is the first one that we have been in that is actually under Canadian management. We had cocktails in the lounge, then went to the dinner dance. Food was delectable and music great. Later we did a round of the night clubs. It might have been Montreal or New York. Everything bright, gay and gaudy. Not very good floor shows, postage stamp dance floors—all terribly expensive and definitely designed to catch the shekels of the poor unsuspecting Yanks and Canucks. It was really fun, and the kind of evening that you couldn't stand very often, but get a kick out of every once in a while.

Must tell you about the hotel where Laura and I stayed. One that had been commandeered by the government—one of the nicest in town. And when you stay in these hotels, you simply get a chit, and stay free of charge. We ordered breakfast in bed, had toast, butter, jam and coffee, and it was 180 francs, about $2.50 each! We nearly died. Rather an expensive breakfast, when all we had was toast and coffee. The lads called for us in time for lunch and then we wandered around Ghent, and back to the Officers' Club for the Tea Dance. Then it was time to go to the station to meet Lyle, one of our unit boys who brought us home.

Will write again soon.
Much love, Lois

March 11, 1945

Another Sunday and time for a short note. Last night we went to the wedding of the Sister who married one of our unit boys. It was a very nice ceremony and quite a few of us attended. Then there was a Regimental Party—Canadian, one of our regiments, just back from the Med. front, so a very gala affair. Went with one of their squadron leaders, a very nice chap from Belleville. It's such a thrill to have the Canadian Army united. They told us that when they were taken out of the line, in Italy, they had no idea what their destination might be—perhaps England, maybe Canada or even Burma! When they were all loaded in the ships and ready to leave, the news broke that they were joining the Canadians in Belgium, Holland or Germany. They said a mighty cheer arose and with one accord, they all sang and danced around the decks. They are thrilled to be here and we are surely happy to have them.

It was my Sunday to sleep in—fortunately, as I was tired after the party. Laura crawled out at 6.30 am, and I rolled over, feeling quite snug and luxurious, thinking I would get up about 9.30. Imagine my surprise, when I woke up and it was 12.30. I certainly had a good sleep and felt quite rested. Got up quickly, had lunch and off to the hospital. We are so busy these days. Even cots in the corridors again. We have had so many lads in lately who were patients not long ago, perhaps only two or three weeks ago. It's so funny—we walk through a ward, and someone screams "Hello Sister", or a pair of familiar-looking eyes peer over the top of a blanket. There are so many boys and they come and go so quickly. There is little Joe, who had his face badly burned but made a miraculous recovery. Then "Mat Head", because of his brush cut, and Curly Top, one a Black Watch boy and the other, Royal Regiment. Both have been with us before, and Curly Top is going back again—after 3 wounds. They are all so young and are bound to get it sooner or later, when they keep returning them to the front.

Now March 13th. Mail was very good today. There were letters from both of you, as well as Margy Byrne, a cable from Grandmother and Grand-daddy and letters from Mrs. Simon and Aunty Olive, all for my birthday. My birthday parcel was there, too, and I opened it. It was so beautifully wrapped, I hated to tear it open. Anyway, am delighted with everything. The shoes are great and will surely be most useful. And the underwear and stockings, films and candy. Everything I needed. Also the lipstick and lotion.

Life is very busy again, with the hospital overflowing, and the social whirl has picked up now that the troops are here from the Med.

Mrs. Simon has had my clothes out and sent some to the cleaners, so all is ready for my arrival. Aileen and the baby had been there for a week and had just left. Aileen was going back to Liphook to pack for Canada. I was hoping to see her before she leaves.

There are such nice boys in the hospital at present. There are three of the cutest lads, sitting up in a row in one ward, and am sure not one is over 19. One reads "Westerns", the second, "Detective Stories", and the third really goes for "Love Stuff". The other fellows call him "Bobby the Kid", and he gets so disgusted and really hurt. He told me that his name is Robert Eugene, and would I please call him "Gene" because it is more impressive.

Then there is another lad, Ralph, who has been helping us lately. He is very tall and quite handsome, but totally unsophisticated—he is a paratrooper, just twenty, and keeps us in hysterics. He was hitchhiking in Holland with two other lads, and a truck flew by. They all screamed and swore at the driver for passing them. There was a screech of brakes and the truck backed up. The driver looked out and it was Ralph's older brother, who he had not seen for five years! It's almost incredible—but it is astounding the way people meet over here.

Sheila left this morning for her leave in England, amid great excitement. Laura and I will be really rushed until she returns. The patients are always willing to help, so we should be able to manage. Another lad gave me a lovely tie today—am not in such desperate need for one now. It's amusing—we are supposed to be giving them things, and yet, as soon as one of them gets a box, they insist on giving us something out of it, and usually after a good mail day we get back to the room with a surprising collection of stuff.

I laughed the other day; there was an evacuation and I was at the door as they were leaving, with cigarettes, etc., when someone called me. There, on a stretcher, was one little lad, and not more than a few weeks ago I had sewed up a rip in his trousers, when he was leaving to rejoin his regiment. This time he was headed for England, and it is really a relief to see the boys going there. When I get back to Basingstoke, will go to Hackwood. I am sure there will be many of them there.

Enough for now.
Love to you both and all the family, Lois

March 15th, 1945
Dearest Family:

Here it is my 25th birthday, and also my day off, so am being very lazy. Just had my breakfast in bed and will go down for lunch and a drink with Helen, our Home Sister. Bob is coming this evening. He is Tank Corps—just back from the Med. Ruth's beau will be with him, so we will have dinner here in the Mess and then go to Ostende to do some of the night spots.

Have been lying here, doing a bit of thinking—and will try to give you an inside glimpse of our work at the hospital.

On the surface, one might get the impression that we are here, working among the patients, giving a lot and getting little in return. Such is definitely not so. Taking a purely selfish point of view—we are gaining infinitely more than they. Only our gains are perhaps more intangible. It's impossible to work among countless young lads—all types—and not learn much of human nature.

To do our job properly and perfectly, one would need to be a Master of Psychology, a glamour girl, a comedian, a Dorothy Dix, a Florence Nightingale, a Santa Claus, a Fount of Wisdom and Information, with the patience of Job, all rolled into one. This must sound like a pretty tall order, and I don't mean that we attain all these standards—on the contrary, I'm afraid Laura, Sheila and I probably fall short on most of the requirements, but we do try, and one certainly learns by experience.

To learn how to handle people, to get the most out of them—to do as much as possible for the boys—without letting them impose. To let them treat you as a sister or girlfriend, and be gay and friendly, but be able to slap them down if they get fresh. To know when and where to offer sympathy—strangely enough, very few really want it. Understanding goes a lot farther. They like to be babied and spoiled and get extra favours—and are very easily pleased. If you remember that they like Winchesters rather than Sweet Caps, or remember their names, or ask about their favourite son or daughter, or even if you only make a special trip back to the ward with a chocolate bar or gum, when they are coming out of an operation.

It's only the ones who haven't completely grown up or accepted a set of values and proper outlook on life who want sympathy. Most of the lads are young and strong, and while it breaks your heart to see them maimed, disfigured or handicapped, it's fatal to let them know—because they accept our reaction to their loss of limb or disfigurement as the reaction of their loved ones when they get home. If we can look at them, straight, and regard their loss as unimportant, and even joke about it—instead of looking at them with eyes averted from an empty sleeve—they lose their self-consciousness and soon laugh about it too. Perhaps it's laughter from a sense of relief—as the thought of going home and being stared at and pitied really scares them.

Being as gay and glamorous as possible helps, too. Then they figure you are human and regard you as a kid sister or the girl next door. We are set apart even from the Sisters—although the boys like and respect them—but we are not part of the actual hospital machinery. I mean we don't have to jab them with needles and such. We try to promote the idea that we visit them as friends—with a personal interest in each man, and really value their confidence, friendship and trust. Being a comedian goes a long way. One surely needs confidence and assurance, and the ability to make them laugh, to forget their homesickness and personal problems. In this, they do a lot for us. They are truly a mixed, critical and attentive audience. Two years ago, if I had walked into a ward with one hundred pairs of eyes giving me the once-over, I would have been self-conscious, to say the least, but you soon become accustomed to it, and when they whistle at you—just tell them you'll have none of that or ask them where they got the long, furry ears?

They tell us the strangest and most hair-raising tales of their lives and loves—some true enough, but very often embellished with extra details. You get a much broader outlook on life, and realize that everyone has troubles and greater ones than any small worries you might have at the time. You develop the ability to laugh at almost anything and acquire a new philosophy on life. As Sheila so aptly puts it, "Why worry? It won't even matter in ten years!" We offer advice to the lovelorn, sympathize and laugh, too, when their gal at home runs off and marries a Zombie. Tell them to keep writing, even if they are not receiving mail, because we are absolutely sure the folks at home are writing faithfully. Sometimes we write them letters ourselves and toss it in the ward mail so that they will at least get something when the mail is being distributed.

So you see, they do a great deal for us—bring out potential qualities that may have been deeply hidden—tenderness, love and understanding, and certainly make you realize that there is great joy in doing for others and that it really is more blessed to give than receive. They boost our morale and ego by respecting our judgement or decisions, and expect us to be able to settle almost any dispute or argument—whether it is scientific or geographical or a question currently in the news. Of course, they try our patience to the utmost, but that is seldom, and seeing them hurt or wounded, with untold courage and patience, teaches us a kind of patience, too.

Just knowing these lads—watching them day by day—seeing how much they think of each other—how kind they are and ready to help—yet also their complete independence, their courage, their pride in their own regiment, their ability to get the very most out of life, and their constant thought and goal being Canada and home—it really restores your faith in human nature. We really do little for them, in return for what they have given us.

This letter is just for you two, as there are so many things I have thought of but very seldom have a chance to say.

Much love, my dears. Lois

March 19th, 1945
Dearest Family:

Hello again! Received your cable on my birthday, so it was very well timed. Loved everything in the box and also the cable message. Laura and I are surely rushing around, without Sheila. You can imagine what a job it is, when we each have over 500 patients to please. The up patients are always a great help. There are usually four or five in the Red Cross Room, unpacking crates, etc.

Remember, I told you about the little lad called Gene. He is very young, with the most appealing face. He has no family—as far as I can find out—is completely alone in the world, so never receives any mail or parcels. It must be a pretty lonely feeling—not to have anyone back home to care about you. Especially when the boys are wounded, and Gene has been hit twice. He is a pretty independent kid; I don't want him to think I feel sorry for him, so have hesitated to ask him too many questions. When I get more details, I'll send his address, and perhaps you could send him candy or a small parcel sometime.

Lois MacDonald Cooper on the wards

Maybe you could cut back on my parcels, because I seem to get so many, and such nice ones. It must be costing you a fortune to pack and mail so many.

Friday was Ruby's wedding. We didn't get to the church, as we were late at the hospital, but made it to the party afterwards. It was a fine reception in our Mess. The cooks had done a great job, and the cake had come from a Belgian pâtisserie, so was quite elegant.

Thursday night Bob was here. He is in the Tank Corps and is such a nice lad. Great to have Canadians around again. We went to several of the local cafés, with some of the Sisters and his fellow officers. One spot is really crazy. The music is wild and fast and you dance around at a mad pace, while everyone steps on your feet and kicks your ankles.

Saturday night we went to a party at Bob's Mess. Had been there the previous Saturday, too, and they are such a decent group. A really Canadian band. A beautiful smooth floor, and the lads are just back from Italy and very happy to entertain Canadian girls. Make you feel like a Queen. They could surely give the Limeys a few lessons in that department!

Sunday morning Gene came in bright and early to see if I would go to church with him. There was another lad with him, a Dragoon, one of Ian's lads. I had taken them to a baseball game the day before, as the guard would not let them out the gate alone. It was a unit game, the Privates playing the Sgts., so it was quite interesting as we knew all the fellows playing.

Now March 22nd. Another day off, and time to relax and continue my note. Life is very full and busy. It will be such a relief to have Sheila back. She should be here Saturday or Sunday. Yesterday was Laura's day off, so I was alone. Got Earl, Ralph, Gene and Buttercup to help me. Had to go to a tea at a nearby Brit. hospital with the Colonel and Matron, at 3.30 pm, so just had to leave the boys to carry on. Returned about 5.30 and they were all still working. Gene and Buttercup are the cutest pair. They are always together. Both were hit in the right shoulder, and have their right arms strapped inside their shirts—so they have two left hands between them. They work together and get along surprisingly well. Earl is a Dragoon and has helped us so much since Sheila has been away that everyone calls him the new Red Cross Sister. Yesterday he did the Officers' Ward and got quite a kick out of doing the part where the sick Sisters are. He asked me if there was more he could do for them, and am sure he was back in to see them at least six times.

I must tell you about "Louie". He's a Negro from the States. He is in a Highland Regiment, so wears a Glengarry cap! (It's a wedge cap decorated with plaid.) You can imagine how peculiar it looks, perched on a mass of black woolly hair, over a coal-black face. He's awfully funny. Gets a big kick out of life and is always laughing. He adores chocolate, and if you give him a candy, he beams for the rest of the day. Yesterday, he went downtown on a pass, and came back drunk as a skunk. He tottered into the Red Cross Room and collapsed quietly into a chair—grinning at everyone. One of his pals asked where he got the money to buy cognac, and Louie slowly opened his coat, with its carefully turned up collar, and said sheepishly, "I sold my shirt!" He had actually sold the shirt off his back for 300 francs! And a hospital shirt, at that!

I was decorated yesterday with the Order of the Fudge Club! One of the fellows said, "Sister, have you got any black jelly beans?" Anything to be crazy. I said I was sorry, but no. So they said, "OK, you can't belong to our club". The next time they said, "Fudge will do". Luckily, I had some at home, so wrapped it up with ribbon and gave it to them the next day. Yesterday, they said they had a very special presentation to make. I was being awarded the first Order of the Fudge Club. They proceeded to pin the medal on my shirt. A 25-centime piece, bound in ribbon, with a bow on top and a pin in the back. With this outfit and another ward that they call Dogpatch, where everyone speaks with a hillbilly dialect—I begin to doubt my own sanity.

Hugs and kisses. Lois

March 26th, 1945
Dearest Family:

Another week beginning and the last one in March. April brings my leave nearer—I expect to be going about the last weekend in the month.

We are still very busy but not going at the breakneck speed of a couple of weeks ago. Sheila is back from Blighty—much to our relief. We have time to enjoy our work again. The lads are just as crazy as ever and keep us laughing all day long.

Have been getting our Red Cross Room spruced up. Had a basin installed, so now have hot and cold running water. Also many new shelves, for our supplies. Have covered the chairs in the blue and white checked fabric from the Jerry mattress covers, and are having curtains made to match. We bought gorgeous rosy azalea plants for the windowsills and it does brighten up the room.

Buttercup had returned to the front. Was with his regiment only one day, when he was hit again, so he came back very quickly. Poor kids, it is a rough life for them. Fortunately, not too badly hurt this time. Have I told you about "Provost"? Another interesting lad, with more than average intelligence. He always draws you into a discussion and before you know it, you have been standing by his bed for half an hour, talking earnestly about any one of a hundred subjects—from world politics to love and marriage! Another interesting pair are "Butch" and "Oswald the Rabbit". Butch is from Cornwall, is French, with the most unusual accent. He always pushes my cart when I am in his ward. Oswald the Rabbit was badly burned when he came in, so was swathed in bandages—one that tied on top of his head, and two ends stood up like large ears. He did resemble a rabbit. Has made an excellent recovery. His name is Joe and he has such an infectious laugh. Then there is George, a stocky little blond who says he is coming back to marry me! He worked so hard, helping us, when Sheila was away. It all started when I met him in the hall one day, and he said he had his ticket back to Canada. I said I wished I could go with him, so he promptly said, "Marry me and come too!" It has been a standing joke ever since.

Sunday, the church service was in the Recreation Hut; as we were all seated, they discovered that the piano was locked and the key was lost. Such consternation! The Padre asked if there was a locksmith or a safecracker in the congregation. Finally, they called out the engineers. There was an RCE type there, so he removed several pieces from the piano and got the keyboard loose.

We have a new dietician—just arrived. I was introduced to her, and knew I had met her before. She said, "I know you, too". I finally discovered that she is Kitty Freeman and had been at "Mac" when I was there. We have had a great time discussing the people we knew there, and catching up on the news and gossip.

Yesterday was a crazy day. It was Good Friday, so the boys began to swarm in from Convalescent Depot. Soon our small Red Cross Room was just a shambles. They were sitting on the windowsills and on the floor. Buttercup was on the top shelf, with his head rubbing the ceiling, and Gene—sitting cross-legged in our oversize waste paper basket!

Into the midst of this came two Red Cross ambulance drivers, and said they were being attached to our hospital—were taking over from the Royal Army Service Corps drivers we had previously. The only difference—they are our Corps girls! Peggy Lee and Patty Spence, both of Toronto. We were quite surprised, and our Colonel and Registrar, really amazed. There was the problem of where to put them. They each have their own ambulance and are more or less mobile, carrying their personal kit with them and living in their ambulance or wherever else they happen to be. It was decided that Patty would be allotted to our Mess, while Peggy would go to a nearby British hospital.

As this was being sorted out, two electricians arrived in the Red Cross Room, to connect the electric plate. They were busy with their noisy drills, and in walked two officials of the Brit. Red Cross, a man and a woman, who are responsible for Patty and Peggy. They battled their way into the room, the woman carrying a sheaf of papers in her hand. That was a sad mistake. In the confusion, she lost her "Petrol Slip", which is very precious. In the meantime, one of our Belgique workers came in to empty the waste basket. He evicted Gene and carted it out of the room. Our British lady caught a glimpse of the huge basket disappearing out the door—was certain her missing "Petrol Slip" must be in it and made a wild lunge for the Belgique and basket. They landed in a tangled heap in the corridor. She was pawing wildly through the rubbish, when one of the boys found the missing paper under a chair.

Then, in bounced a Dragoon DR just down from the Deutchland. He had been in Ostende with a group for the celebration and dedication of "Manitoba Square and Avenue", in honour of the regiment who had liberated Ostende. He was higher than a kite, had letters for several of us, and orders not to return without replies. We still had to complete our work in the wards, and it was 7 pm when we were finished.

Patty had to return to De Haan for their equipment. I went with her and had supper in the hotel with Corps girls who are now living there, where we had so many parties with the Dragoons. We headed back to Bruges, and that is a hectic job, driving one of those lumbering ambulances, in all sorts of weather, night and day. It was dark, and then we had to look for the Brit. Hosp. and then find Peggy. After much difficulty, we finally located said hosp. And then Peggy. Back to our Mess and unloaded Patty's gear; then we had to find a place to park the blooming ambulance. We are right on the main town square—you cannot park a vehicle on the doorstep. The nearest car park was a mile away, so we found it and left the old monstrosity there and walked home. By this time, it was close to midnight and when I walked in, Laura's hair was just about standing on end, as she had no idea where I was.

Again, I thank my lucky stars that I am not a driver. What a lonely, thankless job. However, the girls that do it seem to love the life and wouldn't change. Guess there is a certain pride in having their own vehicle and maintaining it. They are on 24- hour call—so are very seldom free, but sometimes sit for hours without doing anything. They sit in our Red Cross Office, and were there almost all day today. We are quite happy to have them, as it is nice to have someone in the room. We try to be there on weekends as some of the ex-patients come back to visit.

Tonight I am going to a party at Bob's Mess, so guess I should hop to my feet and get ready, and not keep him waiting this time. Expect they will be moving up soon. Will hate to see them go.

Parcels still coming through very well. Box 89 arrived safely and we all thank you so much. The tomato juice is such a hit. Also loved the pickles and mayo. Sheila got some Heinz ketchup, and those things really brighten up our hospital meals. Received 16 dozen bars of chocolate from the Met Red Cross recently. We save it for the incoming convoys. Must write and thank them.

Now April 8th, and the Easter Box arrived in just two weeks. I was delighted with it. Just the kind of a parcel to boost the morale. Such gay, bright lipstick and nail polish, those beautiful stockings and darling earrings. Laura and I had come home, nearly exhausted, and there was my parcel! We were almost frantic and both beginning to think we were developing "war nerves". Saturday night, Laura got word that her cousin, who had lived with them and was like a brother to her, was missing, with the RCAF, so that surely shook her.

We were both tired Sunday morning and didn't hear our alarm at 6.15 am, and first thing we knew, it was 8 am. We got to the hosp. about quarter to ten—locked our door, while we took off our coats and combed our hair. I had my hat on the back of my head and had two pips on one shoulder and none on the other, in my haste. There was a great rattle at the door and stamping of feet. There was nothing we could do but open the door, and in waltzed General Montague and a whole parade of Big Bugs. We nearly had a fit. Was it ever thus. Practically every other day we would have half a day's work done by 10 am, but not so when the General breezed in. However, he was very nice—fired the usual questions at us. "What is your name?" "Where are you from?" "Do you like your work?" etc. They left as quickly as they came. We heaved a sigh of relief, collapsed into chairs and had a good laugh.

Goodnight, my dears,
Much love, Lois

April 11th, 1945
Dearest Folks:

Tomorrow is your birthday, Mother. Do have a very happy day. Hope I'll be there for the next one. I mailed your present several weeks ago, so it should have arrived safely.

We are still pretty busy. We expect Sheila will be back on the job the first of the week. The leave list was up today, and I am scheduled to go to U.K. April 15th. Can hardly wait. It is almost too good to be true. Will write to cousin Bill at once and let him know. Also, I have had several letters from Jack Cooper lately—so will get in touch with him, too.

So many of the boys are coming in as patients again. Remember I mentioned Blackie? Well, yesterday, late in the afternoon, I was on one of the wards and a very dirty, bedraggled creature appeared. A patient, just struggling in. He spoke to me, and it was Blackie, under inches of mud and grime. The poor kids—they take such a beating; however, he was all in one piece, this time, and still had his grin. They seem to age years in just a few weeks. Of course, he probably looks much better today, after a good rest. They just sleep for hours when they first arrive.

I walked through another ward, and a lad called me by name. His face was scratched and bandaged, but it was Stuart McGarvey of Ottawa, who I worked with. It's a strange thing—but in all this time, both here and in England, that is the first time I have ever walked into a ward and seen someone who I actually knew before. Others have been patients, but usually someone else has told me they were here, and I went especially to see them.

Hope tomorrow will be another glorious day, as I will be off. Ruth and I are planning to rent bikes and ride out to the coast. It will certainly be a help when Sheila gets back to work. Yesterday, I was alone, and supplies arrived. Twenty-three crates to be opened and stowed away. Fortunately, the boys do most of that for us, thank goodness!

The main thought in my mind, now, is leave at Coombehurst. It should be perfectly beautiful there. When I think of how lovely it was last spring. We played golf and tennis in April and lay in the sun. The flowers will all be in bloom—even the magnolias and the wisteria. It is the prettiest of all. It is a deep lavender and hangs in great gobs on one wall at Coombehurst.

Last evening, Laura and I went to the unit boys' dance. The Padre took Laura and Ad took me. Have I told you about Ad? He is one of our pharmacists and has become one of my best friends in the unit. If I ever had a brother, would have imagined him to be just like Ad. The dance was great fun. We sported our new Mess dresses and they are really smart. A lovely shade of blue gabardine, with long full sleeves, and white collars and cuffs. Open neck, shirtmaker style, with fly front and flared skirt. So much more feminine than our khaki.

I have been hearing much of Spike Rochon lately. He is with the fighting Chaudières, and that is a regiment that holds the respect of the entire Canadian Army. The boys just worship Spike. He is a Major now and a Company Commander, so is doing exceptionally well. It's difficult to believe that screwball kid of Gauvreau Lake days has accomplished all that. I asked one day if anyone knew him or had heard of him recently, as the last word I had, he was with the Régiment de Hull. The Chaudière boys just leapt to their feet and said he was their Company Commander, and ever since, they have been telling me about him. Do hope I will get a chance to see him, and will write him a note letting him know where I am in case he gets down this way.

Today was particularly hectic. We'll surely be glad when Sheila recovers and returns to us. Laura and I have not had a moment recently.

Well, enough for now. Must get to bed.
Much love, Lois

LEAVE IN ENGLAND

April 26th, 1945
Dearest Family:

Here I am, back again, and quite safely, too. It was a marvellous leave. I had such a good rest, and a wonderful time. Guess I should start at the beginning and tell you all about it.

We left here Sunday morning. One of our M.O.s was on his way to Paris, so picked me up in a transport. We got to the local station and had missed the train, so nothing to do but take the transport to Brussels. The M.O. had a box lunch his Batman had packed for him. Just a small snack for one that turned out to be a huge box of sandwiches, cakes and a dozen hard-boiled eggs! Had lunch at the Atlanta with Chub, the M.O. Then we parted and I went to Red Cross HQ. Later, checked in at the Palace Hotel where I was to stay. No sooner got into the elevator than I met a chap I had not seen since England. We had dinner together and then did Brussels. The biggest thrill of all was riding in a beautiful car. He is aide to a Maj. General, so we had a Staff car. Such complete luxury. We visited various night spots. A fun evening. I was up bright and early and they picked me up and whizzed us to the airport.

It was a glorious summer day. So warm and bright. I got such a thrill out of flying. As we crossed the Channel, could see a row of white clouds ahead, and suddenly, they took shape and became the White Cliffs of Dover! Seemed no time until we were over England. The landscape of France and Belgium is fairly flat, while England is rolling and full of twisting roads. Somehow, I got separated from the other Sisters, who were all Limey, and got in an aircraft full of Brass Hats. They called out all the names,

Brigadiers, Maj. Generals, etc., and then an ATS officer and me. There was an RAF steward on board and he was busy the whole trip, showing us points of interest and looking after us. First he passed coffee, then sausage rolls and sandwiches, cakes and cookies. Then chocolate bars, then gum, and finally, boiled sweets. He passed around maps and charts of the flight, so it was very interesting. It was exciting to land in England. Everything looked just the same and all the signs were in English!

We went right to the Transit camp in the heart of London and checked in. We had been met at the airport by a Canadian station wagon, so we were well looked after. Then I went to Red Cross HQ, saw some of the girls and called Mrs. Simon and said I would be right out to Basingstoke. As London was terribly hot, I had but one thought, to get to the country, and fast.

Called Naval HQ to see how I could get in touch with Jack. Surprisingly, he was right there, so he came and took me to the Ontario Services Club for tea. It's a fine club and one we may be very proud of. Was delighted to see Jack. We met oodles of people we knew. Then on to Waterloo Station and I proceeded to Basingstoke.

Mrs. Simon had sent a taxi for me, and I got to the house quickly. Could not have chosen a better week for leave—we had nine full days of sunshine and it was summer heat. I arrived in time for dinner and it was just like being home again. Ruth and Hoyle were there, and another Canadian girl who has been living there, as her RAF husband is a POW. She is Olga Lane—charming—went to Queen's with some of the Ottawa friends. Got out of my uniform as soon as I arrived, and wore civvies the whole time. Mrs. Simon had them all ready for me. She is so very thoughtful.

Tuesday, Mrs. Simon and Ruth had planned a day in London, and I slept in, then Elsie brought my breakfast up and I looked through my clothes and decided what I wanted to wear, etc. Had a quiet lunch, then put on my bathing suit and spent the afternoon lying out on the lawn, reading. It was just heavenly and I certainly enjoyed and appreciated it.

Mrs. Simon and Ruth had felt badly about dashing off to London and leaving me the first day I was back—but truthfully I was delighted to have the opportunity to rest. Then Olga came home about 4 pm and brought a girl from the hospital that I knew, so we had tea together.

The days just flew past—I had breakfast in bed every day, and got up when I felt like it. Went over to the hospital one day and saw a lot of people. Also some of our patients were evacuated there, so saw them, too. Went out to Mrs. Reford's for tea one day. Various people dropped in to see me. Miss Sturgess, the Matron of the Civilian Hospital, whom I knew. Also Dr. Weston, who used to live at Coombehurst, and Mother Hubbard and Shirley, who also live elsewhere now. We saw a couple of shows, and I had milk to drink! I think that was the biggest thrill of all—it was just like liquid gold and I practically purred over the first glass. Mrs. Simon was simply wonderful. She cooked all the things she knew I liked and was so very good to me.

I took her a box of chocolates and perfume and a bottle of champagne, which she is saving for V-Day. Will send her something for her birthday, which is in May. The night before I left, she gave me a beautiful present, a gorgeous pair of Wedgwood candlesticks. They are really lovely and I will treasure them. You can imagine how thrilled I was. She said they were a belated birthday present, because she knew my birthday was in March but was not sure of the date.

Ruth Campbell is leaving shortly for home. She hates to go and leave Hoyle, but was told that if she did not go home very soon, it might be a year before she could get passage, so she is packing now, and taking the dog.

I just missed seeing Aileen and the baby. She had been there, shortly before me, and they all said that the baby was so sweet and that Aileen was marvellous with her, and also wonderful about her great loss of George. The morning I was leaving Coombehurst, we had word that Aileen had arrived home safely. Colonel Blythe was in a POW camp that was liberated before I got there, and Mrs. Simon was very excited—every time the phone rang, she fully expected it to be news of him. When I left, they still had not heard, but there are so many thousands of POWs to be repatriated and it will all take time.

Oh, I almost forgot. I bought Ruth's bicycle and am having it shipped over here. It should be on its way now. It is a Raleigh and such a nice one. Will be wonderful to have one over here. We will be able to ride back and forth to the hospital. Mary's is here and Sheila has one on the way. Laura will see about one when she goes on leave. She goes very soon.

Friday morning I went up to London, arranged about my passport, got some money and arranged for the bike to be crated, etc., then had lunch with some of the Ottawa girls. After lunch, got a cab to Paddington Station just in time to catch the 1.15 pm train to Bath, as I was going down there to spend the weekend with Jack.

Weather was super. He lives in a hotel in Bath, and was able to get a room for me there, too. We saw every part of the town and it really is charming. Very quaint and quite historical. Has been a naval town for a good part of its history. We went out of town to lovely old inns for dinner. Two of his good friends from Ottawa were also there, Bev and Bert. They had a couple of British WREN friends, and the six of us had a wonderful time. We had a very good weekend and then Jack went back to London with me on Sunday, as he had just received word that his sister's husband—who had been in a POW camp for three years, since Dieppe, had been liberated and was at Jack's uncle's, in London. He was evidently quite safe and well, although he had lost quite a bit of weight. These "Repats" have the most amazing and hair-raising tales to tell—almost incredible, the things that happened.

Don't remember whether I mentioned that we had a surprise visit from Madame Vanier, wife of General Vanier, the Canadian Ambassador to France, recently. Such a gracious lady. She was touring Normandy and this part of France and Belgium with an aide, seeing the dreadful devastation in Normandy and along the route where the Canadian Army had fought, visiting some of the Canadian hospitals along the way. She was visibly upset by what she had seen in Normandy and wondering if, later on, a Canadian Relief Effort could be launched. She spent a little time with us, saw our Red Cross Office and our Recreation Hut. Then, as it was late afternoon, offered to drive us back to the Mess. We felt quite privileged, riding in the Embassy vehicle, with the Canadian Flag flying.

Your loving daughter, Lois

(Ambassador and Madame Vanier did follow up on her idea and approached the Canadian Red Cross Society about a Relief Project for Normandy. In 1946, the Canadian Red Cross Civilian Relief Depot was set up in Normandy, near Bayeux. Three Corps girls, headed by Marian Bigelow, set up the Distribution Centre and huge shipments of household supplies, clothing, blankets, hospital dressings, milk, vitamins, etc., flowed in from Canada. The shipments continued from July through to the end of 1946. The Vaniers were very helpful with this endeavour. The people of Normandy were extremely grateful and our three Corps members were awarded medals by the French Red Cross.)

April 28th, 1945
Dearest Family:

To continue, I went back to Basingstoke to gather up my things. Jack met me at the station, with my bike and baggage. Took the bike to be packed and then met Janie Church, my longtime friend, now a Nursing Sister. She is the first close friend from home that I have seen since leaving Canada. Marvellous to see her. We hardly stopped talking. Reminisced and laughed so much about the days at Pontiac and Gauvreau Lake.

The three of us had lunch at the Royal Automobile Club, then went to Kew Gardens. It was absolutely glorious at this time of year. Jack has a new movie camera with coloured film, so the pictures should be fantastic. The rhododendrons were magnificent and the wisteria all in bloom.

We went back into London; Janie left to catch her train and we went to the ballet, and saw Swan Lake. *Had been wanting to see it all winter. It was breathtakingly beautiful and I loved it. Jack really enjoyed it, too. We had dinner at Oddineno's and saw so many people we knew. Gerry Hanson, the gal who had roomed beside me at "Mac", was there with her husband. We stared at each other, then dashed up and both started to talk at once. She is CWAC and it was such a thrill to see her.*

That was Tuesday, my last day, so Jack deposited me at the Transit Camp where I was to stay the night. It was a big hostel and they broke the news, none too gently, that we would be wakened at 5.00 am. However, the bed was so hard that I was quite ready to get up when the time came. I was sharing a room with a British Nursing Sister, Hilda, who was very pleasant. The trip home was uneventful and I arrived in Bruges for lunch.

It was a marvellous holiday and I surely enjoyed it. Wonderful to have the time in Basingstoke with Mrs. Simon and Ruth and Hoyle and to get over to the hospital again. Everyone gave me such a great welcome. Time in London was fun and I loved going down to Bath. It is a such a quaint lovely old town and I had such fun with Jack and his friends.

Much love to you both, Lois

FAREWELL TO DRAGOONS

April 28th, 1945
Dearest Family:

When I got home there was a letter for me, with news of the regiment. The Manitoba Dragoons have evidently done a marvellous job. Liberated town after town with amazing speed and received various and sundry congratulations and honours. One of their "DR's", Markasino, who we had come to know, was sent out with a message to one of the squadrons, and on the way was surrounded by twenty Jerry troops. After a little persuasion, he got the 20 Germans to throw their weapons into the canal. Then he locked them in a garage, returned to the Regiment HQ, got some scout cars and went out and brought them all in!

It's now May 3rd, and another day off. Life was very busy when I returned. It was almost a week before I even unpacked my suitcase, and then only because Ruth wanted to borrow it to go to Paris. Just heard that Bob Graham, the chap I went out with quite often about two months ago when his Tank Corps Regiment was stationed near here, was badly shot up. Have not been able to find out many details or where he is, but guess he was evacuated from up front, right to England. Paul, his friend, and fiancé of one of the Sisters, was killed in the same encounter. It's very sad—lads who have fought up through Italy, and through the Hitler line, and then get it so near the end.

It was only yesterday that it dawned on me with full realization that the war is practically over. We have talked about it for weeks and months, but somehow I never really believed it or thought seriously that the end was close at hand. I never see a newspaper and very seldom hear a complete news report on the radio. We have a radio in the Red Cross Room and in the wards, but all I hear is snatches of news. Then yesterday, after it was given out quite authentically that Hitler was dead and Van Runstead had been captured, and Berlin had surrendered—our Sgt. Major fairly danced into the room and said it was just a matter of days. He is a typical RSM; nothing ever excites him or even changes his expression. That did make me think, and realize that in another couple of months our job would be finished, and perhaps a few months later I might be home.

Oh, Jack Cooper called last night from Ostende. He had just landed. Had no idea he was coming over here but he will be along for lunch today. He is on his way to Paris on a mission for the Navy, and will be here for a couple of days at each end of his journey. Glad it is my day off.

Now May 5th, and at this point, I am so excited, I can hardly see straight. You probably have my cable by now, about Jack and me becoming engaged. We had talked about it when I was in England, but I had not given a firm answer. It seemed important to me that the war be over before making a commitment. As I said earlier, I didn't think things would come to such a fast conclusion. He decided to come and convince me, which he did!

Now May 6th. Jack and I went to Ostende last evening, to the Officers' Club for dinner and danced there later. We had an amphibious Jeep—better known as a Duck. Now I think I have ridden in most mechanized vehicles, except a tank, although I am quite familiar with armoured cars. He left this morning for Paris on naval business. Wanted me to go too but 48 was not granted. I was torn between going and staying here, to celebrate with our unit and the patients.

I didn't tell Laura last evening. Then this morning at the hospital everyone was in such a dither anyway, I just had to tell her. Laura has not even met Jack, so when I said I was going to be married, she nearly collapsed and wondered who? Have not said much about it here at the hospital because it won't be for some time. Probably long after we leave this unit—not until we get home.

Marion Crawford is being married on Thursday. She certainly surprised the Mess. We are all so happy for her. She is marrying John Barr. They will have a Mess wedding and all the frills. Everything is happening at once and I am just so excited.

Realized that I have not told you very much about Jack. Well, you know quite a bit about him, and you did meet him, very briefly, Dad, in the ski cabin. He is an Engineer Officer in the Navy. Lt.Cdr. now. He plans to take his discharge from the Navy after returning to Canada. Now that hostilities are over, will look for a job. Jack did work in Northern Ontario for several years after graduating from U. of T. in engineering. He joined the Navy in 1941. His parents are both dead. Lost his mother while in his early teens, then his father during his final year of university. He has five sisters and a younger brother. I am looking forward to meeting them. There are many things to work out and we have not looked that far ahead. He will be back from Paris later in the week and here for a few days. Then I will hope to get back to England before he leaves for home.

(In the fall of 1942 a group of girls, eight of us, rented a ski cabin near Camp Fortune in the Gatineau Hills, north of Ottawa. We spent many winter weekends there. One of the girls knew some naval officers and they would drop in occasionally. Jack Cooper was one. In January he had an unfortunate fall on the hill, dislocating and breaking his left shoulder.

Those years there was no road into Camp Fortune. Everyone skied in over the mountain to the valley where the camp was located. That particular

Jack

Sunday the Governor General and his wife, Princess Alice, their aides, and Prince Bernhardt of the Netherlands had gone in on a horse-drawn sleigh, on an old logging road. The head of the Ski Patrol asked if they would take Jack to the highway where he could be transferred to a waiting ambulance. They graciously agreed, so he was put on the sleigh, wrapped in buffalo robes. Prince Bernhardt skied along behind, to make room for him on the sleigh! They chatted as they bounced along. Jack being in considerable pain, he later said conversation was difficult.

Worst part of the scenario was, Jack had requested and waited ages for a sea appointment. It had just come through and he was due to leave the following morning for Norfolk, Va., to join the ship. Instead he went to Rideau Military Hospital for eight weeks. I did not know him very well, so did not visit him in hospital. Then, in mid-June, after I had received my overseas appointment with the Red Cross, and was just finishing up at Met Life, we met by chance on Sparks Street. We were delighted to see each other and I learned that he was leaving very soon for Norfolk, as his ship, the Queen Elizabeth battleship, was still there, undergoing battle repairs. He was interested to hear that I was going overseas also, and said he would try to get in touch. They were quite a while reaching England. Were delayed getting away, then went on to Bermuda for a short stay. Then to Scapa Flow in the Orkneys for an extended period. He finally came ashore and was posted to London and Bath with the Admiralty. Then it was March '44, when Jack contacted the Canadian Red Cross to get my address, and our friendship began to blossom.)

Everything is so exciting. Monday, May 7th is the gigantic May Day celebrations in Europe. The Belgians have been talking about it for weeks. The patients are getting special passes to see it and we are all having a half-day off. We are also planning V-day celebrations—it is to be just like Christmas, only more so—everything for the patients, special food, dances, all-day passes, transportation, and special care for the drunks, and they deserve it too, because they are the ones who have helped make it all possible. Who knows, we may be in England again before long.

Just had some very sad news. One of the Chaudière Regiment boys came all the way back to tell me that Robert Rochon has been killed. I feel very badly, because, of the nine Rochon siblings, I knew Spike the best. He was such a good friend in my teen years, and we used to dance up a storm on the cottage verandahs, with the old wind-up gramo-

phones. His DR came in, practically in tears, because we had often talked about Spike and he knew I would want to know. Remember, not long ago I mentioned how well he was doing, and that his men just worshipped him. They said he led every attack himself and was always well ahead of any of them. His Sgt. Major got it, too. If it has been officially announced at home, please let me know, and I will write to Mr. and Mrs. Rochon. I'm sure they would want to know how much his men thought of him. It seems especially sad to have it happen so close to the end. That seemed to be the last straw for all the tears I had stored up. Went back to our hotel, up to my room, threw myself down and sobbed. It was not just for Robert, but for the many friends, all the fine young men that have been lost.

Much love, Lois

May 7th, 1945
Dearest Mother and Dad:

Well, here we are on the Eve of V-E Day. We know now that it's official that tomorrow is the big day. It's a restless evening. Somehow, I can't be very gay. There are a few people down in the Mess, making quite a racket, but most of the girls are just sitting in their rooms, not knowing what to do. The last years have been too tense and we have seen too much and lost too many friends, to forget it all so soon. The only way anyone can be very exuberant is to drown their sorrows.

The boys at the hospital are happy, but very quiet about it all. They don't even want to talk about it very much, and their one thought and joy is that they won't ever have to go back into the lines again. They say, in complete and utter wonderment: It's all over at last—and I'm still alive! We feel especially sad about the lads killed in the final month. To think that many of them came onto those bloody beaches and fought their way through France, then Belgium and Holland and into Germany, and lost their lives when Victory was in sight. Of course, their sacrifice was just as necessary as the very first ones.

Today was the Parade of the Holy Blood. Bruges is the centre and it's quite an event. Evidently a relic of the Holy Blood was brought from Palestine to Bruges in 1150 AD. So the tradition began. The first one in six years, although it is usually an annual occurrence, but they could not hold it during the occupation. As our hotel is on the Main Square, we had ringside seats. It started at 11 am and continued until 1.45. It was a lengthy parade. We looked out the windows in the front of the building. In peacetime, people come from all parts of the world to see it.

It was a pageant and began with Adam and Eve, then the birth of Christ and it depicted his entire life, with all the characters in Biblical history represented. The costumes were beautiful—it was all so colourful and gay, but rather pagan and unreal. It was a good thing the war was over—for us—as we certainly couldn't have enjoyed such a pageant if our troops had still been fighting. It is such a blessed relief to know that not another Canadian lad will be killed by enemy action. True, there will be snipers—but perhaps they will be able to round them up quickly.

At this moment, we too feel that our job is finished, and are quite ready to fold up and go home. However, it won't be that easy. It will probably be several months before we reach England.

It is now May 11th, and I will continue. Tuesday, May 8th was V-day. The patients were excited, but a quiet excitement. It seemed to take them 24 hours to realize just what it meant. I know I could not grasp the significance of it all at once. The lads had all-day passes on Monday, for the parade, then again Tuesday the passes were issued and they all headed for town and really painted it red. Right after Churchill's speech, the partying began. Champagne corks were popping all over the wards. Everyone began to feel very high and happy. Bed patients got up, boys on crutches threw them away and they surely celebrated. Laura, Sheila and I went home about 5 pm, so we could be ready for the party at night. We commandeered a coal wagon and got him to drive us into town. The weather is beginning to get very warm. We had ten days of cold wet weather.

The party at night was in the hospital. They cleared the beds out of one of the largest wards. We got flowers to decorate in the afternoon and they had an orchestra. Such a wild bedlam. Patients, Other Ranks, officers and Sisters. We all wore our blues, and the patients never see us except in khaki, so you can imagine the result. The Sisters were just mobbed and we were practically torn to pieces. It was a regular free-for-all, but everyone was so happy and excited that they didn't care. It was definitely the patients' night. The Medical Officers didn't stand a chance and couldn't get a dance. If they did manage to fight their way in and grab a Sister, before they could go three steps one of the patients would call a Tag-dance and the poor M.O. would almost be swept off the floor.

We went around and visited all the bed patients. They were in a merry state, too. Guess the Sisters on duty had their hands full, but no one seemed to mind. It was a great success; however, I am sure we couldn't stand one of these evenings very often. Laura, Sheila and I were black and blue to the knees, and exhausted all the next day.

Wednesday I dragged myself home in the heat and just got to the door when the Dragoons arrived. They had driven down from Germany, 500 miles, so were awfully hot and tired. Ian had captured a car, a Ford Deluxe American-built, so is very swish, flying around in his own vehicle. Later we went to Ostende to the Officers' Club, then to the Circle Club. It was really thrilling, driving along the waterfront, all the ships and fishing vessels had their lights on, all colours, and they were twinkling against the water. It's such a pleasure to ride in a real honest-to-goodness car, after bouncing over the cobblestones in the back of a truck for so long. Ian and another chap liberated a town, all by themselves, hence the car, and various other things.

Thursday dawned bright and beautiful. Marion Crawford's wedding day. The wedding was at 12 noon, so we all rushed home and got into our blues, climbed into our truck and off to the wedding. It was a lovely setting. Quaint little church, Church of England. All the M.O.s in khaki and the Sisters in blue. Marion looked perfectly sweet. She is quite tiny. Violet Shea from Ottawa was her Maid of Honour. It was such a nice service; then we all got into our trucks and back to the Mess. Our Mess is most attractive. The lounge is a great square room, with dark red tapestry walls, and an open-air garden, horseshoe-shaped, with high walls around it but no roof. There are French doors leading to it. The lounge was filled with flowers and there were masses of food, a gorgeous cake and any amount of champagne. It was a buffet luncheon, with hot biscuits and chicken à la King, french fries, then fruit salad, all sorts of pastries and the cake. It was over by 2.30 pm, so we all got into our khaki and back to the hospital to await a huge convoy.

Ian (Dragoon) called for me at 6 pm and we drove for hours. As it was extremely hot, we went out to the coast and toured the places that his regiment had liberated. It was quite a thrill now that hostilities have ceased, to go through these towns again—Zeebrugge, Blankenberghe, Knocke, Den Haan, etc. The White Brigade was in action, burning out the collaborators' houses—and as we drove through the streets, there were great piles of charred household goods in the middle of the road, where they had been thrown and burned. Some places, they were still at work—so we stopped to watch. They were smashing the windows, ripping the curtains, and heaving everything out the win-

Marian Crawford and John Barr's wedding day

dows. Articles of clothing, beds, chairs and tables soared through the air, from the upper stories. Willful destruction, yet no one seemed to stop them.

We had supper in Knocke, as Ian had spent the summer there before the war. These resorts, although so badly battered now, must have been absolutely beautiful before. Perhaps someday I will come back and see it all again, when it is rebuilt, but at this very moment, I have no desire to see very much more of Europe.

We returned to our Mess, joined Sheila and her friend and went to the fair, presently situated in our Main Square, just in front of our hotel. We rode everything from the Merry-Go-Round to the Shoot-the-Shoots and played the games of chance. There were sky rockets shooting up all over the place and it was très gay! Then the orchestra arrived in the Mess and the party got under way. The personnel in our unit has changed greatly since we joined it last summer—there are so many new faces and many old ones have left. We are among the long-time members. However, they are still a grand crowd and we always have such fun at the Mess parties.

Ian had breakfast with us in our Mess this morning, and then left for Ostende to catch the boat and on to England for his leave. Jack called from Paris to say he would be delayed and return to Bruges tomorrow. He will stay for the weekend, then has to get back to England and over to Ireland for a few days. Was relieved that he will not be back until tomorrow, as it will give me a chance to catch up on my sleep!

Saturday was my day off, so I slept in, then went up on the roof to lie in the sun. Jack arrived in the afternoon after a tiring trip. The train had broken down between Brussels and Ghent, and they were there, in the heat, for hours. The Cosy Corner is the coolest spot in the area, so off we went, for dinner. They have marvellous gardens, huge shade trees, masses of rhododendrons and lilac, such a heavenly scent. Tables under the trees. A very attractive spot on a hot evening. We returned to the Mess to find another party in full swing. Evidently the M.O. who had won the pool, guessing the Date of V-day, hired an orchestra with his winnings. We joined Laura and Sheila and their respective beaux.

Sunday, I worked until 3.30 pm. Then Jack and I went boating on the canals. That is a popular pastime here in Bruges as it is a maze of canals. It was a gorgeous day and the first time I had a chance to do that. There was another party in the Mess that evening, in honour of four M.O.s who are leaving on very short notice. One is Col. Ross, the 2nd in Command—one of our favourite people. We will miss him.

Monday was my day off. As Jack was staying until evening, we rented bikes and rode out towards the coast. Wind proved too much for us, so we turned back, and found an ice cream parlour instead. Made it back to the Mess for dinner and then he had to leave for Ostende and back to England. He does not expect to be back here again and heaven only knows when I will get to England. Perhaps by July or August if we are lucky. Evidently, besides filing his report on the naval business in Paris, he mentioned that he had become engaged! You can imagine how amused his co-frères were and wondered which mission had really inspired his trip to the Continent!

It is now May 17th, and we're much busier since D-Day than the weeks previously. Running to capacity again; however, it can't last forever.

As yet have not had a letter written since you got my cable about Jack and me. We have made very few plans—it's so hard to tell just when we will get home. Jack expects to be in England until late summer, so hopefully I will make it before he leaves. We would love to have time to take a quick trip to Ireland. He goes there frequently on Navy matters, and I have always had a yen to see the land where Grandmother Kelly was born.

Laura left for Brussels this morning, for her leave in England. She is hoping to spend a few days at Coombehurst. Last evening just as she was packing to go, she received a cable from home, saying that her cousin Art was safe and would contact her in London. It was almost too good to be true. He is RCAF and has been missing for over two months and Laura had just about given up hope. There was great rejoicing and she went off all smiles.

Much love to you both and wish I could be home for your anniversary.

Lois

May 24th, 1945
Dearest Family:

The last week has been busy, to say the least. Ian (Dragoon) was due back from England Sunday at dinner time. When he didn't appear, I assumed he missed the boat, and had dinner and went to the movie in the Mess. About eight o'clock, he called from Ostende—to say that he was there, stranded, because the Navy had lost the keys to his car! It was a long story—but dated back to the morning he left here. I suggested that he come to the Mess for breakfast, knowing it would be the only place he would be able to get food so early. Good idea, but I overslept and nearly made him miss the boat. He almost flew to Ostende and got to the dock just as the boat was pulling out. There was a Limey Naval Lieutenant there who offered to put the car in a garage and look after it. All well and good and he caught the boat.

However, the Naval Officer decided to use the car during the week and was out on the dock one day. He pulled his handkerchief out of his pocket and the keys with it, and they flopped into the sea. There was great consternation. Said Naval Officer was most embarrassed about the situation and had the Port of Ostende in utter confusion—trying to get it fixed up before Ian should return. He sent a diver down to scrounge around in the mud, he had all the Ford dealers in the area rounded up, also locksmiths, safe crackers, mechanics and engineers. However it is one of those Ford V-8's that the switch locks on the steering wheel, so there was nothing they could do. When Ian arrived, they still had not accomplished anything.

They drove him to Bruges Sunday evening. Monday was my day off so we went back to Ostende—by bus. Checked out the car, still firmly locked, saw a movie then back to Bruges—still on the bus!

In the evening, I put on my Blue dress and we went to the Officers' Club. The only one here in Bruges is run by the English and is typical. Had not been there for ten days and in the meantime they had changed it around. We had always danced upstairs—so we went up there, wandered into the lounge and found a place to sit, and waited for the music to start in the adjoining room. The waiter took our order and we were sitting there quite happily until we began to notice that the lounge was filled with staid and austere British officers and not a Sister in sight. Of course, we soon realized that it was strictly the Men's Lounge—so quickly drank our drinks and departed. We certainly had a good laugh. In a Canadian club it would not have mattered so much—but to nonchalantly brave the icy stares and glares of a British club, especially their private lounge—is not done. You should have seen their faces. It was priceless.

Tuesday morning, Ian went out to Ostende and got the car, in running order—minus the lock—and picked me up after four and we went to Blankenberghe and enjoyed the beach for a couple of hours. It is a perfectly beautiful beach. So wide, and it stretches for miles. Unfortunately, these waterfronts are a shambles now. All the marvellous hotels, just shells—if you sit and look out to sea it's quite beautiful—the lovely beach, people sunbathing and swimming, ships in the distance, but if you turn your head and look behind you, there is nothing but ruin and rubble. They will rebuild these places eventually, but it must be heartbreaking for people who knew them in peacetime.

And to think that they did so much damage to Halifax, merely to celebrate V-Day! That was perfectly disgraceful. Too bad some of those ruffians couldn't have had a look at some of these places, and then they might have been thankful that their own city had been untouched by war.

Ian left early Wednesday morning as he was going back via The Hague to see his brother, who had come from Italy, and they had not seen each other for several years.

Jack is in Ireland; I had a note from Belfast yesterday. Will hope to get to England by July. Received Jean and Ted's cable, also numerous nice notes from various people, with good wishes.

I also wrote to the Rochons. Spoke with a Chaudière Lieutenant recently and he was able to give me a few details. Evidently Spike and his Sgt. Major were hit by an 88. So just did not have a chance. Said he had been buried in a Canadian cemetery near a large German seaport. Spike had been awarded the M.C. shortly before his death, so sent them a clipping from Canada's Weekly.

Hugs and Kisses,
Much love, Lois

May 25th, 1945
Dear Ones:

Laura is still away and I'm practically talking to myself at this point. I've hardly been in the room at all in the past few weeks. It's been fun but pretty hectic. The wedding yesterday was just the last straw as far as I was concerned—I mean, I was so tired. The wedding was at 11 am, followed by the buffet luncheon in the Mess. Sheila and I went back to the hospital at 2.00 pm and by the time I finished that last ward, I was barely dragging one foot after the other. Even the boys said I looked completely beaten and thought it was a big joke. The Padre had asked me to go out to dinner with him, but I just couldn't—so came home and crawled into bed at 7.00 pm. Next thing I knew, it was 7.00 am, so hopped up, feeling quite rested.

Just received both your letters about wedding, etc., and was thrilled with all your suggestions. Certainly plan to be married in Ottawa. That is my home and I surely want you two to be there, so the wedding will not be in Bruges or London, when we expect to be home fairly soon.

It is now May 27th, and instead of getting rid of patients, we just admitted well over 350 Canadians. Guess our sojourn in the good city of Bruges will be lengthened. We are fortunate to be here, as reports from hospitals up front say that it is a pretty tough life with few of the comforts that we have here. It was rather funny today, watching the boys come in. Laura is still away and Sheila was off, so I was alone. Three of the boys helped me. They were all ex-patients who had returned for the day. Butch, Blondie and Slim. We carted all the cigarettes and chocolate bars into the A & D (Admitting) and set up there. There were about 250 walking cases and as they came through they were given their papers, etc., then chocolate bars and cigarettes, then pyjamas etc. and assigned to a ward. There were Belgie workmen who grabbed their luggage and escorted them to their room, where they received a good slug of Scotch and a chicken dinner. They were all coming from a British hospital—so were practically speechless by it all. I think what really impressed them the most was the Belgie "bell hops" carrying their luggage! There were stretcher cases coming in two other doors, so we toured the corridors and caught up with them.

With all these new patients, we just cannot tell from day to day what will happen. Yesterday, we closed wards, then today, with such a large convoy, the same wards had to be re-opened. We are hoping we still may get to Paris. Rumour has it that 48's are in order next month, so we are keeping our fingers crossed. I would surely like to see Paris with the lights on!

Hope Laura got to Coombehurst and will have news from there. Mrs. Simon is having a house built just within sight of the place so will be living there, in the same neighbourhood. Coombehurst itself has been sold, but the Blythes will probably live there for a year until they find another home. Such a lovely place and very stately.

Much love, Dears. Lois

June 10th, 1945
Dearest Family:

It was a year ago today that I left Basingstoke. It has been quite an eventful year. We had a Mess Dinner tonight as 23 Sisters are leaving for England and Canada tomorrow. Sheila will go on the 19th. Many of our unit boys, who are Burma bound, are going this week, too. But still the convoys continue to arrive, one yesterday and another lot tomorrow.

Good to have Laura back. We have been biking a lot. On our day off we went to Blankenberghe. Took a picnic and our bathing suits and lay on the beach. It was a wonderful day. Then we bicycled up the coast through Zeebrugge, Heist and Knocke. It's such a funny feeling to see the great German West Wall at such close range. To sit at the base of a big gun, amid a maze and network of the enemy's means and methods of defence. It was quite a miracle that our troops and Allies came through all of it in less than a year. The whole West Wall is a pretty sorry-looking sight. Beautiful summer resorts completely battered and smashed. Hordes of Jerry prisoners at work, cleaning up and beginning repairs. Not a very subdued-looking lot, either.

Jack was so pleased to hear from you, Mother, and is hoping that his sister Win will get to see you soon. I just know he won't be able to get over here again, as the Canadian part of the Navy have left Ostende.

It's now June 14th. Life has been a little dull of late, and Laura and I were beginning to get a little browned off—nothing exciting was happening and there seems little prospect of getting home, and seeing Sheila pack made it that much worse.

Then yesterday, I walked into the Red Cross Room and Laura was beaming from ear to ear, and said, "How about going up into Holland to a Dragoon Party Saturday night—why not?" I thought she was kidding, but there was Markasino, their special DR. They had sent him down with letters, re: the party, so you can imagine how thrilled we were.

His motor bike had died a few kilometres from Bruges, and he had acquired a Limey jeep and driver, so was cruising around in style. He is the one who captured the 20 Jerrys not long before V-Day. I guess they had told him not to come back without an affirmative answer, as he almost pushed us into the Matron's office to get permission.

Sheila is going to a wedding in Holland tomorrow, so will have a trip in that direction, too, before she goes home. We are surely going to miss her. I went to dinner last evening with the Padre. He is an extremely nice person and has been a very good friend to us.

Captain Legate was in from Brussels today. We were delighted to see him and had a long talk. He said that Laura and I could leave and be returned to Canada as soon as our priority number comes up, or wait until our unit closes and then go to England and have immediate priority for Canada. At present we will stick with the unit and finish our job, unless it drags on too long, and then we can ask to leave. It boosted our morale. As did the thought of the coming weekend!

Then the door opened and in walked Chuck Hanson, a Sgt. with the H.L.I. and just about our favourite patient of all time. He was the one who helped us so much and played Santa at Christmas.

He left us months ago and we had heard since that he had been killed and all felt so badly. There he was, large as life and perfectly healthy, although he now wears three wound stripes instead of the single one he had when he left here. You have no idea how happy and relieved we were to see him. We were so glad he arrived before Sheila left. Much love, Lois

June 20th, 1945
My Dear Family:

Well, here we are back again, after a wonderful weekend. Beginning of the regiment's farewell to Europe. The fellows had arranged to meet us in Nijmegen on Friday evening—thinking we could take the morning train out of Bruges. However, we could only get off on Friday afternoon at 3 pm, and have Saturday and Sunday, so it was useless thinking of the train. We had told them that we would meet them at the RTO (Railway Transport Office) in Nijmegen at 9 pm on Friday, so there was nothing for it but to use the old thumb!

We took our haversacks to the hospital in the morning, and were all ready to leave right at 3 pm. We were quite lucky, got to Ghent very promptly, then headed for Antwerp. We rode in all sorts of vehicles—at one point were perched in the back of a truck, on a bunch of old sacks. It was warm and sunny and I was tired, so stretched out and went to sleep. First thing I knew, we were in Antwerp. The most difficult part is crossing a town, and knowing where to find the road you want. We went through Breda, Tilburg, Hertogenbosch, and finally, Nijmegen. All this, with one wary eye on the watch—but believe it or not, we arrived at quarter to nine, which was fair going for 250 miles. We had ridden in trucks, staff cars, jeeps and station wagons. The last one was a Canadian truck, and they asked us where we wanted to go. We said the RTO, which must be in the railway station. They drove us to the station, or what was left of it! A great empty shell, completely gutted and shattered. We stumbled through the rubble and found the RTO, about the only organization left operating. The lads had been there, and left a note for us, saying they would return at 9 pm. We decided to look for the washroom and found the door, but surprisingly that was all that was left! There just wasn't anything on the other side of that door!

We had not told them that we would be hitchhiking, because we knew they would be horrified, but Markasino told them, so they thought we would be hours getting there. They came barrelling up in the Jeep at the appointed time, and there we were, sitting in the rubble of the ruined station. We all laughed and laughed, to think of all the very nice places we might have chosen to meet them, and we picked that!

We left Nijmegen and drove through the hills of Arnhem and through the ruins of the city. Quite battered, but no worse than France. Then on to Apeldoorn—one of the loveliest towns I've seen. Although Holland, for the most part, is extremely flat, Apeldoorn is in a valley and the highway into it is down a long hill. Really a large country town—beautiful homes—and we were especially impressed with the large bright windows—and flowers, every window is full of them! The architecture is marvellous—supposed to be the finest in the world, and quite easy to believe. Ian, being an architect, is fascinated.

Apeldoorn is full of Canadians—such a thrill to be back with our own countrymen after living in a Limey-controlled town for so long. It's all very gay. Huge signs everywhere, and arrows to the Haymarket Club, Club 99, The Stork Club, The Brass Hat. We went to "The Haymarket Club", a Canadian Officers' Club, where they had booked their room and one for Laura and me. Had a wonderful evening there, then started right after breakfast for Leeuwarden. I was really enthralled, driving into northern Holland. We stopped and took pictures of blown bridges—such colossal bridges—it seems such utter waste that they were destroyed.

We saw huge storks and got out and took pictures of them in their nests. They have tremendous nests built on the tops of tall trees. They all laughed at me when I asked if they built their own nests. Then we drove into Friesland, the oldest province in Holland. The women wear a national garb—very colourful—with close-fitting caps of a shiny silver fabric. They all ride bicycles, and I wanted to get a picture. We drove up beside one woman on a bike, Ian jumped out to get a snap, but by then she was yards up the road. We made a second attempt and got well in front of her before we stopped. She turned around and headed the other way! We finally caught her and made her understand what we wanted, and she agreed to pose for some cigarettes. But it had been pretty funny, watching Ian chasing up and down the road with the camera.

The Dutch people will do almost anything for a cigarette. It's quite incredible—if anyone throws a butt down on the street, there is a wild scramble and often several casualties. Jack left Laura sitting in the Jeep and she pulled out a package of cigarettes and the next moment, a crowd appeared from nowhere. They gathered around the car, never uttering a word, but simply staring with large round eyes, never blinking an eyelid.

Staring and curiosity seems to be a natural instinct and national characteristic of the Dutch. Grownups and children alike stand by the hour—not saying a word—just looking. Quite disconcerting at times!

We arrived in Leeuwarden at noon, and went to the Regimental Mess for lunch. It was such a thrill to see them all again. In De Haan each squadron had their own Mess, but it's different here. They are all together in a beautiful big hotel, the Amiticia, with about 100 members, some of them new, but we did know a good many of them. After lunch Jack had to go to Groningen on business so Laura went with him and Ian took me sailing.

We went to a lake about three miles out of town. A very attractive Yacht Club—restaurant upstairs, with huge windows overlooking the water. There was a good breeze blowing so we sailed all afternoon. It was quite different from our lakes at home that are usually surrounded by steep, tree-covered shores. In this very flat land the shores of the lake were only a couple of feet above the water, with open fields everywhere. It was a glorious summer day and wonderful to be on the water. We had tea in the club before going back to meet Jack and Laura for dinner. Laura and I were staying in another hotel, near the Mess, where Ian was living. He had been acting as Town Major for several weeks—relieving the Brit. officer who was on leave. Strangely enough, the Limey Town Major is the rather disagreeable one who had been in Bruges.

We had dinner at the hotel where we were staying—excellent food and nicely served. Met Captain Cahill at dinner and we were so very surprised to see each other. Had not seen him since I was first in England, before he went to Italy as Padre for one of the regiments. He looked very fit and wished to be remembered to you both.

Then it was time to go to the dance. We had donned our Blue dresses and we went over to the Mess. It looked simply beautiful. An elegant ballroom, one of the local decorators had done it up for the occasion. All the Dutch girls were in long dresses, and we were the only Canadian girls there. Some of the Dutch girls were very attractive, although they lack the chic touch seen in France and Belgium. More wholesome-looking but perhaps the lack of available make-up accounts for that. They managed to give us the once-over, looking us up and down carefully.

Everyone was there, and Laura and I hardly had a chance to dance with Jack and Ian. Needless to say, we had a merry time. They are a very fine group of fellows and we have been privileged to have become a small part of their social gatherings, and get to know so many of them. These continentals have their own style of dancing—which consists of much noise, stamping, marching and general mob scenes. They did a couple of numbers for us, and they surely put everything into it—although I must admit I was weary just watching them.

The lads' CO, Pat Black, was quite amazed when he heard we had hitchhiked part way, and said he was much ashamed to think that they had not sent transport for the girls of No. 12. He said they must certainly take us home and would they please take his Jeep! They couldn't quite believe it and thought he would forget in the morning—but no—we went to the Mess for lunch, then sat on the terrace in the sunshine. Pat appeared and said they were both to drive us home and he would not expect to see them for several days. They were moving the following day.

Leeuwarden is the capital of Friesland and a very attractive town. Many canals, and beautiful homes—so well-kept—lovely landscaping and brilliant flowers. They both had so many things to do before we left, as they would not be returning to Leeuwarden, but meeting the regiment in its new quarters in Deventer, near Apeldoorn. In the midst of it all, Ian's batman, Scottie, appeared, almost in tears, saying that he had just received notice of a transfer and he was having a fit. He had been with Ian for well over four years, and hated to leave now. However, they managed to get it cancelled, so we went off and left Scottie quite happy.

We finally got home, fairly late, but we made it to Bruges that night, and we were very glad, as Sheila was leaving the following morning, Monday, for England, and we did want to see her before she left. We had breakfast in Sheila's room and Laura and I surely hated to see her go. We have not had a chance to miss her yet, as Ian and Jack were still here. But now that they are gone and we are back to work again, we are going to miss her a great deal. It's a shame that the three of us could not have gone together.

Tuesday, the four of us went out to the coast, to those marvellous beaches, for another picnic. Back to the Mess for dinner and later, off to Ostende to the new Circle Club. I had told you about the original Circle Club; well, this is a new one, like something out of a Hollywood set. Looking out over the beach and ocean. A magnificent room, exquisitely decorated, excellent band. A heavenly spot.

Music has been an important part of life over here. Many of the bands play the pre-war favourites of the Big Bands at home, "Stardust", "Deep Purple", "String of Pearls", "Moonlight Serenade", "Sentimental Journey" etc., also the recent ones—"White Cliffs of Dover", and "Lili Marlene", that the troops brought back from Italy. And now, the newer nostalgic ones have all come to mean so much, especially as the war draws to a close, and we will all be leaving, getting on with our lives, knowing in our hearts that we will probably never see many of these war-time friends who have become so close and dear—"I'll See You Again", "We'll Meet Again", "I'll Be Seeing You", take on a poignant meaning for all of us.

Laura and I are beginning to get the urge to go home. We have been hoping to wait until our unit closes, but that seems to be so indefinite. Every time we evacuate and the place begins to look empty, we admit another huge convoy and begin all over again.

Every once in a while, this life all seems like a fantasy. I know it will surely seem like a long-ago dream after we have been home a couple of months. There are so many amusing little incidents. When Laura and I were walking through Antwerp, debating about our directions, two Yanks bounced up in a Jeep. They were floored when they heard we were going to Nijmegen, and screamed from their Jeep that if we would join them for supper, then they would take us. We were not interested, as we were in a hurry to get there and were not going to waste time. Whereupon the Yanks shouted across the main street of Antwerp, "Do you know what we are going to have for supper? Delicious, juicy pork chops!" We laughed and almost drooled, but continued on our way.

Time to get to bed or I will never get up in the morning.

Much love, Dears, Lois

June 24th, 1945
Dearest Mother and Dad:

So very glad you met Jack's sister Win, and liked her so much. I had a lovely letter from his sister Dot, in Toronto, so must answer it.

To get back to this week, I made another trip to Holland, strangely enough. You see, when Ian and Jack returned to the regiment after being here, they took Ruth and Pearl with them, for a couple of days. That made it necessary for Alec and Hugh to bring the gals home—so they were here for a couple of days, and in the meantime, word arrived that various officers were going to Canada, leaving Monday, Ian included.

Alec and Hugh insisted that I go back with them this weekend. After a little persuasion, I grabbed my bag and went. We didn't have so far to go this trip as the regiment is now set up in Deventer, near Apeldoorn.

What a beautiful spot that is. We can certainly learn much from the Dutch. Their cities are really a picture. So beautifully laid out—wide streets and boulevards—trees—most modern and attractive houses, with large bright windows. All so well kept, freshly painted and neat and trim. Attractive terraces, flowers everywhere, garden furniture and bright umbrellas on the large lawns.

It was a gorgeous weekend, hot and sunny the whole time. We had dinner at the Haymarket Club and I stayed there again. It must have been a popular peacetime hotel. Then we went to the Stork Club. I do wish you could see it. A country club, on the outskirts of Apeldoorn. The clubhouse itself is on a hill, with a beautiful stone terrace, then in front it is all sand and pine trees—rolling sand, with great lagoons built into the natural setting. These lagoons are really huge swimming pools—equipped with slides, spring-boards, rafts, etc. So much more attractive than the usual small tanks we have at home.

It's all very picturesque and certainly a popular spot for Canadians. We danced there, too. A lovely floor, and I saw so many people I knew. All the 17th Hussars and the R.C.D.s and other regiments we know well, too. Was very glad I had gone back to see the lads again before they leave. They will not all be going just yet, but the whole regiment, the 12th Manitoba Dragoons, have been part of our life over here, especially this last year on the continent. We shared something with them that nowhere will we ever have again. Days when we were all busy, tired, scared, with death all around us, and the guns thundering not too far away. They were in combat, and we were here, seeing it all from a different angle—but still able to understand how much a few hours' relaxation could mean to them. A very precious and vital part of our lives that we will all leave behind when we leave the continent. Ian and I have been dear friends, have had so many good times and laughs, something like Gerry and I last year in England, but am so glad he is going home to Vancouver, as he has been over since the very first.

To get back to the weekend, I had intended to come back on Saturday—some of the unit gals were up there, too, and had promised to bring me home. However, Ian said if I stayed till Sunday, he would send me home by air. We had another evening to dine and dance at the Haymarket and once again saw so many familiar faces. Then this morning we went to the airport and met two friends of his, both from Montreal, and flying to Brussels too. We all went on the same plane, then Johnny and I went to the Atlanta for lunch. My train to Bruges did not leave until 4.40 pm, so we had a couple of hours to walk around Brussels. Then headed for the Gare de Midi (station) and on the way found a fair, so we rode some of the rides. Then I caught the train and got to Bruges for dinner. Air transport is surely the way to travel. The drive to Apeldoorn took six hours, steady driving, on Friday, and we came home today in 50 minutes.

Had a letter from Gerry today. He is back on the Continent again, after an extended leave in Oregon and California. He is in Bavaria, so a long way from Bruges. Am so thankful that he made it through the war.

Do hope we can get to England before too long. All I want now is my leave to Paris and then I will be ready to go.

I am not sure how long Jack will be there and I certainly want to get to London before he goes to Canada. We are planning a trip to Ireland together, if we have leave before going home. Am surely looking forward to some time with him.

Now June 28th, 1945. Letters from both of you today, and you mentioned Portland, that we might have a holiday at the cottage if Jack and I are home in time. That would be heavenly if we make it before the end of August or early September, and have a chance to loaf and rest before we think of the wedding and shopping, etc. The thought of being out of uniform and perfectly free to do as I please—is quite a thrill. True, it's been wonderful being here and we have had a great many advantages and been able to go places and do things, in uniform, that we could not have done otherwise. Still, it will be great to be free again—though I've no doubt we will all feel a little lost.

Ian called me last night from Ostende. He was there with two other Dragoons—on their way to U.K. and thence to Canada. They were so disgusted—so near to Bruges and yet they were strictly C.B. and unable to get here, as they were to leave this morning. The regiment was parading this morning in Amsterdam, it was a shame they had to miss it. Then the regiment is coming to Ostende on the 7, 8, 9 of July. They liberated this part of Belgium last fall, now are coming back to be honoured and entertained. It should be quite exciting—they are having a dance in the Circle Club, then later in the month, "C" Squadron is visiting Bruges to open Manitoba Bridge, when it's completed.

Much love, Hope to see you soon. Lois

July 2nd, 1945
Dearest Folks:

Yesterday was an interesting day. Laura and I went to a Belgian affair with Chub and Ad, two of our M.O.s. We went to the Hansons'—did I ever tell you about Willey and Susie Hanson? We have been to their home several times before. They are a charming couple and live in Ste. Croix, a suburb of Bruges. Yesterday, Ste. Croix had a victory parade. It was mostly the Resistance groups taking part in it and Willey was one of them, so most interested. We went to their place at 4 pm, saw the parade and had tea. There were numerous people there and their two little girls, Nicole and Jacqueline. They are the cutest pair. Especially Jacqueline, the baby, just two, blonde with the most engaging grin. We left them and went to a street dance, all very gay and colourful. Then back to Willey and Susie's for supper, then rolled back the rugs and danced. The two little girls sat at a small table in the dining room for supper. They are very well behaved. Then they went upstairs and came down in their housecoats and said goodnight to everyone. Jacqueline liked Chub especially, and they speak French, so she called him Chobbie. It was lovely to see the Hansons again. They are such friendly, nice people, the kind I would like to remember and be able to see if we ever come back over here.

Thursday we went to Brussels to see the Navy Show. It was excellent and we all enjoyed it. Twenty-five of us went from the hospital. Friday was my day off so, Goody, Barb, Eleanor and I stayed over. Goody was just mentioned in despatches; suddenly, we have a celebrity in our midst. She is a great person and we are all so happy for her. We were having lunch at the Atlanta and there was Captain Legate, our Red Cross Commissioner, with Anna Neagle, so we were thrilled to meet her.

(Anna Neagle was a British film star of that era.)

Letter from Ian (Dragoon) from England and they expect to be stranded there for two months! You can imagine how fed up they are, when they were yanked out of the regiment on such very short notice, just now, when the Dragoons are being feted and entertained everywhere. They are in Aldershot and say that shipping is badly tied up. They all applied to return to the continent, but I guess CMHQ must think they are quite crazy, so turned them all down.

We go to the coast whenever we have time off. The beaches are marvellous and the surf delightful. So much warmer than the North Sea was last summer. The back of the beach is lined with small cabins. You rent one for the afternoon, so you can change, and they are equipped with deck chairs and U.S. Army blankets! Strictly Black Market!

You certainly see the briefest of bathing suits on these Belgian beaches. My green suit and also my white one are positively old-fashioned. These models are tiny bras and very skimpy tights. Most of the children don't wear suits at all, but just run naked.

Did I tell you about the Dutchmen in Leeuwarden? We were quite amused. Many of them speak English very well, but they do get mixed up. They greet you with outstretched hand, smile and say enthusiastically "Goodbye". A trifle disconcerting. We were leaving the hotel where Ian had been living, as Town Major; the regiment was moving, so Jack and Ian explained to the maître d'hôtel that they would not be back—whereupon he stuck out his hand and said "You are leaving? I won't see you again? Hello, Captain!" I suppose we would make more mistakes if we tackled their lingo, but they speak very well and are quite nonchalant, so it surprises us when they mix up the "hellos" and "goodbyes".

The former Manitoba Dragoon Colonel, who led the regiment when we first met them, Colonel James Roberts, is now a Brigadier, heading up the brigade. He is to be married to a Dutch girl shortly. We met her at New Year's. Quite charming. Many weddings in Holland and Belgium.

July 10th, 1945
Dearest Family:

Jack is going to Ireland again. He has been travelling quite a bit. Was down in St. Ives, Cornwall, for several days' leave, with Bev McCauley and Bert Simmons. It sounds like a glorious spot, and here am I, on the wrong side of the channel!

Have read several articles recently, on war criminals, etc. As yet, it seems that not very drastic measures are being taken against Germany.

Remember, we said that when we won the war, there would no longer be a Germany! What a futile hope that was! Surely hate to think of what might have become of all of us, if they had come out on top! I guess it is just not in us to be cruel and tough—or perhaps the real truth lies in the fact that we are all sick of the horrors of war, and just cannot be bothered taking the time and trouble to settle Germany once and for all. All the dilly-dallying about trials for war criminals seems so utterly useless, when the stack of evidence of crimes committed during the last six years, and before that, is tremendous. Enough of this, but it certainly causes much resentment over here.

Much love, Lois

July 13th, 1945
Dearest Family:

Tomorrow is the big celebration for the Dragoons in Ostende. The dance is at the Circle Club. The bar is "Le Manitoba" and the town is really doing it up in a big way.

It's now July 16th. Another convoy is arriving today. Do wish people would stop getting in accidents or getting sick—so we could go home!

It was a busy weekend. The Dragoons arrived on Saturday and we went to the parade in Ostende. It was a beautiful day and the whole town turned out for the occasion. Quite a thrill to see the regiment, all marching through those streets—between shattered buildings—where they had fought so valiantly, not so long ago. They had turned in their armoured cars and most of their armoured vehicles, so were all on foot. They looked great and we Canadians were so proud. Everywhere there were great signs—"To our Canadian Liberators"—the boys always get a kick out of it. They were treated magnificently all weekend by the people of Ostende. That town is under British occupation, so they were doubly glad to welcome the Canadians back.

After the parade, we went swimming, then back to Bruges to get dressed for the evening. There was a special dinner for the officers and men, so they dropped us six ladies at the Officers' Club and we had dinner there, then went down to the beach for another swim. It was terribly hot and seemed the only way we could get any relief at all was to head for the ocean. The party lasted well into the night and we all ended up with another swim. The water was so phosphorescent. If you splashed, it was like a thousand fireflies. Quite spectacular.

Sunday we had the afternoon off, so we went back to Knocke, to cool off again, in the surf. There was a Mess party for Ad in the evening. He is leaving tomorrow. It's rather sad to say goodbye to so many friends at No. 12, both the M.O.s and the Sisters. We have had a marvellous time together, especially our original group that came over from England. There has been a great sense of camaraderie among the girls, and will hope to see or keep in touch with some of them in the years ahead; however, it will be difficult, as we all go our separate ways.

It was a great weekend, but an exhausting one.

Good night, dears, Much love, Lois

LEAVE IN PARIS

July 17th, 1945
Dearest Family:

Since my last letter, Capt. Legate and Col. Frost paid us a visit. Evidently, No. 12 will not be going as soon as we hoped. I am disappointed and hate to think of Jack going home before I get to England. We are in a beautiful spot for the summer. Of course, it can't compare with Canada, but the Belgian coast is a very popular summer resort area. We have transportation to the beaches three or four times a week, and there is always the street-car, which is a 45-minute run, so very handy.

Now it is July 22nd, and I will continue. Appreciated your note about the wedding, Dad, and am so anxious to get there and plan it all. I hope to have a little time when I first get home, to rest and relax. Don't want to rush. Seems to me I've been rushing for two years!

Laura and I are leaving for gay Paree this Wednesday. We will have four full days there, so are very excited about it and so glad we are able to go together.

We are quite busy again. The hospital is filling up rapidly, and we are back on the old hours. Although I hate it when we have only a few patients—the wards are so dull then. Some of the boys are so funny—guess I have not told you much about them recently. One little Winnipeg Rifle told me some tales yesterday. He's a cute lad, about twenty, and a tough little egg. Before V-Day they were fighting through Germany—picking up loot where they could. He captured five mink coats, brand new, from a fashionable German fur shop. Three were jackets and two full-length coats.

His regiment was going into attack and he had the coats in a bag on his back, and carried them all through that attack and finally came out alive—complete with coats. He sent them home in five separate parcels and his mother nearly had a fit each time another coat rolled in. His whole family will be sporting mink this winter.

Mary is coming back to work with us tomorrow. Her job in the OR is finished, and this will enable Laura and me to have our Paris trip together. We had a cable from Sheila and she is safely back in Montreal. Lucky gal.

Had a letter from Mrs. Reford, from Basingstoke. No. 1 Canadian Neurological and Plastic Surgery Hospital at Hackwood is closed, as Lord Camrose wanted his estate again. She said they are smashing all the Nissen huts with bulldozers. There must have been twenty or thirty of them.

Much love, Lois

July 30th, 1944.
Dearest Family:

We have just returned from Paris. It was an absolutely marvellous five days. We left here Wednesday at noon. Went to Brussels and saw Capt. Legate at Red Cross HQ. Then to the Canadian Club, the Atlanta, in Brussels, for dinner. We were sitting there quietly, when in walked four Dragoons, all Canada bound. We were thrilled to see them. It seems the Dragoons always turn up and look after us. We had much luggage, so they took it to the station and checked it for us. The train left at 10.30 pm, and we danced at the Atlanta for a while, then wandered into a sidewalk café near the station until it was time to board.

Capt. Legate had reserved a sleeping compartment for us several days earlier, and we assumed we would be all set. However, when we got to the

RTO, we were informed that a Matron, carrying a crown on each shoulder, had out-ranked our priority. We still had one berth left, but it was an extremely hot night, and they are very narrow. The continental trains are quite clean and comfortable, and have two bunks, upper and lower, in each compartment. Laura had an upper above a French-Canadian matron, and mine had been the upper in the next compartment. When we discovered that I had lost my priority, we asked the Canadian Sgt. at RTO to keep us in mind if the Matron did not show up.

We were hoping she would not appear, but about ten minutes before train time, she rolled up, with a Brigadier and Colonel in tow. We gave up hope and were both preparing to climb into the single upper, when the Sgt. dashed up and said there had been a cancellation, and I could be "Mrs. Ferguson". We never did find out who she was, as the French Matron very kindly offered to take Mrs. Ferguson's accommodation and let us have the compartment to ourselves. It would have been tiring sitting up all night, and as it turned out, we had a good sleep and arrived in Paris at 9 am, all set to do the town. There were buses waiting to take us to the leave hotel, the Metropolitan. Then we made appointments to have our hair done and manicures, to get all glamoured up.

We spent the first morning in the beauty parlour, then off to Canada Corner, the Knights of Columbus, to arrange our itinerary. That organization is surely doing a good job. Over here, they seem to be non-denominational and have a wonderful set-up, both in the hospitals and in their various centres. They have a shopping service, arrange all sorts of tours, get theatre tickets, arrange hospitality and a hundred and one other small things. Provide French girls for the Canadian lads. One Essex Scottish Corporal was sitting patiently while they found him a Baroness. It seems that his pal had taken a Countess to dinner and he was determined to go one better! They found him one.

We arranged our leave, then wandered around town—up the Champs Elysées—what a beautiful street! Parisians may well be proud of Paris—such a blessing that it was spared. It's hard to believe that any one city can be quite so lovely. It is wonderfully laid out with modern stately buildings.

We went to tea at the Canadian Officers' Club. The Canadians have done very well for themselves in Paris. It's a very fine club, with large lounges, dance floor, dining room, bars, etc., all exquisitely furnished and attractive. We met two chaps that we knew, 3rd Anti-Tank. One was Mickey Phair, whose family have a summer place near Curriers, at Stoney Lake. His sister is one of our Corps girls. Last year I met his brother Bill at Basingstoke. His friend Rae was very nice too. They have a Jeep, so they took us around Paris.

Thursday night Laura and I went to the Opéra Comique, to see Tosca. *It was excellent and we loved it. Friday we had the morning to wander around, and did some shopping, although prices are exorbitant. Had lunch with Mick and Rae, then Laura and I went to a fashion show at Paquins, in the Rue de la Paix. What a thrill that was! Of course it really broke our morale, in our old khaki skirts and shirts. Beautiful clothes of all types—but quite out of the question. I priced one smart grey suit and it was 20,000 fr., roughly $500. We wondered if they ever sold anything, but guess they do as the people on the streets are beautifully dressed.*

Rue de la Paix and Place Vendôme are truly fascinating, as most of the well-known cosmetic houses are in these streets, also Rue Royale. We just had a hey-day. We were in Molyneux, Schiaparelli's, Dana's, Renoir, Elizabeth Arden, Molinard's, Ciro's, etc. There were Yanks galore, all stocking up on perfume. We wore our Blue dresses most of the time, as they were cooler, but we seemed to cause quite a bit of interest, as no one knew what we were. In our khaki, without jackets and Canada badges, everyone thought we were British. The Fashion showrooms are magnificent, and such gorgeous things. Molyneux is fabulous, and Schiaparelli, so exciting.

We met the lads at the club, for dinner, and then planned to do the hot spots. Evidently no one goes to Montmartre or Pigalle, the night club districts, until midnight, so we danced at the club first. Then the Canadian Provost Marshall, a friend of theirs, took us around the town. A marvellous escort, as he had complete entrée to all the spots, and believe me, there were plenty. Do wish you could have seen the hair and hairdos—every colour imaginable and stacked in great high pompadours on top of the heads. It was the bright pink hair that really shook me.

We began at the Shanghai, a completely Oriental atmosphere. A huge stained-glass front, in Chinese design, with the light shining through from inside. Most striking. All very gaudy, gay and artificial, but fun. The usual floor show. One number was a tap dancer, in black face make-up, wearing a bright Scottish plaid zoot suit, and singing with a French accent, in Oriental surroundings.

Champagne seems to be what everyone orders. It is about 1,000 frs ($25) a bottle. Touring the night spots could be expensive, but most of the lads are loaded down with Buckshee (loot) money, so it doesn't mean a thing to them, because they cannot change it into English or Canadian funds, but can only spend it over here. It's just like handing out pieces of paper. We went from one night club to another, all a little different, noisy, colourful, crowded. Saw the Can-Can in several places. It's a great dance and so much a part of Paris. Music is so gay and fast, and costumes bright and pretty, and the dancers so enthusiastic and talented. Our Provost Marshall friend knew all the best places and *we were fortunate to have him guiding us around. So many Yanks with fascinating French girls. Pigalle is quite a place—a world of its own. Then we hailed a horse and carriage and bounced home, in the early hours of the morning. Surely an evening to remember.*

Saturday morning we slept in. Then went out and hiked around again. We went along the Rue de la Paix, across the Place de l'Opéra, down Rue des Italiens and off into the side streets. Then down Rue Royale, Rue Rivoli, the Concorde and eventually across the Seine to Quai D'Orsay. The weather was beautiful and it was rather thrilling to be able to walk around Paris. We stopped at a couple of sidewalk cafes. They are fun. It's just like a passing show, to sit in one for half an hour. We met Mick and Rae for lunch again. Then they got the Jeep and we did a tour of the city—with guide book clutched in one hand. We saw Napoleon's Tomb—really a magnificent edifice—the Trocadero, the Eiffel Tower, Cleopatra's Needle, the Louvre, Le Tuileries, Notre Dame, the Madeleine, Sacre Coeur, etc. Also drove through Montparnasse and the Latin Quarter. We didn't have a chance to go into the Louvre, and I was disappointed about that, but will definitely come back to Paris sometime, with Jack, and we will see all those things then.

Paris is surely in a class by itself. I am truly grateful that we had the opportunity to have leave there before going home. It is such a fantastic city. Utterly charming, but almost unreal. On the surface everything is so lavish and absolutely luxurious, but underneath, I'm sure the majority are actually starving. Food and cigarettes are at a premium and the black market flourishes.

We had stopped at the railway station to see if we could get sleeper accommodation for the trip back to Brussels. There was already a long list ahead of us, so we did not have much hope. They dropped us at our hotel for a quick rest and bath, before they returned to take us back to the club for dinner. Rae's brother had arrived from Brussels and was with them. He had a staff car, and was returning to Brussels very early Monday morning, so he offered to take us. It was just too good to be true, and certainly solved the problem of having to sit up all night on the train.

Laura and I suddenly remembered that we had tickets for the Folies Bergère for Sat. night. They had already seen it, and we said we would not bother going, but they insisted, saying we must have wanted to see it, if we had the tickets. After dinner, they drove us down to the theatre—thinking it was a huge joke, the gals going to the Folies, while the lads went back to the club for a quiet drink! Arranged to pick us up at 10 pm, figuring we would have seen enough by then.

I was always under the impression that it was a night club, but it's not. It's a theatre and a truly beautiful one. A gorgeous lobby and bar, all decorated in light and bright colours. We were both really thrilled with it. The costumes were marvellous—so lavish, with very tall and elegant headdresses. Silks, satins, sheers, glorious colours. The girls were tall and stately, in spike heels. It was really a treat to see a show like that. It was all so well staged, the scenery was fantastic and the lighting seemed to make the whole thing. Very professional. We were just spell-bound. It was 10 pm before we knew it.

There were two G.I.s standing behind our box, and we had told them we would be leaving before it was over. They looked surprised and said in Brooklynese, "Oh yeah, who are you kidding!" When we got up to leave and gave them our seats, they eyed us strangely, as if we were definitely wacky—walking out before the finale of the Folies Bergère! The dancing did not have strict precision and the routines were not remarkable, but the whole effect of colour, lighting and staging made it quite spectacular. When we came out, Mick, Rae and Cecil were waiting—still most amused about the whole situation—of escorting us to the door of the Folies and then meekly coming back to call for us. We had another evening of night clubbing. I thought we had seen most of them, but no, we had barely scratched the surface. Was quite delighted to see a few more performances of the Can-can.

I must tell you about the wedding in Paris. One of the Sisters from No. 10 Hospital was in Paris on university leave a short while ago. She met a Parisian family and when they heard she was being married soon, insisted that she have the wedding in Paris, so they could have the reception at their home, for her.

It was all laid on and the bride and groom were to come from Holland, the day of the wedding. Bud Hoffman, who was with us in the days of Bayeux, is now Head of the Educational Services in Paris for Canada, so he arranged most of it for them. He got a bus and gathered up a load of Canadians who were taking the university courses and transported them to the church, then it would be full of Canucks and have a friendly atmosphere.

There was no sign of the bride and groom, and everyone waited and waited. Finally, after a very long time, they arrived. Everyone waited again, while the bride washed her face and got into another dress. The groom had been in a Jeep accident during the week, so he hobbled up to the altar, on crutches, with one leg in a huge cast! The Minister was all set to start, when he realized that they had overlooked the necessity of a best man. After much whispering and mumbling, the Minister asked Bud if he would do the honours. Whereupon he was introduced to the groom, who by this time was a nervous wreck. They proceeded with the ceremony, and from then on it went beautifully, and the reception was wonderful. This had happened just before we got to Paris, and Bud filled us in on the details. Said he was almost a basket case before it was over!

Sunday morning we slept in again. Had a lazy time and lunched with the boys at the club. Cecil was with us, so took us all for a drive in the afternoon. We went to Versailles. It was a warm sunny day, and a wonderful time to see the palace, in all its glory. Almost beyond description—the graceful Louis furniture and exquisite tapestries. Very ornate, and surely depicts the luxuries of life at court in France, during the reigns of the Louis's. The gardens, terraces and landscaping are marvellous, everything so carefully trimmed and manicured. We spent most of the afternoon exploring the interior and enjoying the walks through the gardens and ornamental ponds.

The Bois de Boulogne is the loveliest spot. It is on the outskirts of Paris, on the way to Versailles. Country and woodland, close to the city, yet it is quite wild and natural looking. Acres of wooded territory with walks, lakes, trees and flowers. Versailles is a quaint old town. We were there last September, but at that time did not see the palace, but went to the American 12th Army HQ.

Cecil had his Sgt. Major with him and he didn't know anyone in Paris, so one of the other lads loaned him a jacket and he became a Captain for the evening, and came with us. We had dinner and stayed at the club for the dance that evening. In Paris, you really have to dine at the leave hotels or Officers' Club. Food is very scarce in civilian establishments.

That was our final day in Paris and Cecil picked us up at 5.00 am Monday morning. It was pitch black at that hour and as we sailed up Champs Elysées. There was a great crash and bang, as we ran into a chair in the middle of the road. Fortunately, there was no one sitting in it! Such a strange place to leave an iron park chair, in the middle of the Champs Elysées!

It was a very pleasant drive in the staff car, which is quite a luxury, when one has become accustomed to Jeeps and half-tracks. The countryside was beautiful in the early dawn, with the sun shining on the grain fields. We arrived in Brussels in time to take the afternoon train to Bruges. It took us Monday evening and most of Tuesday to recuperate, and it has been a hectic week.

A letter from Jack says he is going to Germany for several weeks, to inspect Marine machinery in the Kiel area. That will delay his trip home, and he sounds excited about the trip to Germany, too. He is flying to Hanover, but said that he might be able to return to England via Holland and Belgium, so am keeping my fingers crossed.

Went to a party in Ghent, for our Quarter Master, Bill Thurwell. Twelve of us went from the hospital, to the Canadian Club in Ghent, as we bid farewell to yet another good friend.

Thursday night, Chub (one of our Medical Officers who has been a very good friend) took me dinner dancing at the club here in Bruges. At the next table was a large party of British Tank Corps officers. They were leaving shortly for Burma and were surely celebrating. Being regimental types, they were more human and nicer than the ones we usually see in Bruges. They insisted that we join their party, which until then was strictly stag. Every once in a while, I realize that the war is far from over and that the Eastern situation will be pretty tough. Unless you have something like that still ahead, you lose that urgent feeling that every moment is precious and that you must get the very most out of everything—living each minute to the fullest. These lads, going to Burma, still have that feeling and were making the most of their last few nights in Belgium.

We got a big kick out of them. They were singing all sorts of songs and when they got to their own regimental one, they all got out on the dance floor, on their knees, one behind the other, forming a chain, with their hands on the shoulders of the one in front of them, and went around the room. There was one very nice lad, Don Collie—I called him Junior, as it seemed to suit him. He was from Guilford, not far from Basingstoke, so on the strength of being almost neighbours, we decided to have dinner together on Saturday.

But I seem to be getting ahead of myself. Friday I went out with an officer patient. He was being discharged the following day. He picked me up at 5 pm. It was a glorious day, so we drove to Blankenberghe. He let me pinch-hit for his regular driver, Elmer, and again I had the fun of driving a Jeep. He is a very nice lad. A Sports officer with an armoured regiment in Groningen. Usually I stay strictly away from the officer patients, because the officers' ward is the hardest to look after. Perhaps because they are used to giving orders, usually they are quite demanding, expect the most and show the least appreciation. We walked miles along the beach, climbing the sand dunes.

We had dinner at the Officers' Club, then went on to the Circle Club for the dance. It was a fun evening. He is returning to his unit tomorrow.

Saturday, I kept getting messages all day, saying that "Junior" would be calling at 7 pm. It seemed to be the joke of the switchboard as well as the Mess. Two of his friends, lads that had been at the party on Thursday, wanted to come too, so Laura and Marg Simmons joined us. We all went to the club for dinner and had a very good evening. They were extremely nice fellows and we surely had many laughs. The chap Marg was with turned out to be Sir Philip, no less. But what's a title here or there? We brought them back to the Mess and all went to the kitchen and fixed coffee, toast and eggs.

First thing I knew, Junior had the Matron's table napkin tied over his head, babushka fashion!

They were leaving Monday morning for Ostende, en route to England for leave, before going East. They were CB (Confined to Barracks) in the Transit Camp, so promptly climbed the wall and returned to Bruges. We all went to the club again for dinner and danced and more or less repeated the evening before. It was really a thrill to meet some Brits who were polite and easy to get along with. They are still totally different from Canadians and I guess they will never understand our sense of humour.

Got into bed at 6.30 tonight. The night life is beginning to catch up with me. However, here in Bruges, everything seems to come in bunches, and it will probably be quite dull for weeks now.

Jack is on his way to Germany. Wish I could join him for a couple of days. I miss seeing him. We have hardly seen each other since we became engaged. He is a pretty special fellow and I am anxious for you to get to know him. I need more time with him, too. We have never had much time together, but suddenly, I realized that he was the person I wanted to spend the rest of my life with.

He is hoping to see Mar in Germany. I had a letter from Mar. Had tried to get in touch with him when I was in Brussels for the Navy Show, but he had left that very day. Strangely enough, he had seen me at the Navy Show the evening before, and couldn't catch my eye. I had written to ask him if he could find out anything about Webb, Laura's Air Force beau, who was reported missing. Mar said that there is very little hope, as he got a report from one of Webb's squadron, who had seen him go down in flames. Laura felt very badly, but I guess it is better to know the worst, as "Missing" is so indefinite. (Mar Sherwood was an old family friend, also a ski friend of Jack's.)

Well, it is high time for me to get some sleep.
Much love, my Dears, Lois

August 8th, 1945
Dearest Mother and Dad:

The yellow bathing suit arrived on Monday—quite a speedy trip. It came before the blue form saying it was on the way. I just love it and it fits perfectly. Now all I need is some good warm weather, so I can sport it at Knocke. Weather has been rather miserable of late—cold and rainy. We were lucky to have those marvellous warm bright days in Paris.

I had a letter from Jack today and he will be on his way to Germany later this week. Then he should return at the end of August, so if I can make it to England, we could go to Ireland early in September, so it all may work out. A large evacuation went out today and hoping to send more on Monday; it looks more hopeful.

Evidently, Lease-Lend with Belgium ends the end of October, and after that we will have to pay for everything—buildings we occupy, heat, light, water and local labour. Now, it is all taken care of by the Belgian government but that all ends 6 months after the cessation of hostilities—which should be November 8th.

We had intended to go to Utrecht this weekend. Rae and Mickey Phair had asked us to come up, but Mary has been sick again and is still a patient, so Laura and I could not get away together. They were going to send transport for us, and we had to call them last evening to tell them we couldn't go. It took us about an hour to get the call through. We had to go through so many places—our own military switchboard, then Ghent, Antwerp, Eindhoven, Nijmegen, The Hague and finally Utrecht, and then their Mess. Twice, after we got right through to Utrecht, we got the wrong number!

It's now August 14th. A year ago today we landed on the beaches of Normandy. Laura and I were laughing about it last night, because, secretly, we had both expected to be shot at, then we landed on that peaceful, sunny French Peninsula, with the fighting a good 20 miles away.

Is the Japanese war really over? We get so little news, and then it is hard to tell if it is authentic. I imagine it is now just a question of days. The lads here who did not volunteer for Burma are surely kicking themselves, as those who did are almost all in Canada and now will not have to go.

The Churchill rebuff was a little difficult to understand, but quite typical of his country. They don't seem to appreciate a good thing when they have it.

It's now August 15th, and another V-Day, and the final one, too. Guess I haven't grasped the full significance of it. It all seemed to happen so fast, and I certainly thought that the Japs would fight to the last man.

Imagine being in New York or, better still, San Francisco today. Such excitement, and now the Yanks can really celebrate freely. I'm sure they couldn't have celebrated the European Victory wholeheartedly, as they still had so much ahead of them. Now we can all quite truthfully and humbly say—God Bless America!

It was a quiet day at the hospital. In fact we had been there for an hour before we even heard the news. The Medical Officers had heard it in the middle of the night. Their Mess is in the hospital, while ours is downtown. From all reports, they evidently had a wild celebration, so the Sgts. and NCO's felt quite justified in getting all steamed up today. We had a church service this morning and then everyone went back to work. Somehow or other, V-Days depress me more than anything, as I can't help thinking of all the lives lost.

We still have many patients—but our job was really finished when the last battle casualty left the hospital. Now they are all accidents or medicals, many with VD. Some of the lads are so young, it's a shame. Thank goodness for penicillin so they can get it cleaned up before they go home. So we will be glad to leave. There is a possibility that we may have a short leave in Amsterdam before we go back to U.K. Of course, what we really want, more than anything, is to get home. Perhaps the Eastern situation will release more ships for all of us. I certainly hope so. Boys coming down from Nijmegen, the Canadian Repat. Depot, tell stories of how their sailing dates are set and cancelled again and again.

Then the Maple Leaf *is full of accounts of thousands of English brides, and more thousands of children, going to Canada. While we all sit and wait. There is plenty of resentment, especially from the lads who have been away from their Canadian families for five years—while these English babes probably saw their husbands within the last year, yet they are getting the priority.*

Unfortunately, this war, instead of uniting our nation with the mother country, seems to have widened the gap, has served to create a much greater nationalism for Canada. The U.S. and Canada should have such marvellous futures—so much potential. Surely hope we don't waste our opportunities!

Canada has always been inclined to be overly modest, perhaps because we had a small population and did not have enough confidence or belief in our own capabilities. The Yanks have always patted themselves on the back and were never slow to tell you what a great country they have. Sometimes we resented it and thought they bragged unnecessarily—but after this war, they have surely proved themselves—with the great flood of men and material given so generously.

Britain, on the other hand, did not blow and brag so openly as the Yanks—but rather by subtle means managed to instill in the minds of the peoples of the world, especially the dominions and colonies, the fact that Britain was definitely superior, and anything British made was certainly best. It never occurred to us to question any of the nonsense that was part of our education, but merely accepted it and placed Britain on a lofty pedestal. At the same time, being away from our own country, we have been able to view it in a different light and new perspective, and realize with surprise and a good deal of pride, that Canada, in relation to the size of her population, has done a tremendous job—both in men, materials and organization. So now it is time for us to wake up and tell people what a wonderful country we have, because if we don't, no one else will!

We are having a cocktail party and buffet supper and dance in the Mess tonight, to mark our anniversary of a year on the continent. Ad is coming back for the party and it will be great to see him. He has only been able to get back a couple of times since he left the unit.

We have our Amsterdam leave approved for August 30th for 6 days. Am afraid Jack will not be able to make it over here, after all. In yesterday's letter, he said that his trip to Germany had been delayed so long that now it was almost out of the question. Said if I could get to England, early in September, we would probably still be able to make it to Ireland. We will try to go to County Cavan. Please ask Grandmother if she knows the name of the town where she was born. I know she was only four when she left, so it would be difficult for her to remember much about it.

You asked about the wedding. Not too large an affair. In Chalmers United Church, then a nice reception, wherever you decide. You did mention the Quebec Suite at the Château Laurier. Sounds marvellous. I realize that a date is very important for you to line up these places, so will cable as soon as things become definite over here.

Bye now, and much love, Lois

HOMEWARD BOUND

August 22nd, 1945
Dearest Mother and Dad:

Laura and I are coming home! I still can't believe it is true, but word came through today, from Brussels, that two girls will arrive on Friday to replace us. We had asked Capt. Legate, when he was here, to see what he could do to get us home—because there seems little hope of the unit closing.

Our Amsterdam leave has gone out the window. However, we would surely prefer to be heading home, and leave the day after tomorrow, August 24th, for Brussels, then hope to fly to London the next day. I just can't get over it. It's too good to be true, and we will get there before Jack leaves. We should have a week together in England, and may get to Ireland, after all.

Will cable from England, when we get our sailing date, then will call from Halifax or New York or Quebec, wherever we land, so you can get to Montreal to meet me. If we arrive in the evening, we could stay with Aunty Marjorie and family overnight and drive home the following day. Will express my luggage right through to Ottawa, as I am sure we would have a problem getting it all in the car.

We are really thrilled to be leaving together. We finished our work this afternoon. Marion Bigelow called from Red Cross HQ about 3 pm to give us the good news. We saw the Matron and Colonel Fraser immediately and will take tomorrow off to pack, then come back to the hospital Friday morning to do the rounds and wish the patients, the Sisters, the O.R.s and the M.O.s farewell. Isn't it exciting? My stomach does a flip just thinking about it! Will surely hope to see you by the end of September.

Everything is going into that old trunk in quite a hurry.

So much love to you both—can hardly wait to see you! Lois

August 30th, 1945
Dearest Family:

Here we are, safely settled in London. Seems ages since I have written, but with moving about there has been little opportunity. Marion and Margie Ambrose, her driver, arrived Friday about noon bringing Ginny Cook and Val Kerr, the two Corps girls who are replacing us.

Laura and I had done a mighty quick job of packing and settling up everything. The thought of going home surely spurred us on. I was able to sell my bike. Our Batman looked after it for me. The maids in the hotel were all fighting for it.

We left so suddenly—after looking forward to it for so long. What made it easier to bid farewell to our beloved No. 12 Hospital was the fact that many of our original and dear friends had already left. Our comrades of the Bayeux days and early days in Bruges, when we shared so many laughs and some tears, as the casualties flooded in, are already back in Canada. Our original C.O., Colonel Fraser, is still with the ship, and we bid him a very fond farewell. He had been so kind and helpful to us always. As we said goodbye, he thanked us and remarked that in almost eleven months in operation, the hospital had admitted over 20,000 patients. He said, "And you Red Cross girls knew them all!"

We showed Ginny and Val around the hospital, and Mary will still be there to guide them. Ginny belonged to our Ottawa detachment. They seem thrilled to be there, for a term on the continent. Were moving into our room in the hotel.

We left for Brussels after lunch, and they had reserved a room for us at the Plaza. It is a British Officers' Club and a very swish hotel. Marion had arranged a little dinner party for us at the Rendezvous, the Canadian Club, that evening. It's a perfectly beautiful Club and we always enjoy going there. They met us for lunch on Saturday, then took us, bag and baggage, to the airport. We boarded the freight plane with two trunks, two bed rolls containing folding cots and a few bottles of champagne, two huge dunnage bags, six knapsacks and two suitcases, plus the coats and jackets we were carrying. It was a good thing there were only a couple of other passengers. Luggage was all heaped in the middle, and we sat on long bench seats along the side of the plane.

Arrived in Northolt, on the outskirts of London, and went through customs. Such confusion. We had so many papers and so much luggage, we tied up the whole establishment. Finally got into London on the Air Transport Bus. They dumped us out in St. James Street, in front of Byron House. Laura sat on top of the luggage, while I phoned for transport. Sue Edwards came for us. We had not seen her since Bayeux. She is leaving for home with a draft of girls tomorrow. We should be able to go with the next group. We missed this one as we did not have our exit papers processed in time. It takes about ten days to get them through.

Jack was out of town, in Ireland. He had no idea I was coming so soon. Sunday, Laura and I went to Basingstoke. I was so glad to see Mrs. Simon and it was a thrill to be at Coombehurst again. We had a wonderful day there, then lugged the rest of my clothes back to London Sunday.

Monday morning we reported to HQ and spent the whole day getting our papers in order. Had to have our passports renewed and found, to our amusement, that we had not even been admitted to the country, as we had entered by Air Freight and here we were applying for Exits! However, it was soon rectified.

Jack called first thing Tuesday morning. I had managed to locate Bev McCauley on Monday, so he was able to contact Jack and let him know we had arrived. I met him at the Ontario Services Club and we went to the Criterion for lunch. Then we went shopping and got my ring. It's really a beauty and I am so thrilled with it. Dying for you to see it. It's very plain but so pretty. A narrow platinum band with a solitaire diamond, set quite high. I've spent the last two days just admiring it!

We arranged our trip to Ireland, had tea and carried on to Naval HQ to see his friends that I knew and meet some of the others. We saw a show, Happy and Glorious Happy and Glorious, *a George Black production—quite light-hearted and colourful. Great music. We had dinner at Oddenino's and came back home to show Laura the ring.*

Wednesday, Laura and I went back to Coombehurst, as Jack had to go to Bath for the day. Mrs. Simon is going away for ten days and we wanted to say goodbye, in case we are gone before she returns. We stayed overnight and returned to London on Thursday.

We have decided to be married as soon as possible. I did want to have a month or two, to relax, but Jack will be on leave before his discharge, so if we can have the wedding about three weeks after I arrive, then we will have almost a month for a honeymoon, and he is anxious to start looking for a job. Jack sails on September 9th, so should be home by Sept. 15th or 16th. He is going right to Ottawa, to HQ, and will get in touch with you soon after he arrives. Hate to rush, when I have been away for so long, but do want to have Jack's leave. Hope to have Laura and cousin Jean as attendants and would like to wear white. Thought at first I wouldn't, but then, you only get married once!

We are off to Ireland tomorrow. We had hoped to fly and it was arranged, but we lost our priority, so will take the overnight train to Scotland and the ferry across to Larne and on into Belfast. I am excited about going to the Emerald Isle. We will spend a couple of days around Belfast, then go down to the Free state.

More on our return. *Much love, Lois and Jack*

September 5th, 1945
Dearest Family:

We arrived home from Ireland last evening, after a glorious leave. Ireland was simply heavenly. So tranquil, everything so green and lush. Rolling, with hills and mountains in the background. Tommy Fyfe, also Canadian Navy and a good friend, met us with Jeep and driver. As we drove along, Tommy was giving directions to his WREN (lady) driver, and addressing her as "Love". After hearing this four or five times, we began to think he was being rather familiar, then discovered that her surname was Love! They took us to the Crawfordsburn Inn, in Holyhead just out of Belfast. Completely charming old inn. Lovely setting. The dining room was fascinating—a beautiful room with gorgeous antique tables and chairs, all different sets, each a treasure. We had two idyllic days, walked and swam and enjoyed the sunshine, the wonderful country air and the delectable meals.

(We never returned to Ireland, but in February 2000, I accompanied daughter Diane to visit with granddaughter Christy, who was on exchange at Queen's University, Belfast. After much searching, we found that marvellous old inn. It was more attractive than ever, built in the 1600s, and it has been carefully maintained. We had a memorable lunch there. Such a thrill for me to walk through the lovely old rooms again.)

Tommy and Love took us for a tour of Belfast one morning. Such an interesting city. Someday we will return and see it all in more detail. Walked along the coast, looking out over the Estuary and then the

Sea, as we headed for Bangor. There was a huge swimming pool there and we climbed the ladder for the water slide and down we went, into the very coldest water I ever remember!

The following morning, we caught the train for Dublin. Crossed the border, and did run through County Cavan, but did not have time or information to stop and pursue Grandmother's roots. Guess we will have to save that for our next visit.

Dublin was quite fascinating. A large busy place, with the River Liffey running through it. Our hotel was right in the middle of town, very nice and so convenient. We went to the race track and that was an experience, watching the bookies giving their hand signals. Enjoyed the races. Won a small amount, then managed to lose it, but it was great fun. We had glorious weather the whole time in Ireland, so were very fortunate. Rode in a Jaunting car, a horse-drawn conveyance, and saw many of the points of interest, then it was time to catch the ferry over to Holyhead in Wales. The ferry trip was lovely—always fun to be on the water. Then by train through Wales, and what wonderful country! And on to London. The food in Ireland was marvellous. So many delicious goodies that we had not seen for months. We ate so much chicken, thought we would sprout wings.

Jack is leaving for Scotland on Friday, and sailing Sunday in a destroyer, should be in Canada by September 14th or 15th. He will wire you, then go on to Ottawa. He will possibly be there for three or four days, and I would like him to stay with you, if it won't be too much trouble. Then he will go home to Toronto. If only I could come with him, but of course, that is not possible. However, it will not be very long before we sail, too.

(Jack did go home in a destroyer. The only bunk available for him in that crowded ship was in the Sick Bay. A fellow officer, in a bunk across from him, was taking a Scottish Terrier puppy home for his wife. It took a great liking to Jack and each morning he awoke with the pup curled up on his chest. There was a steady parade of young sailors, day and night, being jabbed with penicillin needles, to clean them up before they got home. It was not a very restful journey.)

The Red Cross have been very decent to us. We have had eleven days' leave and are going to help out in one of the clubs for a while, starting tomorrow. It will be Maple Leaf II, only a block from Corps Gardens, where we are living. It is just about a block from Corps House. They are all in the same area. No definite word of a sailing date, but we have been promised the next draft, probably before the end of the month.

We had thought we might like to go to the West Coast on our wedding trip, but have pretty well decided against it. Both feel we have travelled a good deal in the past two years and think we would both enjoy a week or so in the Laurentians, or somewhere like that. It's now September 11th, and we had hoped that we might have a date by now. Rumour has it that the first possible date with passage for us will be Sept. 25th. Of course, something may turn up in the meantime, so we are keeping our fingers crossed.

The irony of it is—there are ships going on September 15th and 17th, but they are completely filled with English brides. You can imagine how the Corps girls feel about that!

Sunday, I went to Cambridge and spent the day with cousin Bill. He came in from Oakington and met my train at noon. It was such a thrill to see someone of the family and be able to talk about home without explaining and describing everything. Bill looks very well and hasn't changed at all. We had a lovely day and he showed me a good part of Cambridge. My train left about 9.15 pm and should have reached Liverpool St. station by 10.45 pm. However, somewhere along the line, in the wilderness, the engine died and we stood on the track for two or three hours. When it looked as if we might be there for the night, I stretched out on one of the seats and went to sleep. We eventually got going again, and first thing I knew someone shook me and said we were in London and it was 2 am. Fortunately, the cabs were still running, so I got home safely, to find Laura practically organizing a search party.

At present, I am working in HQ. At first we were both sent to No. 2 Maple Leaf Club, but my posting was incorrect, as there are two Miss Harveys, and I was sent to the wrong one. Today, I was posted here, to the Hospital Supplies Dept. Miss Harvey is going on leave tomorrow, so I will be looking after the Dept. The fact that I know nothing whatever about it doesn't seem to matter a bit. Am sure the hospitals will begin to wonder just what goes on at Headquarters, when their supplies flow in, all mixed up.

Jack should be with you soon. I will write him a note and send it home, so he will get it soon after he arrives.

Had a pleasant surprise this morning, when Gordon Rolfe called. He is married to Jack's sister Isobel and has been a POW since Dieppe. He, too, is awaiting a sailing date. He dropped in after lunch and I was delighted to meet him. We had a wonderful chat. He stayed for tea in our canteen and helped me struggle with a few of the hospital supplies. He expects to be here over the weekend, so if Jack's sister Marjorie, the WREN, gets down from Scotland, we will all get together.

Love to you both, and to Jack, if he is with you.
Lois

September 17th, 1945
Dearest Mother and Dad:

The good news just came through that we should sail on the Ile de France *from Southampton on Sept. 27th. We should land in Quebec and that will save that long train journey from Halifax. There will be 25 girls going—the two of us and three other gals we came over with—who are just about the last members of that group of forty.*

Yesterday was quite a day. I tried numerous times to get Joan on the phone, without success. The last letter I had, she had moved to the vicinity of Tunbridge Wells, after being bombed out in London. I had mislaid the phone number, and as it was not under her name, could not contact her. Decided to go to Tunbridge Wells and take a chance on finding them.

When I got there, I found that she lived 10 miles farther on. Got on another train and went to Ticehurst. There I found that I must walk a mile and a half to Stonegate. There was a fine gentleman and his wife, a Major and Mrs. Anne, and when I enquired, they said they, too, lived in Stonegate and would take me. The final straw was when we finally found "Bramdear", Joan's home, only to discover that she had moved two months ago. Mrs. Anne insisted that I join them at their home for lunch and then could go back on the train with her in the afternoon, as she was going up to London to meet her niece. She is perfectly sweet. From Ireland, and really an Irish type, with bright blue eyes and black hair. They have a dream of a home. Set on the crest of a hill, so that you could see for miles across the valley. It had been a very old farmhouse, and is long and low, with panelled walls and low beamed ceilings. Acres of gardens, beautifully kept, and smooth green lawns. We came back to town on the afternoon train and had tea together before Mrs. Anne went to meet her niece. Charming people and certainly kind.

It is now September 20th. Only four more days! We are going on board on Tuesday the 25th, so should sail that day, or surely, on Wednesday the 26th. I'm so excited about going home!

This afternoon am going to Basingstoke for another goodbye with Mrs. Simon. Will stay over until tomorrow evening and then come back to London and go to Kelvedon to see Jack's grandmother on Sunday. She lives with his aunt and uncle. Monday we will get our luggage ready and receive our last-minute instructions.

Last evening I was out to see Joan and Alec Reid (Joan's married name). Finally found them, in London! After travelling all over Kent and Sussex on Sunday, looking for them. They have moved into another house, in Barnes, not far from the place that was blitzed. Alec is home for a few days' leave and was busy redecorating. He is a fine fellow and the little boys are adorable.

Sunday evening, went to South Harrow to Jack's aunts. Three families live in the same street, so they all got together for the evening. They are a jolly group and have been very good to me. They are Jack's mother's relatives, while the ones I saw in Kelvedon are his father's people.

We have no idea when or where we will dock—possibly Sunday or Monday. Perhaps you will be able to find out when the Ile de France *is expected. And where!*

I imagine Jack has gone to Toronto for Winnie's wedding. I am so disappointed about missing it, but delighted that he can be there—to give her away.

Hope Jack will be able to be with you to meet train or boat.

Heaps of love, see you soon. Lois

LEAVING LONDON

We left Corps Gardens, having said goodbye there, also at Corps House and at HQ, to the gals we knew. There are so many new faces. We had been in the first 90 Corps girls Overseas, so 551 had followed. Most of our first friends had already left.

Caught the train for Southampton. The *Ile de France* was waiting when we arrived at the docks, and we boarded with much excitement. It surely was not the luxury liner of pre-war days! We were twenty to a cabin. Ten sets of bunks, crowded in. Sharing a bathroom with another twenty! Lounges were stripped pretty bare. Little or no furniture. We sat on the floor to play bridge or cribbage. Only time we sat on a chair was in the dining salon. We were informed that we would have two meals a day—breakfast and dinner, with three sittings for each. We were encouraged to take an extra bun or roll at breakfast, fill it with bacon or whatever, and have it for a snack at noon. Meals were few, but extremely good.

The ship was simply crammed with service people. Seven thousand on board! Walking on deck, one moved in a solid mass of bodies, surging along together. Fortunately we had a fairly smooth passage. Three or four days out, the engines ground to a halt and we were "dead in the water" for several hours. What a frustrating time that was, when no one knew what was happening or how long we might be delayed. Luckily, it was almost a flat calm; we might have been in real trouble, in a rough sea, with so many on board and no power.

We sailed triumphantly into Halifax on October 3rd, 1945, greeted by a deafening chorus of sirens and whistles, flags waving, and firehoses shooting skyward. Quite a dramatic Welcome Home. It was pretty exciting and emotional to realize that after over two years in war-torn England and Europe, we were finally, and safely, home in Canada.

We took the *Ocean Limited* to Montreal, arriving in the morning. As the train rolled along, many thoughts flashed through my mind. What a fantastic two years! I had seen so many places, and met so many fascinating people. It had been a fabulous experience: the beauty of southern England, with our very dear Mrs. Simon; the great camaraderie with the group at Corps House and the personnel in the hospitals; the wonderful patients who had taught me so much about life and giving and caring for others; our memorable experiences and wonderful friendships of those incredible years.

There had been moments of great sadness, frustration, stress and downright fear and horror, but also much fun and laughter along the way. Unforgettable people and moments were etched forever in my memory. I would not have missed a moment of it for anything. With a whole new chapter in life about to start, I was ready to step off the train and begin.

Crawsfordsburn Inn near Belfast, Ireland
Mrs. Cooper, at the doorway, revisited the Inn in 2000.

I had called home from Halifax, so Mother, Dad and Jack were there, with my Montreal relatives; also Laura's family, and our dear friend Sheila. Again, it was exciting and emotional. There were tears of joy flowing freely as we all embraced and everyone talked at once.

WAR ORGANISATION
OF THE
BRITISH RED CROSS SOCIETY
AND
ORDER OF ST JOHN OF JERUSALEM

Presented to
Lois J. MacDonald.
Canadian Red Cross Society
in recognition of devoted service to
the cause of humanity
during the second world war
1939~1945

George R.I. — Sovereign Head, Order of St. John of Jerusalem.

Elizabeth R — President, British Red Cross Society.

EPILOGUE

Going through all these letters, trying to decipher and copy them, has surely been a trip down Memory Lane. Quite an emotional roller-coaster, as I recall all the dear friends who were such an important part of my life in those two very special years. I picture them as still very young, in their 20s and 30s. Now, of course, they would be in their 70s and 80s, if they are still alive! No.12 Hospital personnel had become our close friends: the Sisters and the Medical Officers, plus all the young men that bounced in and out of our lives!

Our wedding took place in Ottawa as planned and we honeymooned at the Seigneury Club in Montebello and the Laurentians. Then we settled in North Bay, where Jack had accepted a position with the Ontario Northland Railway. It was a new and exciting experience for me, as I had never been in Northern Ontario.

The wartime friends, most of them, I never did see again. Unfortunately, we all just drifted apart, as we returned to civilian life. We had families and many new responsibilities. Ours was a busy household, with four daughters. Jack travelled five or six days a month. We both belonged to various local organizations, but still managed to spend much time with our daughters. Summers we lived at our beloved log cottage on Trout Lake, nine miles from town. In winter, we skied as a family, as soon as each one became old enough to wear skis. We travelled both as a family and, sometimes, just the two of us. It has been an extremely happy family life, and we celebrated our Fiftieth Anniversary in l995. Then, sadly, in 1997, we lost our dearest Jack.

I imagine that similar things happened to those hundreds of dear friends, as they got caught up in their new lives, and our paths just never crossed.

We corresponded frequently with our wonderful Scottish Mrs. Simon, sending pictures of our growing family. Jack and I had a final visit with her in 1967, in her home near Coombehurst. Sadly, she passed away in 1969.

I have kept in touch with the Red Cross Corps girls, through our Overseas Club, which a few stalwart souls initiated, at the close of the war. As I always worked in the hospitals, I did not know them as well as the girls who all worked and lived in London. Then, living in North Bay, a smaller community, we did not have a local branch as did the larger centres across the country. They have held a reunion every single year since 1945, and I have managed to attend a few of them, more recently. In June '99, we met in Toronto, 80 strong. There were a few wheelchairs, walkers and canes, but they made the effort to come and all had such a glorious time, just seeing each other.

Of course I am still in close touch with Laura, Mary and my dear friend Aileen, who did marry again, a few years after the war. With much sadness, we lost Sheila two years ago. Laura and Sheila had spent a lovely week with me in Florida shortly before that.

Laura married Bill Rowbotham, an American, several years after the war, and they lived in St. Louis. She bred Standard Poodles and became one of the top breeders in the Midwest. Now widowed, she has returned to the Oakville area. Laura and Bill and Jack and I had many happy visits together over the years.

Sheila married her wartime beau, Laird Bovaird, soon after arriving home. They made their home in Montreal and raised four fine sons. Then they retired to Toronto, where I saw her frequently.

Mary was our career girl, becoming an Executive Assistant to Prime Minister Lester Pearson, and later, working with Pierre Trudeau. She has taken a long-time interest in the Red Cross Overseas Club and has convened several of the Ottawa reunions.

Aileen married David Howes after the war and they had two sons. They lived in Toronto and had a charming country home in Claremont, moving there in retirement. We keep in close touch.

Ruth and Hoyle Campbell lived in Toronto, where he had a very successful career in Reconstructive Surgery. They have twin daughters, both married and living in California. Both Ruth and Hoyle are gone now. Aileen and I visited Ruth in a beautiful retirement facility a couple of years ago, then were very sad to hear of her death recently.

Over the years we have visited back and forth and kept in touch by phone. We all share a very special bond, forged during those war years.

I have attended the reunions recently—the fiftieth at the Château Laurier in Ottawa was memorable. Since then we have had fun "gathering" in Toronto, Ottawa, Charlottetown, Montreal, and now back in Ottawa in May of 2005 for our glorious 60th!

It will coincide with the 60th Anniversary of VE Day and we are to be included in the ceremonies at the National War Memorial and opening luncheon at the new War Museum. Our numbers are dwindling, however; there were over 60 in attendance in Montreal last year.

We all look forward to the coming "Gathering" in May with much anticipation. It will officially be our "Last Hurrah."

Lois MacDonald Cooper

Lois MacDonald Cooper was born in Ottawa in 1920. She was educated at the Ottawa Ladies College, then MacDonald College of McGill University. She enjoyed many sports and loved the outdoors, spending much time in the Gatineau Hills. Her parents, Elwood and Mabel MacDonald, were always very supportive. She worked for the Metropolitan Life Insurance Company before going overseas with the Canadian Red Cross.

Soon after her return to Canada Lois married Canadian Naval Officer John Cooper. They settled in North Bay, Ontario, where he worked with the Ontario Northland Railway.

Jack and Lois took great pride and pleasure in their four daughters and enjoyed many activities as a family. In retirement in 1977 they bought a home in Cape Haze, Florida, a small community on the Intra Coastal Waterway south of Englewood. They spent lovely winters there before moving in 1995 to Sarasota, always returning each spring to North Bay and Trouth Lake. Lois's husband Jack passed away in 1997.

Daughter Carolyn and her husband Chris Kofler, and daughter Laurie and her husband Steve Wilbur, reside in Sarasota. Daughters Marcia and her husband Barry Pond and Diane and her husband Don Wallace and families live in North Bay. Lois feels very fortunate to have family in both places.

Quebec, Canada
2005